Mobile Media Learning:
INNOVATION AND INSPIRATION

Mobile Media Learning: Innovation and Inspiration

Copyright © by Christopher Holden, Seann Dikkers, John Martin, Breanne Litts, et al. and ETC Press 2015
http://press.etc.cmu.edu/

Design Direction by Shirley Yee

ISBN: 978-1-312-98125-6
Library of Congress Control Number: 2015935860

TEXT: The text of this work is licensed under a Creative Commons Attribution-NonCommerical-NonDerivative 2.5 License (http://creativecommons.org/licenses/by-nc-nd/2.5/)

IMAGES: All images appearing in this work are property of the respective copyright owners,
and are not released into the Creative Commons.
The respective owners reserve all rights.

Mobile Media Learning:
INNOVATION AND INSPIRATION

EDITED BY

CHRISTOPHER HOLDEN, SEANN DIKKERS,
JOHN MARTIN, BREANNE LITTS, ET AL.

TABLE OF CONTENTS

INTRODUCTION

1. *What:* Innovation and Inspiration in Mobile Media Learning 9
   Christopher Holden

2. *Why:* Mobile Media Learning As Progressive Educational Technology 15
   Christopher Holden

3. *When, Where, and How:* Practical Considerations When Designing Your Own Mobile Media Learning 27
   John Martin, Seann Dikkers, Breanne Litts, and Christopher Holden

MML PLATFORMS

4. Traveler: A Digital Journal for Enhancing Learning and Retention in Field Trips 45
   Lohren Deeg and Kyle Parker

5. MIT App Inventor: Democratizing Personal Mobile Computing 59
   Shaileen Pokress

6. ARIS: Augmented Reality for Interactive Storytelling 67
   Christopher Holden

CONNECTING TO CLASSROOMS

7. School Scene Investigators: A Collaborative AR Game for Middle School Science Inquiry 87
   Denise Bressler

8. Building a Student-Centered Classroom with AR 101
   Tim Frandy

9. Introducing an Neighborhood: Mobile as a Springboard for Exploration 109
   Kim Garza and Jason Rosenblum

10. Experimenting with Locative Media Games and Storytelling in Fine Arts 123
    Fred Adam and Veronica Perales

CONNECTING TO COMMUNITIES

11. "To Have Fun and Display Our Awesomeness": Mobile Game Design and *The Meaning of Life* 139
    Bob Coulter and Ross Stauder

12. Project Exploration's Environmental Adventurers: Amplifying Urban Youth Agency, Identity and Capacity with Mobile Technology 145
    Jameela Jafri et al.

13. Civic Engagement and Geo-Locative Media: Youth Create a Game to Discuss Political Issues 157
    Juan Rubio

14. Technovation Challenge: Introducing Innovation and Mobile App Development to Girls Around the World 171
    Angélica Torres

CONNECTING TO CURATED SPACES

15. Quest for the Cities of Gold 199
    Gianna May

16. *ParkQuest:* Mobile Media Learning as a Large Group Activity 211
    Seann Dikkers, Ryan Rieder, and Tamala Soloman

17. *Lift Off:* A DIY Addition to a Smithsonian Space 219
    Christopher Blakesley and Jennifer McIntosh

18. *Horror at the Ridges:* Engagement with an AR Horror Story 229
    Rebecca Fisher and Seann Dikkers

DISCUSSION

19. What Have We Seen, What is Missing, and What is Next for MML? 245
    Christopher Holden

CLOSING 255

EDITORS AND AUTHORS BIOGRAPHIES 257

ACKNOWLEDGEMENTS 265

SECTION ONE

Introduction

1. *What:* Innovation and Inspiration in Mobile Media Learning
2. *Why:* Mobile Media Learning As Progressive Educational Technology
3. *When, Where, and How:* Practical Considerations When Designing Your Own Mobile Media Learning

CHAPTER ONE

What: Innovation and Inspiration in Mobile Media Learning

Christopher Holden

On behalf of my co-editors and our authors, thank you for joining us in our explorations of the space of Mobile Media Learning (MML). The bulk of this book consists of reports from the mobile frontier: students, educators, and researchers who have explored many educational contexts by inventing with mobile technologies. This is bookended by some editorial material to add context. The first chapter situates our book as part of a continuing conversation about MML and sets forth our mode of presentation, a co-edited volume of individual stories. The second chapter positions the study of MML within a larger historical picture, where we consider Seymour Papert's take on the computer as a tool for educational self-determinism as analogy and history lesson. In the third chapter we descend from theoretical to practical consideration of MML, providing a short manual for those who wish to design their own learning projects using mobile technology. Together, this introductory matter gets at the what, why, where and how of MML.

As we get to the who of MML, we have grouped the contributed chapters in this book into sections.

- MML Platforms - Projects showcasing software that enables regular people to act creatively in the name of MML.
- Connecting to Classrooms - Projects where the main context for MML is a formal educational setting such as a classroom.
- After Shool and in the Summer - Projects whose main setting is informal or semiformal learning such as a summer program.
- Fields of Dreams - Stories that focus on the development and use of a single exploratory MML design. These are all Augmented Reality games designed for public audiences.

However, this grouping is for the sake of your digestion, not an attempt at taxonomy; our authors' work is relevant outside and across the boxes we have chosen to put them in. For example, we chose to include *Traveler* in the Platforms section because it is a general purpose mapping tool you can download in the Google Play Store right now. But the authors of that chapter also describe the app's first uses in two very different field study courses. So the chapter could also easily fit in the section

Connecting to Classrooms. Since it is also the story of a design that was made for a specific setting and the first test of that device, it would also fit in the final section, Fields of Dreams.

A glance at our Table of Contents shows the diverse range of inspiring explorations shared within these chapters. The subjects cross divides between the Humanities and the Sciences, politics and architecture, and even honey bees. Our authors include an undergraduate, PhD students, educators involved in community outreach, and University technologists and professors. Their work takes place in classrooms, parks, museums, summer programs, an international program for girls and a creepy asylum. We hope that all of these stories—regardless of discipline, grade level, or context—inspire your own explorations.

The final bookend to these stories is a brief reflection. We share a couple of the most prominent themes we saw or didn't see and a few thoughts about where MML is headed next. We hope this next chapter is one you help write.

A SERIES OF BOOKS ABOUT MML

Perhaps you have already read the first volume of *Mobile Media Learning: Amazing Uses of Mobile Devices for Learning* (2012). In many ways, this book is a sequel.[1] If not, you can go read it right now, and I'll wait here for you.[2]

Done? OK good.

A couple years ago, the editors of Mobile Media Learning: Amazing Uses of Mobile Devices for Learning—Seann Dikkers, Bob Coulter, and John Martin—assembled several educators who were doing interesting work with mobile media and learning and asked them to share their stories with the world. The book documented forward thinking work with mobile and that MML was doable by normal educators, without exceptional technological skills or investment. These educators had found ways to begin exploring the educational spaces opened up by mobile: a loose term we use again here to refer to the many manifestations of handheld, networked computers and data collection devices (e.g. smartphones, digital cameras, GPS devices, and tablets). The voices and projects contained in the book from 2012 are some of the early educational forays into a world already transformed by mobile.[3] By sharing the stories of these pioneers in mobile learning, the editors said, "Yes, you can try this too!"

---

[1] Hopefully more like *The Empire Strikes Back* than *The Matrix Reloaded*.

[2] Go order it here: press.etc.cmu.edu/content/mobile-media-learning, and read the free pdf while you wait for the print copy to arrive.

[3] Early is a funny word to use here. As mentioned in the last volume and again heavily referenced in this one, Klopfer and Squire for example have been thinking, writing, and working in this space for more than a decade. Myself and the other editors have been involved for quite some time as well. Yet, these do still feel like the early days of mobile because the pace at which the world is changing in terms of this technology has only increased.

The previous volume also implicitly made the claim that there is something special about the uses of mobile for learning that come from the ground up, through small experiments and communities of practice. Each chapter represented work done at a grassroots level, not unified by a field, age level, job description, or methodological similarity. Together those stories provided a rich snapshot of a few corners of the world where educators were finding ways to take mobile into their own hands to produce new kinds of learning opportunities. It was an early statement in a conversation we hope to add to here about the use of mobile for the aims of educators of all stripes, not just within specialized research programs. It has inspired new projects, and helped to connect others who were already involved with similar work. It is now time to check in, in this book, on the progress of MML.

"All well and fine," you say. "Soooooooo, is this book just a few more stories?"

Yes and no.

Yes, once again we have brought together a wide array of designers and given them a chance to share their stories. Yes, again we want you the reader to be able to see something familiar and inspiring, and say "me too!" However, no, this is not merely an addendum.

The few chapters in the previous volume could hardly have overseen every possibility for the uses of mobile media for learning or constituted a complete representation of who was out there, doing this good work. That territory is vast and constantly growing. The projects described in this volume cover new ground and different goals, contexts, and constraints. At a minimum, the growing diversity of participants, approaches, and agendas you will see in this volume gives a more complete picture of what is out there. As a reader, it should be even easier this time to see an experiment, context, or idea that you can connect with.

Moreover, after putting together this round of stories and working with many more explorers whose stories are not yet in print, we can speak with more conviction to a theme that guided the first MML book. Across all these differences in context and goals, there really is something shared, the active interpretation of mobile technologies to enact the ideals of progressive education: learning as a meaning-making activity, self-determination as a goal and value, learning that is co-constructed among its participants, and learning that happens through making new connections. In this book, we reveal more of the shape of MML, in breadth and depth, than was shown or existed at the time of the previous effort.

This volume should also help you to check in with a conversation that is evolving in pace with the swift embedding of mobile technologies into all aspects of life. Two years is a long time in the world of mobile. Newcomers are able to cheaply and quickly produce truly fascinating work that would have been hard to imagine emerging into practicality from inexperience two short years ago. Between the two volumes then, we can see an evolution in thought and action taking place as the tools have themselves progressed and found their ways into more hands.

Finally, the best reason for more stories is quite simply that they are inspiring. All of the authors have invested their hearts and souls in their projects and their commitment shows. None of them know all the answers (neither do we), but they all see something on the horizon and are unafraid to follow that vision. It is a wonderful thing to see so many people embracing the opportunity to play an important role in the development of their own intellectual destinies. These authors have given us a lot to think about and make us want to do more. They will do the same for you.

WHAT IS MOBILE MEDIA LEARNING?

I have a confession to make. The term Mobile Media Learning hasn't always felt very clear or helpful to me. MML is a fine enough acronym, and certainly a good acronym is one of the keys to the realm, but what does MML mean? It was quite a while before I realized that it is more about an attitude than about anything else. So before going any further, I'd like to clear up how we think about MML.

For a long time, I thought about MML something like this: Okay, mobile, like mobile devices. Media, now I'm thinking about multimedia and all the conversations going back to the 90's about multimedia in education, like the promise of the CD-ROM. And learning, well at least I think I know what that is. Soooooooo... MML is what we get when we put those together, right? Media delivered via a mobile device for the purpose of learning?

There is quite a lot of activity involving mobile and learning that satisfies this simple definition. However, this definition does not quite fit with the conversations about MML that I've been a party to. For example, nowhere in this book or the previous one is there a chapter about using a Learning Management System to administer reading quizzes online or deliver them via phones as if this were progress. The kind of MML we are talking about is somehow supposed to be about more than the usual formula: school + mobile device = learning. So, what was missing in my initial definition of MML? How can I do better for you than simply saying, "I know it when I see it"?[4]

The definition of MML from the first book is really very helpful, though it flew under my radar until I began to put together this chapter. "Mobile media learning includes the instant and ongoing connection of handheld devices to online information and communication for personal growth and increased agency within professions and communities of practice."[5] What is importantly included here that is missing from a more generic interpretation of MML is the bit about "increased agency." This is why taking quizzes on your cell phone instead of on paper doesn't fit. Thinking about mobile technologies in terms of managing persons and their doings contributes more to the bureaucracy of education than learning itself, and simply reproducing existing forms of instruction on a small

---

[4] The characterization of pornography by Supreme Court justice Potter Stewart: "I know it when I see it" (Jacobellis v. Ohio, 1964).

[5] Dikkers et al, 2012, p. 21.

screen instead of paper also misses the point of what is really possible with mobile: going somewhere new, seeing something you have never seen before, sharing a deep interest, doing something you had no idea was even possible, telling stories in new ways, making something you care about, connecting new ideas, and generally taking ownership of who you are going to be through what you choose to do and think about.

MML is a broad concept but it retains meaning. Despite the many purposes, contexts, contents, and disciplines represented by people using MML, we usually have something to talk about together. As a loosely confederated set of thinkers and practitioners in MML for example, one of the desires that is frequently expressed is to use mobile to help unpack learning from all the little boxes we have squeezed it into. Educators seek to free ideas that have been isolated through disciplinary walls and rigidly defined roles. They use MML to push back on the traditional boundaries of School to connect learning to the real world. In aligning with efforts like these, our commitment is not to mobile itself as a set of tools for improving learning as it has already been constructed within educational structures, but to explore how mobile enables us to make learning come alive in new ways.

We are not interested in all outcomes the abstract affordances of mobile technologies provide, but with how individuals and groups can interpret mobile technologies to achieve a higher degree of self-determination in the learning they create or engage in. We are people who see the mobile revolution as a chance to make instances of education more about what learning should really be about. That's MML.

Let us not forget too that mobile itself is a big deal. It is the fastest spreading, most thoroughly adopted technology in history. It has taken two previous destabilizing innovations—the computer and the internet—and has put them in the pockets of most everyone.[6] At this moment in history, so many ideas are suddenly possible, or so much easier as to feel newly possible, *because of mobile*. Disregarding the influence of this context on our world and work would be careless.

To represent progress in the exploration of mobile learning, the editors felt strongly that the most appropriate and useful format for continuing the conversation started in the first book was to again have practitioners tell us their stories, and—through the mangling known as co-editing—to produce a plural account that still strives to make some sense of the chaos. We believe that this format can move forward conversations about the roles mobile media can play in learning because it productively and honestly addresses the following issues:

Preserve diversity. If there is one obvious finding of the innovative approaches to mobile learning presented here and generally, it is the way MML transcends typical divisions between age and experience level, subjects or disciplines, job classifications, and educational contexts such as

---

[6] comScore reported in May 2014, on data from March, that 166 million Americans have smartphones for example. This is a market penetration of over 68%, up from 54% the previous year.

classrooms and summer programs. Writing separate books for each learning context encountered through MML misrepresents both the reality of these situations and hides what is one of the strongest indications we are on to something more than the same old thing. It is refreshing to see people working together across traditional divides. Above all we seek to faithfully represent the diversity of participants and approaches taken.

Avoid authoritarianism. It is common for researchers to act in the capacity of an interpretive filter, representing alone upstream what happened on the ground among many. But it can be more honest, and in this case it is only a bit more trouble, to let everyone involved have their own voice. If all this work is about increasing the agency of those who participate, doesn't it make sense to let them tell their own stories? We present the plurality that exists across MML without contorting these authors' ideas to fit a pre-programmed moral, except in our editorial chapters (which we cannot stop you from skipping entirely). This way you can better help decide whether the central themes we see emerging ring true to you. Hopefully too, you will find others we have missed.

Simplicity of storytelling. Writing about learning too often hides meaning within specialist jargon. Myself, the other editors, and our authors have tried our best to avoid this trap, describing the relevant goals and approaches in each project in everyday language as much as possible. These stories should be accessible to those without significant technological expertise or degrees in Education.

Provide conversations. Because our main goal is to provoke further conversation, we proudly and straightforwardly share these stories as they are. We hope they pass a simple and honest test for validity, wholly appropriate for the exploratory mode of research we have witnessed and participated in: does anything you see here seem likely enough to have value that you might try something similar yourself? Can you discover enough of what was actually done to give it a go?

As we dive into MML, it is worth reflecting on how the artifacts we produce in the name of research or conversation aim to represent the activity that preceded their creation. In a day and age when so much conversation happens outside books, we should be even more thoughtful about when, how, and why we put one together. We think this one was worth it, and we hope you do too.

CHAPTER TWO

Why: Mobile Media Learning As Progressive Educational Technology

Christopher Holden

The previous book in this series framed Mobile Media Learning (MML) by connecting the present and future to the past of progressive thinking about learning. John Dewey served to embody the perspective of someone who cares and knows a great deal about creating strong opportunities for deep learning and who is thrust into a world redefined by mobile technology. This perspective also helped to unify the diverse experiences shared in the chapters themselves. Here, rather than going back to the dawn of universal education during the industrial revolution, we can once again establish common context through an earlier technological and social revolution: the computer. Just as Dewey was a voice for humanity rising out of a system of education created for good but often doing evil, the computer has a progressive champion whose words are even more relevant today: Seymour Papert.

Papert is well-known for his role in the creation and promotion of many technologies to support learning, especially Logo and its later variants and derivatives[1], but the truly progressive nature of his views about the learning he wished to support through technology are perhaps less widely remembered than they should be. I remember encountering his work under the guise of cosntructionism—for me then just another -ism—regarding the how of education, not realizing he had a lot to say about why until I read some of his work on my own. He championed software like Logo not to improve student performance in existing math classes, but as a way for students and teachers together to begin to explore a new kind of mathematical thinking that went far beyond math class and made explicit connections to non-mathematical parts of life. He saw this as a subversive act that demanded creative input from its participants to function as intended and, when taken seriously, might form the basis of liberating learning from the limiting perspective of School.[2]

---

[1] Logo is an educational programming language and graphical environment with a rich and interesting history. The homepage for the Logo Foundation has a brief history of the software and its use: http://el.media.mit.edu/logo-foundation/logo/index.html.

[2] Along with Papert, I will use "School" here and in later chapters to refer to the well-earned stereotype of formal educational environments. Certainly not every school, or every experience within a school, is characterizable using this stereotype.

I would like to revisit some of the major themes in Papert's *The Children's Machine* (1993) as a preface to the work of our authors here. His views on technology and learning can help us better understand the reach and importance of the mobile explorations they have undertaken. Taking a brief look back in time can help us see the broader context to which we hope to contribute and help us possibly avoid some common missteps in our discussion and evaluation of work that makes use of technology to improve learning.

THE CHILDREN'S MACHINE

Although Papert has written significantly in many places, *The Children's Machine* (1993) parallels most closely what we are trying to capture and speak to in the world of mobile and learning here. Papert begins his book with the idea of a visitor from the distant past. This visitor immediately recognizes the vast changes in how the modern world operates since their time, in particular how sciences like astronomy or medicine have greatly advanced. At the same time this visitor does not find himself so out of place in a modern classroom. In fact, little has changed. This hypothetical visitor asks, "Why, through a period when so much human activity has been revolutionized, have we not seen comparable change in how we help our children learn?" (p. 2).

Papert blames the conservatism of School for holding back progress in learning, especially that its participants are expected to fill narrow predetermined roles rather than take active roles in learning. He claims,

> School has an inherent tendency to infantilize children by placing them in a position of having to do as they are told, to occupy themselves with work dictated by someone else and that, moreover, has no intrinsic value—schoolwork is done only because the designer of a curriculum decided that doing the work would shape the doer into a desirable form. (p. 24)

He further explains, "School does not have in its institutional mind that teachers have a creative role; it sees them as technicians doing a technical job, and for this the word training is perfectly appropriate" (p. 70). He echoes Ivan Illich's famous condemnation of School that the main thing it teaches is the need to be taught (p. 140).

In sentiment then, Papert aligns with progressive educational thinkers like Dewey, Friere, Piaget, and Vygostsky. Papert hopes that the changes in learning the hypothetical visitor might be able to see would include greater agency of students and teachers in their roles; learning that is active and self-directed; learning that is expected to happen in evolutionary and emergent ways, instead of according to subject and timetable; and that what is valued as a route to knowledge might be expanded beyond simple individual efficacies within the narrow print literacies typically emphasized in School. He wants the visitor to be able to see learning that resonates with "with a respectful attitude toward children and a democratic social philosophy" (p. 15). To hint at what this learning could look like, he considers powerful learning moments in his own early life, as well as some he has seen in his work with youth and teachers, and laments that these kinds of experiences are hard for School to recognize or support.

At the same time, Papert criticizes the actual actions and effects of progressive reforms to date. He sees the progressive education movement as fundamentally having its heart in the right place, but finds that its proponents too often lack the tools and conviction to initiate real change. He says, "Almost all experiments purporting to implement progressive education have been disappointing because they simply did not go far enough in making the student the subject of the process rather than the object" (p. 14), and "so far none of those who challenge these hallowed traditions has been able to loosen the hold of the educational establishment on how the children are taught" (p. 3).

Regarding conviction, Papert sees little help coming from traditional centers of leadership like education research, educational policy, and—in his neck of the woods—computer aided instruction. These are typically forces and means for assimilation that ultimately serve the system. However he does see rebels doing important work from within the system—yearners—who operate as "a sort of fifth column within School itself: Large numbers of teachers manage to create within the walls of their own classrooms oases of learning profoundly at odds with the education philosophy publicly espoused by their administrators" (p. 3).[3] He believes that together these individual subversive efforts can one day be successful, growing and multiplying from lone voices in the darkness into true grassroots action.

Papert explains that change is not possible until access to powerful tools becomes commonplace:

> Early designers of experiments in progressive education lacked the tools that would allow them to create new methods in a reliable and systematic fashion. With very limited means at their disposal, they were forced to rely too heavily on the specific talents of individual teachers or a specific match with a particular social context. As a result, what successes they had often could not be generalized. (p. 14–5)

He sums up the to-date failure of progressive ideals to change learning, and his optimism in their eventual success, through the parable of humanity's dream of flight. Papert tells us,

> My hypothetical Schoolers said that progressive education has been tried and did not work. I agree that it hasn't worked very well but in something like the sense in which Leonardo da Vinci failed in his attempts to invent an airplane. Making an airplane in Leonardo's time needed more than a creative manipulation of all that was known about aeronautics. His failure to make a workable airplane did

---

[3] Papert does not only count teachers among the yearners. he specifically includes administrators and parents as well. The term indicates an outlook on education, not a place within its hierarchy.

not prove him wrong in his ·assumptions about the feasibility of flying machines. Leonardo's airplane had to wait for the development of some thing that could come about only through great changes in the way society managed its resources. The Wright Brothers could succeed where Leonardo could only dream because a technological infrastructure supplied materials and tools and engines and fuels, while a scientific culture (which developed in coevolution with this infrastructure) supplied ideas that drew on the peculiar capabilities of these new resources. Educational innovators even in the very recent past were in a situation analogous to Leonardo's…When educators tried to craft an actual school based on these [progressive] general principles, it was as if Leonardo had tried to make an airplane out of oak and power it with a mule. Most practitioners who tried to follow the seminal thinkers in education were forced to compromise so deeply that the original intent was lost (p. 15–6).

For Papert, the computer is the first tool capable of enabling individual efforts at progressive change to actually take off. This conviction stems from his early work with computers in 1965 at MIT, long before they were common in the world, where he realized their capacity to do more than calculate. He says, "problems which had been abstract and hard to grasp became concrete and transparent" (p. 13). To explain further,

> It was pure play. We were finding out what could be done with a computer, and anything interesting was worthwhile. Nobody yet knew enough to decree that some things were more serious than others. We were like infants discovering the world. I thought about computers and children. I was playing like a child and experiencing a volcanic explosion of creativity. Why couldn't the computer give a child the same kind of experience? Why couldn't a child play like me? What would have to be done to make this possible? (p. 33)

Learning with a computer was something automatic and authentic for him. Its ability to respond to and provoke his inquiry suggested that others too could use it to find new and powerful routes to knowledge. Of course, at the time he was one of the few people—even at MIT—to have access to a computer. He had to wait until 1980 for the landscape of access to change sufficiently. But when appropriate hardware became available and inexpensive enough, learning with computers began to happen outside specialist circles.

Papert is clear that access to hardware, while necessary, is not sufficient to increase agency in the ways he imagined. He realized that transformative as these machines can be for the few people who will be enticed and capable of approaching their use as such, it is software that is really capable of empowering the majority. Providing access to the power of the computer means making software that enables regular people to use the machine in creative ways. He made Logo so that teachers and youth could use the computer as he did in those early days.

Papert also mentions a third aspect—beyond hardware and software—of putting powerful tools into practice. He doesn't give it a name, but I will call it inspiration. He describes 1980 as a pivotal year for change because enough people had read *Mindstorms*—Papert's first book, an initial plea to get others thinking about how technology could be best used for learning—to get excited about what could be tried using computers and Logo. Finally, these

> three events came together to give a powerful boost to the awareness among teachers that computers could be used in the spirit of progressive education. *Mindstorms* set this out in easily accessible form, inexpensive personal computers reached a level of performance that could support a usable version of Logo, and Logo software became commercially available. The result was a grassroots movement that generated many thousands of classroom implementations of PET [Progressive Educational Technology]. (p. 42)

Papert gives many specific examples of classroom implementations using Logo and Lego-Logo and how they convey what he sees as their promise for enacting self-directed learning. The particulars are not especially important to review here, but in telling these stories he also clearly lays out a set of connected values that characterize these creations.

1. Active, self-directed learning. Students should be subjects actively directing their learning, not objects of instruction.

2. Bricolage. Doing what we can with what's at hand is a valuable way to make new connections between ideas, disciplines, etc.

3. Cultivation. A guiding metaphor for knowledge to be added to the existing ones: construction and acquisition.

4. Concreteness. Reverse the traditional idea that intellectual progress consists of moving from the concrete to the abstract. Computers provide a new kind of concreteness we should value and use as a way to renew value of concreteness elsewhere.

5. Creating publicly. Making things "in the world" is especially valuable.

6. Informal learning. There is inherent value in informal ways of knowing, not just as scaffolds for formal instruction.

7. Time. If it is important, take your time with it.

These values transcend Logo and the early days of classroom computing. They can flesh out the concept of "increasing agency" for us with MML as they did for him back then. In particular, I think the above list of values can help us identify our authors' creative urges and see how even little experiments along these lines might fit into a bigger picture of meaningful change. Although not all of our authors explicitly aim to overthrow oppressive forces in School—or are even working within schools—it is clear that their efforts are in the name of producing learning that is qualitatively different than the norm. They are all looking for new ways to connect young people's abilities and interests to the world we live in. Their work will also help us directly consider the triangle of hardware, software, and inspiration that forms the catalyst for change in a mobile age.

TWO DECADES AFTER *THE CHILDREN'S MACHINE*

So if in retelling *The Children's Machine*, I am in effect saying, "It's all going to work! Just substitute mobile for computer. Papert says so!" you might wonder about the twenty-one years between that book and today, or the thirty-plus years since the supposedly pivotal moment in 1980 when the powerful tools Logo and *Mindstorms* became widely available. Surely, Papert's thesis has now had its chance. How much closer have we got to achieving the progressive dream?

Some look at the current state of School and think back on Papert's moment of optimism as just one more failed progressive dream. After all, here we are—through several rounds of large scale reform including No Child Left Behind and Race to the Top and now the Common Core and huge efforts to purchase computers and implement curricula aware of them and the internet—and the net effect seems to have been to regird School as an institution mostly concerned with pre-defined, standardized achievements as primary goals for its participants and assured in its uniform power over them through those standardizing mechanisms. The computers are no longer just in the lab, but Computer Science is just another one of the disciplines, another subject in which our students seem to be constantly falling behind.

Tyack and Cuban's book, *Tinkering Toward Utopia* (1995) probably contains the most well-known skeptical take on the potential for technology to materially change education. Their claims in part echo Papert's criticism of earlier progressive movements.[4] That is, the supposed changes enabled by technological progress are judged to be simply too small and timid in the face of what they call "The Grammar of School," while the revolutionary character of the reform becomes assimilated to the status quo. I don't exactly disagree with this big picture. Yet, there are yet reasons for optimism that we might miss with a one sentence "State of School" report or if we simply accept Cuban and Tyack's criticism as proof that new tools are an immaterial part of trying to make things better.

But why do we expect School itself, as an institution, to have been changed thus through centralized reform? Recall, Papert doesn't envision change coming from the top or arriving in the form of centralized reform. His story begins from the stubbornness of School to change, and he already saw in 1993 how it works to co-opt the computer in an attempt to limit its subversive potential. School assimilates the computer to its ways, using the computer to aid instruction "without questioning the structure or the educational goals of traditional School" (p. 41). It is then no surprise that

---

[4] See (Papert, 1997) for his own statement of and rebuttal to Tyack and Cuban and other common criticisms of his dream for progressive educational technology.

> School did not let itself change under the influence of the new device; it saw the computer through the mental lens of its own ways of thinking and doing. It is a characteristic of conservative systems that accommodation [change on the part of School in response to the transformative uses of new technologies] will come only when the opportunities of assimilation have been exhausted. (p. 41)

In fact, Papert explicitly doubts the inherent capacity of central action—even reform—to be capable of addressing the needs of progressive education.

Just as Papert does not dismiss what progressives have ultimately aimed for, only the strength and fervor with which they have been able to pursue their dreams, we should be careful to dismiss his work or our authors' with the trite response, "been there, done that". One lesson to learn from this history should be to dissuade us from the incautious empiricism progressives often trick themselves into. If our reports on the use of new learning technologies limit themselves to seeing our work as developing instruments to be applied to the existing problems of learning, we have ceded our ground before the battle begins. If we are instead after whole new ways of thinking about and accomplishing learning, we should remain committed to that interpretation in our measurements and reflections as well as our production and use.

Papert saw the singularity of the computer, the strength with which it changed our sense of what was possible in the world, and saw an opportunity for megachange in education. He saw a chance to avoid the traps we have inadvertently built around learning in the process of putting together School. And while the three decades since Logo and computers in classrooms have not brought about the utopia we might wish for, today there are more and better equipped rebels than ever before. Thanks to the computer and now to two more technologies in the intervening years—internet to connect those computers and mobile to put those advances your pocket—yearners like our authors are able to produce and collaborate together across institutional boundaries.

MOBILE AND THE INTERNET: TWO NEW TOOLS

We have so far hinted at the analogy between the twin revolutions of the computer and mobile and the internet in terms of their similarity. Briefly, it is worth considering some differences between the tools available then and now to see what it is about the internet and mobile that are specific advances for those of us hoping to push forward the ideals of progressive learning. There are of course many differences that have been discussed extensively elsewhere (e.g. Klopfer and Squire, 2008), but three stand out as salient for us: 1) multiplicity of software environments for digital creation, 2) speed of communication, and 3) overwhelming pressure from and connections to life outside School. Many of these are not specifically affordances of mobile, but may more properly be described as the power of people connected by the internet when it is in most everyone's pocket.

When Papert wrote *Mindstorms*, Logo in classrooms and computer labs was really one of the only games in town when it came to large numbers of people having access to the combination of hardware, software, and inspiration necessary to make use of the computer to do something new. Papert describes Logo as not only for doing a new kind of math but for connecting multiple arenas of life. He's especially proud of a collaboration between students using Logo in the name of dance. But we can now look at Logo and see how little of life is touched by its use compared to the programs and services available today. Since then, tools with obvious appeal outside the hard-edged computer culture have proliferated greatly, their reach has been vastly extended by both the internet and changes to how software is bought and sold (e.g. open source, mobile apps). With the incorporation of multiple media forms and advanced interface design, connecting out from a very computer centric interface and programmer mindset has become but one of many cognitive styles grounding these tools and their default uses.[5]

The internet has done more than speed up software distribution. It has fundamentally changed the routes by which people can communicate and collaborate. Back in 1993, when Papert mentioned the thousands of educators who were exploring with Logo, we can appreciate that these points of light were either scattered rather diffusely through the country, largely concentrated in particular areas (say near MIT), or some combination of both. For those trying to do the good work away from a geographical center of the movement, we can appreciate how minimal and infrequent any contact with others nearer the center might have been. For example, my own elementary school teachers, Mrs. Robinson and Mrs. Jackson, were excellent teachers but somewhat disconnected from the technology in use at our school. When I was six, they did like many others and took us to the computer lab for an hour a week and moved into the background. This was my first exposure to computers and Logo. Could their practices have evolved further or more quickly were they more connected with others engaged in similar endeavors?[6]

So today, I take it for granted that I, sitting here in New Mexico just as geographically and maybe socioculturally disconnected from our authors in Wisconsin, New York, or Cambridge as my elementary school teachers were in the early eighties, nevertheless have many ways of thinking and acting together with other explorers of MML across the globe. We are truly working together, only many miles apart. It's not so much that the world is flat, but deep connections can be made across great distances between regular people with tools that are today common.

---

[5] Although I am as likely to think first of fancy software as the next technological idealogue, just consider what has been enabled by Microsoft Word, email, and the humble internet forum in the way of connecting and empowering people to follow their dreams. If we could more consistently realize the value of even simple tools by today's standards for progressive learning, we'd be there already.

[6] All the same, I remember Logo fondly. Those hours with it in the lab were memorable moments of creative power with computers. Our use bore no connection to what we did in math, but I had the freedom to play with Logo there, and enjoyed using it to make abstract landscapes through absurd adjustments of the turtle's parameters. More than most of the official curricula in elementary school, it had a subtle but profound impact on my understanding of myself, computers, and learning that continues to evolve today.

By making it far easier for people to collaborate across long distances, the internet has also altered the ways in which grassroots action can become broader change. Initiatives no longer need to occur at massive scale to be viable because resources, participation, and momentum can be carried through those distances with so much less effort than before. To understand this change in orientation, recall Papert's skepticism that central planning would be willing and able to deliver progressive education. In part this is a simple organizational impracticality: a hierarchical model of delivery and adoption has narrow bandwidth; if change comes from the top, that limits the diversity possible of what is delivered to the masses. It is as true with educational materials as it is for television broadcasts. Some diversity can be accommodated, and this is typically through the usual segmentation of School into disciplines, grade levels, and job descriptions: this stuff for Geometry classes, this other stuff for English AP, this stuff for elementary classrooms, these are the responsibilities of teachers, textbook authors, and so on. In this model, where change comes from the top, its implementation should be capable of directly influencing a great number of people (every 8th grade math teacher) to be worth adopting and its instrumentation should be possible within the bureaucracy (teachers don't have time to write books; they have lesson planning to do). Conversely, when thousands of people can work together not based upon being 8th grade math teachers, but say an interest in locative data collection, they can organize along the lines of their shared interests, taking conversations farther, producing materials, and cross-pollinating without any official means to do so. The work of a few can more easily spread and mature without ever needing to seek the route of the tens of millions.

Finally, and where we begin to see how the promise of the computer and internet are actually made material with mobile, we have the incredibly fast adoption and the thoroughness with which mobile technology has become enmeshed with everyday life. On the one hand, access has already been discussed as a necessary ingredient. We suddenly live in a time of near universal adoption of mobile internet devices.[7] This was never true with non-mobile computers and might never be. On the other hand, even more important than simple access are the secondary effects of widespread use, especially when we consider the ability of School to employ its standard tactics of assimilation.

With the computer, School defended its ways by assimilating the device, creating a new room—the computer lab—and a new field—the computational arts/sciences. Thus isolated, the computer's possible harm was minimized. But with mobile, you cannot relegate it to a special room or a certain field because students are bringing their devices to School in their pockets. Because School does not in most cases primarily provide access to these devices, it cannot limit their transformative uses in the same way they did with computers.

This doesn't mean School won't or hasn't tried to preclude the possibilities of mobile. Within formal educational environments the most common response to mobile technology remains to simply pretend it doesn't exist—"Put away your phones everybody!" The strategy has been to draw a line

---

[7] Serious issues of access remain, but there are several orders of magnitude difference between then and now—most teens and adults in the US have smartphones or similarly capable pocketed devices. Adoption across the rest of the world is perhaps even more fantastically fast. Cell phones are connecting the world as never before.

between productive thinking and use of these devices—"Phones are only used for texting your friends and Facebook! We are here to do real work"—and hence ban the use of them because they *distract students from learning*. As a long term strategy it seems untenable because mobile device use is so prolific outside the classroom, and not just for chatting and gossip. Mobile is pervasively useful for a lot of what we do in life despite time wasted on Facebook (ignoring for the moment the cogent argument that there might be something important to what we do there as well). As people like our authors continue to develop instances of powerful learning enabled by mobile technologies, more and more of the public will realize that learning isn't somehow magically exempt from the influence of this technology. Phones aren't necessarily disruptive to learning, simply disruptive to the order of the typical School classroom. It will become more and more difficult to see School as contributing value to people's lives—not merely acting as an entitled gatekeeper—if it so aggressively ignores such a major part of them.

MAKING THE MOST OF MOBILE

Our—the editors'— job in putting together these stories is to share a common sense of purpose among them, to help you to see them for their similarities and importance. What I see in this book is a cross section of the sort of grassroots action Papert described emerging around Logo three decades ago. Our authors use these tools not to gain simple efficiencies within the existing system but to find new ways to organize and think about learning. This activity is made possible through the existence of robust software, the availability of appropriate hardware, and a cultural awareness that change is possible and can be effected by those on the ground floor. I hope this book can be a part of spreading that awareness and inspiration. Within each discipline or grade level at a single school, there are likely not enough of us to make a dent in the status quo, but together across these contexts, we start to look a bit more substantial.

This is important because as students, teachers, and researchers—participants with each other in relation to School—we have our own choices to make. As Papert maintains, it is the progressives themselves who have thus far been too timid in realizing their vision (1993, p. 14). We are too often willing to stay in our silos or subjugate promises for substantial change to co-option by the status quo by interpreting them as mere instruments of instruction. Researchers should recognize that meaningful change in School is about development work, not imposing new standards (p. 41). And what can hold teachers back is too tight a focus on what their students are supposed to learn while being inhibited to learn themselves (p. 72). The success or failure of mobile media learning to transform learning will be measured not in individual trials, but through our willingness to create with one another to make learning fly.

REFERENCES

Klopfer, E., & Squire, K. (2008). Environmental detectives - the development of an augmented reality platform for environmental simulations. *Education Technology Research and Development, 56,* 203–228.

Papert, S. (1980). *Mindstorms: Children, computers, and powerful ideas.* New York: Basic Books, Inc.

Papert, S. (1993). *The Children's Machine: Rethinking school in the age of the computer.* NewYork: Basic Books.

Papert, S. (1997). Why school reform is impossible. *Journal of the Learning Sciences, 6*(4), 417-427.

Cuban, L., & Tyack, D. (1995). *Tinkering toward utopia: A century of public school reform.* Nation. Cambridge, MA: Harvard University Press.

CHAPTER THREE

When, Where, and How:
Practical Considerations When Designing Your Own Mobile Media Learning

John Martin, Seann Dikkers, Breanne Litts, and Christopher Holden

It can be a daunting task to imagine integrating new media into an existing program or even starting from scratch: Where should I even start? What should I do in my context? What if I don't have a budget for resources? What are the tradeoffs of using one design over the other? These are questions we and our authors also ask ourselves each and every time we start a new project. This chapter is designed specifically as a bit of practical help to support you as you take on the challenge of navigating the uncertain territory of MML.

The first piece of advice we have to offer, one that is thoroughly borne out in the chapters that follow, is that there are many entry points and learning goals to pursue using mobile technologies; there is no one right way, specific class or subject that is a better fit than any other. MML is and should be a place of diverse interactions and development.

IDENTIFY YOUR LEARNING GOALS AND STRATEGIES

The applicable goals for MML are broad, centered around "increasing agency" within the processes of learning. The list of values derived from Papert's work in the last chapter (p. 19) should be a useful, though by no means complete, framework for thinking about the ways in which agency might be increased. There are some specific affordances of mobile that are worth paying attention to when conceiving how you might implement MML in your learning context. Remember, the point of all this is not simply to translate paper instruction to a small screen. Rather, picking up mobile media should be a way of enacting learning you care deeply about. Depending on whether you design a simple content-driven tour or your students are producing interactive content, outlining the bounds of your pedagogical situation in terms of goals, time, and technology will help scope the potential designs you can tackle.

One way to think about the agency leveraged in the design and use of MML is to focus on who is doing the creative work of making. Agency is key in making an experience authentic. If nothing that participants do makes a difference in the experience, then it means they are not really doing anything. Certainly a big step in this direction is the act of designing and enacting learning activities with MML rather than using what is handed down to you from someone else. There are many places to situate the agency you want to develop. Within an activity, participants inherently have less agency as consumers than as producers, but this does not mean the only way to increase learners' agency is to have them constantly in the driver's seat. Mobile media can help support existing high-agency designs as well as be used to develop them from scratch.

Start by asking yourself some guiding questions to frame your design:

Identify a Connection. Do you want players to learn about a historical event? Do you want them to gain data collection skills? Or do you want them to critically engage with place through producing? Approach design with what experiences you want participants to end up with and the objectives of your time. How do you want this learning time to end? How will you know if you have ended there? How and where is your use of mobile media relevant? What unexpected or emergent outcomes can you anticipate or support? Finally, what designs will lead to that ending?

Identify desired results. Should students merely remember and understand concepts? Or use your design to take on the roles of professionals? If so, are they actually contributing to the field, like with citizen science data collection type activities, or does their mimicry have other motivations, like being able to see the world from a new perspective? Should they apply and analyze concepts by reviewing and evaluating each others' examples? Should they know more about a building or park? Should they have 'met' a historical character? Observed something in the world? Or should they struggle with creating artifacts to teach peers? Some results are best met with MML, some may not be. This is an area to look for a good match between affordances of MML to create an experience and what learning you'd like to see happen.

Determine what learners are going to do and how you are going to know they have done it. Do you want to use mobile media to give exposure to content, or are you planning to have them demonstrate a higher order thinking through your design? Could learners build a presentation with data gathered from the field? Will they need to work together to solve a problem that exists entirely within the mobile media? Should they be able to tell a story? The action of learning can take a variety of forms. Consider the verbs your design will enable in the name of learning and how these verbs work across the multiple media in your design.

RESPECT WHO YOU ARE

It is also important to look inward. It is easy to forget that learning opportunities don't just depend on theoretical frameworks but your personality and the specifics of the situations you're working in.

These more personal qualities should be seen as essential ingredients in the making of something new and explicitly reflected upon in the planning stages.

Specifically, start with learning about yourself, as this will influence your design decisions implicitly whether or not you acknowledge such explicitly. It's important to identify a path that feels most authentic to you. Starting here will help you determine your own comfort levels regarding chaos and control—beginning afresh with new media can be intimidating. To own and leverage up front what you bring the table plays a large role in whether and how you continue when you confront challenges.

If you lean instructionist—orienting naturally to the management of the details of what students learn and how they learn it—you may want to begin with a didactic approach to your use of mobile media. Perhaps, make something for students to consume (like a tour) or directly enact (like a story) as opposed to setting up scenario in which the students are doing the creating. Mobile can deliver content and information that builds knowledge. By situating your content in the outside world instead of within a textbook in a classroom, you may be able to transform the learning of specific content and skills from an unwelcome chore into something students really connect with.

If you lean constructivist—always looking for opportunities to give students space to bring prior knowledge, attitudes, and opinions into their learning—you may find it easier to begin with an open-ended approach. For instance, have students collect and create mobile media themselves or ask them to contribute choices and/or creativity framing a subject or challenge around their own interests. This approach can both be empowering for students and remove some of the work you need to put in ahead of time for the production of media.

We mention these two leanings as a way to say that MML can accommodate many personalities, not to further the misconception that the two approaches are mutually exclusive. Within the examples in this book for example, it is common for the actual media produced or interacted with to be rather didactic while the learning activities the media belong to are anything but. Garza and Rosenblum (chapter 9) describe the rather open-ended learning scenario of a design course but where their use mobile media filled a specific, almost rote goal to give students a mobile-mediated tour of a neighborhood.

As you look outward from yourself to your design, remember the power of empathy. Notice how our authors are learners too. Their design and use of MML is not only for the people on the other end of their designs. When we conceive of learning only as transmission of knowledge from experts to novices, we miss the value of empathy that allows teachers and students to share the journey. This also means that the most important quality to have as an educator looking to use MML is not expertise with the technologies, but an interest in learning.

PLAN FOR THE TIME YOU HAVE

Time is always short. It is an unavoidable consideration of designing a MML activity. But many have found it possible to manage. To begin, there are two main units of time that you should consider: 1) planning time—how much time do you have for design?, and 2) play time—how much time are students going to spend with what you create?

If available planning time is minimal, consider shorter designs or sharing the design time with the learners. Regardless of the tools being used, designs get longer when they involve intricate or multiple interactions within software and when you are preparing and producing even non-interactive media for consumption or use through mobile devices. AR games that are meant to be played by learners as exposure to content or participation in an interactive story typically require a lot of research, planning, design, testing, and iteration.

Design time in these areas can be lessened if you are willing to let the experience outside the device, say in the observation of the world, provide the majority of the content you are exposing learners to; creating simpler activity types, say a simple tour or scavenger hunt instead of a fully interactive story; relying upon actions learners may already know how to do with their devices, say taking pictures and video; or even creating structural details ahead of time to be filled in by learners.

Some of these strategies avoid time spent in planning stages by having learners doing the principal production of mobile media. By conducting field research—guiding players to gather data from the world—you can avoid the work of creating a story or digital interactions ahead of time. Another option is to have the learners become designers and create their own projects.

Though learner-created designs can require much less planning time on the front end, they can often take significant play time to frame, guide, enact, and debrief. As with designing any learning activity, time constraints can pose a threat to the learning goals, so it's important to weigh the tradeoffs and be realistic with what you can achieve in the time you have. For example, field research projects often require significantly less time designing, yet require time to debrief and build project work. Asking learners to spend an afternoon visiting a neighborhood (chapter 9) offers a different type of learning experience than taking learners on a 15-week around the world field research trip (chapter 4). Conversely, investing more time in a designed project can create a fairly packaged, rich, experience within a fixed amount of play time (chapters 15-18).

For designs that involve outdoor activities or exploration, time management has additional features. It is important to consider the act of traveling to and between destinations, balancing time spent doing things on devices with other activities like debriefing or walking. It takes time to walk from one place to another, and with MML this should be part of the designed experience. Fisher and Dikkers (chapter 18) suggest, for example, that an outdoor AR game gets a little tiresome after the first hour of play, but they pushed up against this time limit wanting to cover physical distance on the ground and emotional distance in the development of their game's story. Ultimately though, there are no hard and fast rules for dealing with time in MML projects.[1] One advantage provided by mobile technology is to divide attention across time and place in ways others than those given by the industrial schedule followed for most organized learning experiences. MML doesn't have to happen during class time.

Iteration is our final and most important word of advice concerning time. Even though you can never test your ideas enough, find ways to test them early and often. Look for mention of it in our authors' chapters. Every new process is easier and begins to feel natural the more familiar you are with it—seeing the process through a few times helps. The amount of planning that goes into the first version of anything is huge, and there are always so many details you cannot see until you get there. The second time you try something, you have the benefit of less planning time but that is when the bad luck seems to strike. The third time's a charm. By then you start to know what to expect and have hit your stride. Plan to learn a lot from early iterations. Look for student volunteers to play ahead of structured times too, many students are excited to help and can provide valuable insights.

PLAN FOR THE TECHNOLOGY YOU HAVE AND WILL USE

You have identified your learning goals and mapped those onto realistic time constraints, now what? Maybe you do not consider yourself a techy. Maybe you don't have enough devices for your program or classroom. Good news: MML doesn't require the newest, fanciest mobile devices, or any at all. Instead, the goal and main challenge of MML is to connect people to learning.

Just as with time, the point of considering tech is not just to demand more, but to make plans in accordance with what you have and want to use. Consider that there are a wide variety of tools available to you. Some are things, some are relationships, some are ways of doing things. Since the focus on mobile tends to be about devices like smartphones and tablets, it is worth pointing out that you can get started with pencil and paper alone.

Rich learning activities can be produced with greatly varying levels of access (Table 1) to advanced technologies. Incredible locative experiences have long been afforded with paper maps. Indeed papercraft should not be forgotten. Envelopes coded to open at various places can add authenticity and mystery to a locative design.[2] Technology that can be found in most library storage closets (old cameras, audio recorders, and the like) or that which is ubiquitous among your audience (texting to contact learners or have them ping you) can be appropriated with intent. Even as your designs scale in the advanced technologies they make use of, you do not need a full classroom set of smart

---

[1] An exception: Hofstadter's Law, "It always takes longer than you expect, even when you take into account Hofstadter's Law."
[2] See Colleen Macklin and Thomas Guster's chapter in our previous Mobile Media Learning book.

devices; if some students have devices (sometimes this strategy is referred to as BYOD—bring your own device), you can group learners or use the devices you can provide to fill in gaps of access. Also a combination of advanced and simpler tools can be used together creatively (one notetaker with a clipboard, a photographer with a camera, and a navigator with the smartphone). Navigating your local landscape of access can help you find a way to make MML part of your pedagogical toolbox in many situations.

Table 1. Types of technology available for MML to educators.

Old-Tech	Low-Tech	Some-Tech	Class-Tech	Super-Tech
Notebooks Paper maps Envelopes + Notes Plaques	Simple cameras Simple recorders Instant Messaging (i.e. Remind101)	Smart Devices (1/group) BYOD resources Digital text	Classroom set of Smart devices Local WiFi Digital images	3G or 4G connections Battery packs WiFi remote hubs Digital video/audio

That said, there are specific features of the technological landscape worth paying attention to directly. The two main ones are hardware and internet access. Look for their mention in the chapters that follow. Most of our authors have found unique and inventive ways to put together the logistical pieces necessary to get their ideas off the ground. As above, hardware can refer to a large category of things. But as you plan and look forward, we are talking about smartphones, tablets, and (for the moment) iPod Touches. There are two dominant software platforms: iOS and Android. While it is important to pay attention to this fact—apps are frequently available for only one platform or the other, and Taleblazer is the only design tool used by our authors available on both iOS and Android—too many good ideas have been halted by insisting on cross-platform compatibility as a credo. Pay more attention to the ecology of devices available and desirable in your situation. For example, if you are having students explore a neighborhood, a bulky tablet may be unwieldy and feel out of place. In such situations smaller devices may be a better bet, even if that means relying upon those owned by participants rather than those provided by a school or program.

Finding reliable internet access that will satisfy your needs is a bit trickier, but again look for how our authors have addressed this issue. Check your software, your WiFi and/or cellular connections, and the technology your learners have. Mobile software frequently either requires internet access to function or to make use of the features users care most about. Many devices provided through schools and programs can only access the internet through WiFi, meaning they cannot in general access the internet out in the world. Smartphones and some tablets on the other hand can access the internet through their cellular connection (3G or 4G). The reason so many apps essentially require an internet connection is due to the assumption that most people using these apps are doing so on devices like these. The BYOD strategy can often be of help here, but when it comes to filling in the gaps, you can also provide access through mobile hotspots.[3] These are routers that receive an internet signal through cellular towers, just like a smartphone, and pass it on to a handful of devices via WiFi. Another solution is turning on a smartphone's hotspot capabilities. Cellular data is almost always metered, available through different prices, devices, and with varying reliability regionally, and if you are working through organizations, there may be restrictions on which services you can use depending on how you are allowed to pay for or be reimbursed for devices and service charges.

Finally, if all of this is beyond you, ask your local IT support staff for help by asking, "Can these devices use X software at Y location?" They should be able to help and navigate solutions with you easily. Many of our writers did just this and were able to practically move forward with their design ideas. Start with what you have and plant seeds for funding what you want, but don't let this stop you from starting today. Determine what you have so that you don't spend needless time hoping for more technology, writing grants, or setting aside your good intentions to design. Design now. Iterate. Experiment. Dream bigger after you've done a few 'pilot studies' or 'paper prototypes'.

A BEGINNER'S FRAMEWORK FOR MML ACTIVITIES

Certainly, we want our authors' specific examples of subjects, activities, and methods of designing and engaging in MML to inspire you into action. You will see approaches and designs that are worth borrowing heavily from. We also offer in this chapter a framework of three styles of MML activities as a practical lens through which to view these various examples: See, Explore, and Design. Each of these styles or modes has many uses. It may be easiest to get started by following one of these three paths for your first design. Table 2 summarizes our discussion of these styles and indicates examples of them within our authors' chapters. There is also some correlation between these styles and the discussions of how ARIS (chapter 6) and App Inventor (chapter 5)—software for the creation of mobile media used by our authors and useable by novices—are used.

See. Where you produce mobile media for learners to consume or interact with as a way to learn something. This mode of communication is from one (designers) to many (consumers), and because the content can be decided in advance, is often seen as doable without disrupting too much the typical classroom format.

Explore. Where you create opportunities for learners to collect, share, discuss, organize, or report back on observations or acts in the outside world. Similar to many citizen science projects, students can gather data from the world to produce new knowledge.

Design. Where students have a chance to design, create, and often test mobile media for others. Using some of the same tools that you would use to create within the categories above, learners can be guided, in typically open-ended design studios that last several weeks to a full semester.

---

[3] The most popular mobile hotspot for years has been the MiFi. Sometimes you will hear this as the generic term for a mobile hotspot.

Table 2. See, Explore, and Design: Three principal styles of MML and examples of each throughout the book.

Strategy	Explanation	Specific Examples and Create/Play Hours (C/P)
See	Instructor designs mobile media and learners use it to receive content and practice skills.	*School Scene Investigators*—An AR game for young people to play to learn science and how to work together (chapter 7). The examples of ethnography provided to students (chapter 8). Sample apps learners remake before jumping to their own creation (chapter 14). *Quest for the Cities of Gold*—An AR game museum patrons interact with to learn history (chapter 15). *ParkQuest*—An AR game event participants play to get them to explore the outdoors (chapter 16). *Lift Off!*—An AR game to enhance the experience of patrons of an aircraft museum (chapter 17). *Horror on the Ridges*—An AR game to make players scared (chapter 18).
Explore	Instructor designs a framework for learners to explore or document an aspect of the world. Learners use mobile to gather and work with information.	Ethnographic work via ARIS (chapter 8). *Explore East Austin*—AR tour that provides a framework for documenting a neighborhood (chapter 9). *Traveler*—An app for students to document field studies (chapter 4). Documenting and reporting on bee behavior (chapter 12). Students explore political issues to include in a geocaching game (chapter 13).
Design	Instructor creates opportunities for learning through design of mobile media and use by peers or others.	Almost every one of our authors and the editors as they have created their own projects, but specifically Bressler (chapter 7), Stauder (chapter 11), May (chapter 15), Rieder and Soloman (chapter 16), and Fisher (chapter 18) because they worked on their designs as students. Folklore based AR games (chapter 8). Visual design projects (chapter 9). Experimental mobile cinema (chapter 10). Mobile game design camp (chapter 11). Incorporating content into a geocaching game and designing and giving talks to the community about the game (chapter 13). Multi-site 12-week app design program (chapter 14).

An Example of See

MML can help us see what is often invisible. In the service of See, mobile media allows for a particularly rich form of presentation, perhaps most easily suggested by an outdoor AR tour. Tours have always worked by leveraging a real physical context as a naturally motivating setting for content. Tours accomplished through MML can make up for some of the things that can be difficult or less than optimal about tours. The tour guide need not be present, especially useful when you want students to hear the insight of an expert who would be difficult to have there in the flesh (e.g. an art historian in the museum). Content can be delivered via multiple media formats, highly customized, and interactive. Interactive design that is enacted not only on the device's screen but through a player's location and actions can come alive in a way it couldn't before mobile.

In tours and similar expressions of See, participants are situated to be somewhat passive—to listen or read and follow along the instructions and plan that is supplied by the guide. It is not constantly necessary to challenge the assumption that the students are there to master content that the teacher and textbook materials *know already*. Interacting with media in new ways can still be a way to make those ideas come alive and take on new, deeper meanings.

By aiming to make a better, cheaper tour, MML can give us more opportunities to leave the classroom and rejoin the world. A common group experience that provides concrete experience and examples related to course content can be a powerful precursor to class discussion and reflection. If the goal is to get the students to experience a place, and physical interaction is enough to convey course concepts (or to provide an experience for the group to unpack later in class), then a tour can be created cheaply and easily.

However, the experience of being on a tour is largely composed of listening and following. Standalone tours can be more work to make and be less engaging for students because a rich interactive tour requires a great deal of polished media which requires a large budget, premade media assets, and skilled help to create. A tour where content is primarily delivered on screen also typically faces the following challenges:

- Mobile content can be difficult to read due to external distractions, screen glare, weather, etc. Too much text to read on the tour is a common design mistake.
- Absorbing content while walking can be dangerous and distracting.
- Screen content can compete with place-based content. Instead of seeing the example in the world, the tour focuses the learners on what is on-screen).

A few considerations for the design of an MML tour:

- Choose local places/phenomena that are worth witnessing in person (e.g. tree fungus, ongoing protests, architectural examples, hangouts for sub-cultures, etc.).
- Plan non-content parts of the tour (e.g. travel time) as part of the learning experience. Design ways for learners to digest their experiences between moments of delivery.
- The primary goal is to design the experiences you want students to have, not produce another container for content to be absorbed by them.

- Weather tends to turn bad at the least opportune times. Design flexibly to accommodate unforeseen logistical problems and expect to find new ones when you actually run the tour with students.
- Since a tour may not provide much depth of activity for students, design additional activities for students build on their experiences from the tour.

Regardless of how polished the tour, we suggest that you design it to make the best use of the world and the device. Use the screen to provide prompts for them to interact and engage in the environment they're visiting. It makes little sense to bring students outside the classroom if their primary activity is reading or watching a screen, however bringing them to relevant places can enliven class content and engage learners in very powerful ways.

An Example of Explore

Exploring with MML gains benefit from making observation collective and reflective. All you need to do is create a framework of interesting questions to prompt students to engage in meaningful exploration of the outside world. This is not new, and mobile devices are in no way necessary to pull it off. But they do have something to offer. The area of collection and the acts of collection are typically simple and self-contained. The research agenda and collection types can be determined in advance, making it simple for newcomers to get started.

The verbs that we find in Explore—take photos, videos, send notes, look up—are familiar and need little introduction for learners because they are the same verbs smartphone users have quickly grown accustomed to and now take for granted. The Traveler app (chapter 4) was developed specifically to combine some of the existing documentation capabilities of mobile devices into a format relevant to field studies. Not only do mobile devices have an inherent and usually familiar ability to collect many kinds of data, but their contextual awareness permits the easy assignment of relevant metadata (from GPS coordinates of a photo to supplying keywords for categorizing data), and their ability to support communication through the internet can enable data to be quickly shared and worked on together or to be related to bodies of existing knowledge. In chapter 6 for example, Tim Frandy had his students learn ethnography by doing it. Their first efforts—of varying quality—were instantly shareable with the class. This variability of quality became useful for the students to reflect on and improve their practices as junior ethnographers. Others may use these same capabilities to pool information and debrief about what has been found out together by everyone. This is how Jameela Jafri et al. had their students use mobile to document bee behavior (chapter 11).

The promise of distributed data gathering, made easy with mobile, encourages us to think about projects along the lines of citizen science, ethnography, and journalism, where young people with devices are enabled through mobile devices to apprentice important professional activities and find important and meaningful data. But there are also some things to be careful about when Exploring with MML:

- Not all data is important or good data. Spending a lot of time and effort gathering data that turns out to be junk can be a real let down.
- The technology allows for simple data collection, but the automatic tools for interpretation are minimal so far. ARIS for example can know that a person has taken a photo and where, but not what of.
- Gathering data, as simple as it can be to do, is also on its own not always a very deeply engaging activity.
- Data collection within formal educational environments especially can quickly lead to tricky privacy issues. For example, the geotagged videos shared through the internet are not just of bees.

A few considerations for the design of a data collection activity with MML:

- Know what you want to use the gathered information for ahead of time. The focus can be on the development of skills in addition to the value of the data gathered.
- Plan ahead for how and how far the gathered data is going to be shared. Implement appropriate procedures to ensure the limits of sharing are clear and easy to effect.
- Don't just involve learners with the tedious, repetitive parts of the work. Some of what they do should be at the level of interpretation, analysis, and synthesis of the information they collect.
- Find ways for learners to work together, not just as autonomous units.
- Do your homework locating appropriate software. Because data collection is what mobile devices do, there are many, many options of tools that might best fit your particular circumstances.

An Example of Design

You learn the most when you can make something real you care about. Having learners create with mobile media is often the fastest route to increasing their agency in the learning process. It is also the messiest.

Instances of Design will usually involve a perspective or framework of inquiry consistent with your themes or content as a way to make the creation of mobile media relevant to your specific learning context. Students can also be included in different aspects of the design process, resulting in more or less open-endedness in the design activity. Juan Rubio's *Race to the Whitehouse* (chapter 13) had youth largely fill out an existing design by researching and preparing content, but Tim Frandy's students (chapter 8) were given a rather blank slate for several weeks of the semester to develop their mobile media connected to folklore. Design projects allow students to gain knowledge and understanding of course concepts—to be able to reproduce them in their designs—at the same time as they develop media and design skills.

Student-created projects are fairly simple to set up and run. There is need for production teams to painstakingly design and test a complicated media artifact. But you and students should be comfortable with a bit of chaos. To be successful, you need to trust that students are resourceful and smart enough to solve problems. You need to limit the complexity of projects according to students' skill levels and time allotted.

One pitfall to avoid is the "digital native" fallacy: assuming too much about the skills and experiences with media your students already have because they grew up with technology. Despite students' typical familiarity with mobile devices and videogames, they are just as typically inexperienced in the production of mobile media beyond some basic activities like taking a photo or shooting a simple video clip. Something like an AR game is just as alien to them at first as it may have been to you. Having students create with mobile media seems to work especially well after they experience something you or others have already created. A nearby model to work from can be instructional and inspirational. Often learners will want to show that they can do a better job at it than you.

Again, there is nothing about Design that requires mobile media per se. But students can more easily imagine something like an AR game they created having a life beyond the classroom instead of a paper they wrote. This doesn't have much to do with the differences in media but how we are used to making use within educational contexts of student production with a specific medium. Students' typical attitudes to paper writing are developed only after years of writing them only to be read by a teacher and only for a grade. When students think they are working on something real, they tend to put more time and effort in polishing it because it is something they want to share with their friends and family.

Student design sounds from a distance like a rich and conceptually simple way to increase agency in learning. "Make stuff!" just might be the progressive educational mantra of the age. But just as "discovery learning" for example is now disregarded especially for the lack of structure associated with it, we are careful here to note that facilitating student design is a complex and nuanced practice. It easy easy enough to fail by simply saying to your students, "Welcome. Make something cool by the end of the semester. That is all."

Some of the complexities inherent in facilitating student design owe to the complexity of the media and design processes itself. Another source of tension: shoehorning an open-ended process designed to produce diverse, emergent outcomes into educational structures that are not always tolerant of this. Design is messy and School eschews messes. Open-ended design can be uncomfortable for students used to traditional learning environments. Some of the specific challenges you may encounter:

- Fitting design activities in time slots and spaces set up for content acquisition.
- Trying to balance content acquisition, skill development, and attention to process in the time you spend with students, the time they spend on their work, and in how their work is evaluated.
- Developing internal motivation to create in situations where students are already motivated by the grade they will receive.
- Choosing topics for design (see chapter 14 for how Technovation Challenge has struggled to define good topics for their design challenges).
- Organizing student labor (Can people work alone? Do you choose teams?).
- Evaluating individuals based on group effort.
- Helping students to find focus and purpose in an open-ended learning environment.
- Evaluating and facilitating quality media design in avant garde formats (what makes a good AR game?).[4]

Consider ways to make the opportunity for learners to design and produce with mobile media more productive and less terrifying than it sometimes can be:

- Consider offering alternative options when it comes to format (papers, posters, videos, etc.) for them. In Frandy's class (chapter 6), students were given the choice for their final project of creating a WordPress website, a Digital Video, or an MML project; about 1/3 chose each.
- Structure the design process itself clearly. An example: pitch the idea, share rough cuts multiple times with peers for feedback, and a presentation date to share a final version with the rest of the class.
- Your students are not alone in learning how to create with mobile media. Create trust by sharing your struggles as a new designer in this space.
- Find ways to make your students' designs capable of living outside the classroom. May (chapter 15) continued her design work in a class as an independent study and collaboration with a local museum. This can be simple too. Successful designs one year can be used to model design the following semester.
- Complex designs can be better pulled off by a well-functioning team than an individual. Find ways to promote cross-functional teamwork—in how you facilitate and evaluate—instead of having students divide up content and responsibilities equally.

---

[4] Paper writing assignments again provide a good warning. The supposed mechanics of a good paper—especially minimum page length—have been become so prominent in how writing is evaluated that they have replaced attention to actual quality of communication.

- Start small when the situation cannot support larger design efforts. In chapter 13, Juan Rubio describes involving youth in only fulfilling an existing design due to the project's limited amount of time.

CONCLUSION

There are many ways to make use of MML in very diverse learning contexts and content areas. Especially in formal learning environments, increasing learner agency with MML can often be described as making connections outside the classroom. This can be about seeing how content and ideas take on a new life out in the real world, exploring it and bringing it back in together, or making something that might live on outside the classroom. In the following chapters, you will see all these modes in play, often at the same time. The experiences our authors share should help fill out the skeletal framework we have laid out in this chapter and help give it meaning when it comes to thinking about your own work with MML.

SECTION TWO

MML Platforms

4.   Traveler: A Digital Journal for Enhancing Learning and Retention on Field Trips
5.   MIT App Inventor: Democratizing Personal Mobile Computing
6.   ARIS: Augmented Reality for Interactive Storytelling

This section contains chapters whose main focus is the elucidation of a software platform designed for MML. The chapter about Traveler also describes its first real use to help document architecture and planning field studies, while App Inventor and ARIS are used by some of our authors. Each of these three platforms is available to use by the general public for free. Since beginning this book, another platform used by one of our authors— MIT's Taleblazer used by Coulter—has become generally available. Platforms like these make it possible for normal educators to make use of the ideal affordances of mobile media in practice. Not only do they facilitate production of media, collection of data, communication, etc., they are underdetermined, allowing for significant creative and diverse interpretation by their users. Unlike software whose use is more scripted, Learning Management Systems for example, these software platforms allow educators and learners to articulate their own ideas through MML.

CHAPTER FOUR

Traveler: A Digital Journal for Enhancing Learning and Retention on Field Trips

Lohren Ray Deeg
Assistant Professor of Urban Planning, Department of Urban Planning, College of Architecture and Planning, Ball State University, Muncie, Indiana, USA | ldeeg@bsu.edu

Kyle Parker
Senior Software Engineer for Developing Technologies, Information Technology Services, Ball State University, Muncie, Indiana, USA | kyleparker@bsu.edu

---

The sketching trip is a time honored architectural tradition rooted in field-based observation and recording. To learn from great examples of the constructed environment and transmit those lessons to a project-based design studio, students are first asked to experience the spatial, social, and material dimensions and details of a place. The experiences gained by walking through cities and major sites are at the core of our educational approach. A dozen students enrolled in a field study follow their instructor around a corner and down a street, dutifully take photographs of a house designed by Frank Lloyd Wright, and then follow around a bend, up an avenue, and into a church yard to sketch a quaint and contemplative cloister. They'll do this all day long, and, yes, they will be learning. It is a core foundation for formal architecture education and remains a memorable learning experience for generations of students. As P.D. Smith writes, "The city needs to be explored at a walking pace and discovered step by step. For understanding a city is, indeed, a cumulative process not unlike turning the pages of a book" (2012, p. 169).

At the same time, we have seen over and over again that despite the reputation of the sketching trip as a learning experience, our students don't seem to retain much of what they see when they come back to the classroom. After the trip, students will often have no idea where they've been or how those places were connected. By the time they are discussing the trip in class, they usually don't even recall the route they took or the locations where they captured photos and made sketches. Something is missing. With today's technology at our disposal, it should be easy and effortless for students to revisit that step-by-step journey instead of fumbling through a pile of disconnected photos and sketches. If technology could help assist students with recall, they might be able to make better use of what they had experienced in the field.

While there are many mobile apps available for students to use on field study trips—Evernote, Dropbox, Sketchbook, My Tracks, and Google Docs, just to name a few—they lack a single interface to tie everything together. Luckily, Ball State University is fortunate enough to have a dedicated group of information technology staff able to help develop imaginative and creative projects to enhance the teaching and learning experiences of our students. So we set out to make Traveler, an Android tablet app that could help support our field studies by combining mapping with the collection of photos, sketches, and other media.

During the 2012-2013 academic year, we tested Traveler with two different field study programs offered within the College of Architecture and Planning at Ball State University. We started with a small group of freshmen students visiting the Chicago region for four days and ended with a larger group of upper-class and graduate students on a 15-week trip around the world. The trips served as critical in-field and real-life assessments of the app, the use of tablets, and our future desires and goals to embrace a mobile-centric student lifestyle. The union of teaching methods / pedagogy associated with field based learning opportunities with the development of software applications speaks to a commitment on the part of the University to advance and embrace new media in teaching and learning. Traveler is an example of this initiative and commitment.

ABOUT TRAVELER

The central feature of Traveler is an ability to record and visualize the path of a student in the field. Of course a path is only a line on a map. Our students in environmental design traditionally collect a variety of media, so the app was bundled with a variety of recording tools, and Traveler's real power then lies in its ability to pin, or geolocate, photos, audio notes, short videos, and even sketches to this path. This makes each student's path personal and establishes the trip as a series of experiences of movement through time and space. As shown in Figure 1, a student's richly annotated path is layered over a reference map powered by Google Maps.

Figure 1. A screenshot of Traveler in use. Media recording functions are located on the top row in red, an integrated map and recorded path is located in the lower right, and recorded media is referenced in the upper right gallery and right hand column.

Upon returning to the classroom, this annotated path becomes a powerful reference. Students can access the map to remind themselves of where they've been and what they saw. They can play back the pinned media through Traveler itself. Having this personalized travel journey documented gives students a way to engage aspects of the cultural landscape well after the field trip has concluded and may support rich and collaborative debriefings upon return to the classroom or studio.

Figure 2. A screenshot of Traveler in dynamic playback mode, using Google Earth.

The data collected within Traveler can also be used elsewhere, for example with Google Maps or Google Earth. Students can play back animations of their recorded paths in these programs, complete with three dimensional structures and environments. They can access their pinned materials there to relive the field study and recall the buildings, scenery, paths, and even people they saw along the way.

TRAVELER TRACKS WINDY CITY FIELD STUDIES

Our first test of Traveler was with 17 college freshmen on a four-day trip to Chicago. As an accompaniment to a studio-based environmental design course—a class that challenges students to invent, conceptualize, and design spaces for people—the Chicago field trip exposes students to several masterworks by notable designers and planners in history as well as recent trends and issues in architecture, landscape architecture, and urban planning.

Figure 3. Students use Traveler in Oak Park, Illinois.

Notable historic districts, such as Hyde Park, Lincoln Park, and Oak Park, contain small details and several different residential typologies typical of urban living. The Loop and Magnificent Mile contain landmarks that are recognized around the world. It's a trip Deeg—lead author of this chapter and instructor of the course—has taken many times before, always with students armed with an array of paper sketchbooks, pencils, markers, and cameras. However, students forget or do not pick up on the details or general atmosphere of these Chicago neighborhoods. This is particularly clear when we ask them to design a neighborhood later in the semester. We wanted to know if Traveler's recording and playback features could assist in the recall of a district's features.

We provided each student with a project-funded Android tablet pre-loaded with Traveler. Deeg and the software developer met with the students to introduce the functions of the tablet and Traveler app before departure. The students were enthusiastic about having a single device to carry instead of the books, drawing tools, and cameras in past offerings and were quick to learn the ins and outs of using the new app. However, we noticed that in some cases the time required to navigate the interface and menus drowned out their ability to experience place and to hear the history and observations shared by the instructors. As students' familiarity with Traveler increased, they seemed better able to absorb the information around them as well as to interact with the app.

New software requires careful observation of its use and the quick fixing of problems. The decision to send Parker—coauthor of this chapter and lead software developer of Traveler—to travel with the students was a very good one. Parker made some needed changes to Traveler in the field, troubleshooted issues, and enhanced the app to make it easier and quicker for students to access some of its features. Having the software developer travel along with this initial excursion was critical to enhancing the app's functionality and improved the students' reactions to the mobile media platform. For example the students discovered a big problem on the very first day of the field-test. They found that a certain gesture with the stylus erased their sketch without prompting them to save their work. To suddenly and irrevocably lose their work after spending 20 minutes sketching was obviously a concern. The next morning, each student received an updated version of Traveler before heading out for the day's tour. Having Parker there meant we were quickly able to address the issue and move on.

Students were able to capture many digital photographs of places along the field study route, often opting for a panoramic view of their surroundings (Figure 4) or to record short videos of large structures, panning and tilting instinctively to capture large buildings or tree lines. Students responded to different spaces with specific media choices, using a still photograph for most situations, or panoramas when spaces were expansive. When additional sensory information like water and sound were prevalent, students tended to record short video clips. These deliberate choices in media revealed what the students were observing. Wide, expansive views lent themselves to a panoramic photo, much to the surprise of Deeg, who wasn't aware that the tablet could record them. Observations of people moving through space over a period of time are well-represented by a short video or the sketched diagram with notes. As students became more comfortable with Traveler's interface, they learned that different kinds of recordings supported their observation and interpretation of the site. Where the terrain could accommodate a large group for a period of time, we stopped to do more fine, detailed sketches. Overall, we were pleased with how Traveler performed on its first outing and that using it fit in well with our ideas about what students should be doing to pay attention to and document the places they visited.

Figure 4. A student's panoramic photograph of the waterfall garden, Chicago Botanic Garden, Glencoe, Illinois. Photo by Taylor Sheppard.

In past field studies to Chicago, students were given time in the classroom after the field study to create sketches from their photographs. This work was well organized, thoughtfully laid out, and detailed, but because its submission was so separate from its creation, the sketches lacked spontaneity and even accuracy. In contrast, sketches done by this year's field study class, often completed in 30 minutes or less, were more dynamic and more easily became a part of their continued reflection on the trip, a marked difference between working in the field and in the classroom in the past. These activities supported the skills we wanted the students to develop—to see and observe the built environment and sketch it as a form of memory and retention. We feel that sketching from observation richens the experience of visiting a place and has the capacity to inform the later sketching that we encourage as part of the design process. Therefore, to understand architecture, and to later design good spaces and places, students are encouraged to sketch good spaces and places.

Figure 5. A student's sketch of the Mrs. Thomas H. Gale house in Oak Park, Illinois. Digital sketch by Paige Story.

In general, our students liked using Traveler and the tablets during the Chicago field study. We surveyed them afterwards to find out how well they liked Traveler and the tablets and whether they aided their studies and understanding of place. About three quarters said they enjoyed using the tablet in general, as they were allowed to keep them for a three-month period. Almost all either agreed or strongly agreed with the statement "I found the Traveler app to be useful during field trip week in October," which comprised their use on the four-day field trip. However, outside the trip—and during our sessions in the classroom—the students treated the tablet more like a novelty than an essential tool. On two separate occasions in the design studio course, which the field trip supported, Deeg asked for the tablets to be taken out and referenced. On each occasion, only two students out of 17 had brought the tablet to studio that day. Since the tablet was not perceived to be a necessary thing, our hope that the field trip information could be referenced in the studio did not really come to fruition. More activities that specifically integrate Traveler and the tablet will be necessary in the 15-week design studio timeline if we wish to do better.

TRAVELER JOINS THE WORLD TOUR

The second test for Traveler came during a very different kind of field study, one that took 24 upper-level and graduate students to 25 countries and 60 cities over a three-month period. The field study, called World Tour, is an intensive and fast-paced study of architecture, landscape architecture, and urban planning throughout Europe, Africa, and Asia. The diversity, complexity, and logistical limitations of some sites and locations and the trip's duration encouraged us to spend significant time and effort to prep these students to use Traveler. Parker met with the students on several occasions before World Tour to explain the features and capabilities of the app and showed them how to use it flexibly. For example, we knew there would not be reliable WiFi in several locations, so this required the students to save and load maps ahead of time. The training sessions were also meant to address the infrequency of reflective use we observed in the Chicago trip by helping the students see how the tablet and app could be used to review and evaluate their experiences to better aid in their projects and coursework.

Beyond preparing students to make more consistent and flexible use of Traveler during the field study, these preliminary training sessions focused on how the app and tablet might integrate with their tourist and academic activities during their time abroad. Students wanted to explore other apps and how to connect to peripheral devices to contribute to their ability to use the tablets for their coursework. They wanted to see how to integrate this with their other photography of the locations on the trip. Essentially, they wanted to know if they were going to be using the tablet anyway, did they need to take along a laptop too? How could the tablet serve as a functional alternative? Questions like these are of course going to come up and present additional challenges to introducing mobile-based curricula in classroom situations. They inform the continued development and polishing of our app and help us understand the flexibility of the app's possible use across disciplines.

As with the Chicago trip, Parker came along to help, joining the group for the first two weeks of the tour, testing and improving the app based on observational and experiential student use and feedback. The learning curve experienced by both instructors and students was facilitated well by this inclusion. Traveling with the group fostered collaborative discussions and sharing of ideas, leading to a better understanding of what Traveler and the meant for the field studies. We hadn't really planned it this way, but in reflection, those in-the-moment reactions and evaluations were critical in shaping how the app continued to evolve from its initial test with the Chicago tour and how we imagined positioning the app for future trips. The ability of Traveler to work across different devices, including smartphones and Android-enabled cameras turned out to be really useful and points the way forward.

Another recurring theme that came up during the trip was students' desire to share their experiences with family and friends back home. As a result, we added a new dimension to the field study—we came up with a way for parents, classmates, and instructors back home to follow the path of the World Tour students via the Internet. We quickly developed a website, and as network connectivity allowed, tour professor Rod Underwood uploaded his recorded paths in Traveler to the site where visitors could view the travels in either the Google Maps web based interface or the Google Earth application interface. For family and friends, this offered a unique perspective on the trip—one that past participants never had. We were able to upgrade Traveler on the fly to make it easy and attractive for students to share their adventures and thoughts with family as the trip progressed. This did more than help students keep in touch with those back home. We usually think about the learning that happens between students and instructors during the class or trip and the dissemination that happens when we return as separate and unrelated activities. But learning deepens when it becomes something that is shared. Being able to share their experiences so immediately meant students were engaging more deeply with the trip while they were still on it.

Students were also required to maintain personal logs or journals of the cities they visited and things they experienced. On a field study of such magnitude, with each participant taking thousands of photos, one could be forgiven for later confusing photos of Helsinki with Stockholm or sketches of Abu Dhabi with Dubai. With these elements pinned in place via Traveler however, it was easy for everyone to keep track of each location. Traveler was working just as we had hoped it would. All of the media collected with Traveler included time and date stamps, optional descriptions, and GPS coordinates associated with the path recorded from the day's activities. With this information readily available, the review and playback of each travel day included that associated media and provided that direct connection between where the students had traveled and the sights and places they had captured with Traveler.

Most cities on World Tour were one- or two-day stops so it was crucial for the students to hit the ground running and be prepared for the immersion of places and experiences they would encounter. With Traveler, students could quickly download and save a map, record the path of guided tour experiences, orient themselves geographically to the map, and reference their previous day's path. This assistance allowed them to concentrate on absorbing and recording their experiences without fear they'd later be unable to place the photos, sketches, videos, and notes in context. It also gave them a point of shared reference with the instructors (see Figure 6) both in the field and while traveling between locations.

Figure 6. World Tour instructors collaborate with students using Traveler.

REFLECTIONS FROM AROUND THE WORLD

We didn't anticipate it, but Traveler turned out to be a useful tool for those planning the trip as well as for the students. The instructors—and we as authors—now have instant access to over 25,000 media items, hundreds of paths, and countless reflections all stored and waiting without having to take additional steps to produce this documentation. This stands in contrast to past years where harvesting travel media from the students required the optical scanning of slides and sketchbooks. Having the maps, photos, sketches, and short video clips all combined within Traveler will make planning World Tour 6, set for the Spring of 2016, a snap, according to the instructors. Reviewing the media as embedded to a path, enjoying the dynamic playback of the paths in Google Earth, and learning from the geographic and chronological organization of that media, whether successful or unsuccessful, will help them arrange the next tour and hone how they address their learning objectives. Reacting to the types and quantity of media (or lack of) that the students recorded allows the instructors to evaluate the learning and synthesis that occurred in key sites. Viewing dynamic playback of the recorded paths might be of more assistance in making critical decisions for future trip planning than vague memories about how things went. Likewise, in reflecting on our experiment with Traveler, we were easily able to archive the media, organize it by student name, and quickly prepare a number of articles, papers, and presentations efficiently in comparison to previous years. The ability to use student-generated media for synthesis and evaluation, while not anticipated in the development of the app, is a cheerful outcome of the development process and an example of mobile app development yielding more than we intended to put in.

On the whole, the instructors were pleased with students' use of our platform. World Tour Professor Rod Underwood offered one example of the critical thinking skills that can be reinforced in travel, with the example of a Middle Eastern market. Comparing and contrasting the phenomena such as a market's physical layout, placement within a city, and observed human behavior are just a few of the things that can be studied across locations. Examining locations such as the Medina market in Fez, Morocco; the Grand Bazaar in Istanbul, Turkey; and the new central market in Abu Dhabi, U.A.E.; require good attention and retention to understand the significance that ties these places together. Further, to develop a gestalt in a student's mind when referring to such a typology of place requires good notes, discussion, and synthetic ability. On reflection, it may be argued that these were essential learning objectives of the trip. What was interesting about Traveler was that the tablet and app combination was "not changing the way students learn, but adapting to how (the current generation of students) use mobile technology and how they learn now," said Underwood. The app, he said, made the trip's learning objectives that much more achievable in the field.

Leslie Smith, another World Tour instructor, also noted the importance of technology in helping students attain geographic awareness, and understand the layout of a city or cultural site. In an email after World Tour, he said "The Traveler app clearly provided the students with more comprehensive and sophisticated discoveries and conclusions throughout their study travel, as evidenced in the enhanced scope and depth of their required commentary and design explorations as they submitted frequent en-route coursework assignments throughout the semester-long global study." The physical layout of a cultural site, its placement within a city, the neighborhoods around it, and its overall significance to the city were all revealed and enhanced by the recording of a path around and through it. These recorded observations assisted in providing good information for the student to use in the the design process later. For example, the semester long studio assignment included a design argument or proposal for a new or improved public space for a student's hometown. A 15 week tour of the world provides a certain detachment for students in reflecting on their home environment, and it speaks to the changes that occur in the students over the course of the tour. In part, the technology provided the tools necessary to design and plan strategies for improvement in the hometown, in both referencing significant sites, and the ability to map the hometown on a mobile device while traveling.

For this assignment one student was tasked with using the physical layout of the Plaza de Espana in Seville, Spain to influence the improvement of a site in the western suburbs of Chicago, Illinois. He used Traveler to record and visually explain the placement and definition of public space he observed and recorded in Spain (see Figure 7), very different from what he had experienced in suburban Chicago previously. He used Traveler to help him apply the learning, recording, and recall of the concepts he was exposed to in Spain to his design process. It is this application of learned examples in design that make travel such an important and rich experience for our students, and the ability of students to visualize this through Traveler really did seem to help them make that transition.

Figure 7. World Tour student Matt Adams references the layout of the Plaza de Espana to influence an improvement to a retail district in his hometown of Arlington Heights, Illinois.

STUDENT RESPONSES AND FUTURE SOFTWARE DIRECTIONS

The development and use of mobile media for and within field based experiences taught us much about the future possibilities of Traveler and tablets for this and other purposes. The two experimental groups varied not just in age and duration of the trip, but also in the way the students used the application and tablet. The Chicago group was very comfortable taking photographs and attempting sketches with the tablet but did not often reference the paths they traveled using Traveler. The World Tour group preferred their digital cameras and paper sketchbooks, but valued and used the recorded path and GPS navigation features with great regularity. World Tour participants also used the GPS and mapping features to explore cities in a self-directed manner after following a planned, guided tour on arrival. Students could reference where they had already traveled and direct their attention and paths accordingly—as one student noted, "I never felt like I could get lost."

Students have also given us many ideas about how to continue improving Traveler. Although they were pretty happy with what Traveler already does—75 percent of the students on World Tour either agreed or strongly agreed that they enjoyed using Traveler and about the same number recommend it for future tours as well—tech-savvy students had several suggestions for us. One suggestion was to link Traveler to other apps that provide information about nearby WiFi hotspots, and another noted a preference for a different sketching app that offered more advanced features, such as multiple layers, zooming, and a wider array of drawing tools. Of course one of the best reasons to make use of multi-functional devices like tablets is not having to incorporate every good feature. If another app has a desired functionality, we can simply make sure it is available in advance on the devices we provide. Students on both field trips noted that currently tablets are only marginally helpful in completing their other field study coursework, due to frequent unavailability of WiFi, the learning curve of the interface, the cost of a keyboard and other accessories, and access to software based productivity tools and applications.

Survey responses indicated a desire to link a wider variety of digital devices and data sources to Traveler, perhaps as an expression of consumer flexibility which this generation of students expects. They already have many other devices

SIDEBAR: ATTITUDES TOWARDS MOBILE MEDIA CREATION

For those who might consider using digital tools in a capacity similar to a field study, it may make sense to briefly explain attitudes we saw among students towards using the tablets to create media on our trips.

Sketching on a Tablet. Our students have largely grown up with drawing on paper, and most continue to value the tactile and permanent-feeling experience of drawing on paper as opposed to drawing on a screen. That said, the bundled sketching interface incorporated into Traveler is quite advanced. It mimics traditional sketching and painting media well, and some students used it with great aptitude (Figure 8). Their attitudes about where they liked to draw outweighed the technical capability of the tool to be used to produce quality work.

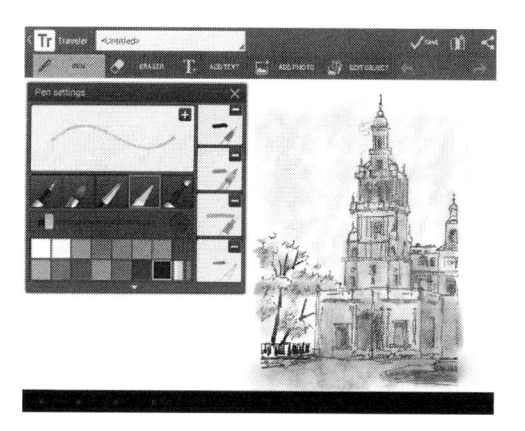

Figure 8. World Tour student Gu Chenyuan's sketch made in Traveler of the Giralda tower in Seville, Spain.

(con't on next page)

like smartphones, digital cameras, laptops, and frequently store and access data "on the cloud." To make tablets we hand out and Traveler feel more usable, they need to not only function but be capable of participating in this broader ecosystem of data and devices[1]. In future iterations of Traveler, we intend to facilitate linkages to high quality digital cameras, smart phones, personal computers, and a dedicated data storage cloud so that students can choose which device records their path in Traveler and not be tied to a single device. Social media is another ingredient of considering the future of Traveler within the digital ecosystem. We saw, but hadn't specifically anticipated, that popular platforms such as Facebook, Instagram, and Tumblr became pipelines and storage of travel media outside of the Traveler platform. In the media backup of the tablets we performed, we saw that students were producing and sharing media with apps like Instagram (see some nice examples of Instagrams in Figure 9).

SIDEBAR
(con't from previous page)

Tablet Photography. The camera on a tablet is a little bit of a different story. With a fixed focal length, little zoom or manual features, and overall rather low quality when compared with high-end digital cameras, it is no surprise students used the tablet minimally for photography. It may take a bit longer, but this too will likely change as the quality and quantity of photography on mobile devices continues to increase. In the meantime, it may make sense to find ways to include photographs made with other devices.

Figure 9. Photos uploaded to Instagram, as archived in the tablet. Photos by Sarah Schinbeckler.

We and our students have also have begun to think of the existing feature set of Traveler not as an end but a beginning of something bigger. Students expressed the desire for Traveler to not just record a path but also inform of attractions nearby. Linking or layering Traveler with other recent developments in location based, augmented reality software looks like an interesting way to address

---

[1] This opens up an entirely different can of worms, but in reality, we should be thinking generally in terms of BYOD—making use of devices students bring themselves—not trying to make loaner tablets "feel" like a personal thing for the students. We think one thing this experience showed is that the student needs to feel a sense of ownership for the device, whether that be a tablet or a phone, and make it a part of their personal life, before there's a chance of making it part of their academic life.

this suggestion, creating an information rich travel experience for future field trips. For example, the Google app Field Trip, released in 2013 for Android and iOS, pushes notifications to users based on their specific patterns of behavior. The ability for other apps to crowdsource travel information to produce user-generated, geographically located markers, verified by databases, and potentially connected to historic and cultural resources, businesses, and institutions has implications for the mapping and sharing of places we are asking students to do. Students will have access to more than just one or two voices of experience with these new places. Examples of interest, like places to eat that are of good value to the university student, the entertainment value that centers on a style of music, hand crafted souvenirs, and the safest public spaces and streets to visit in the evening hours are just the beginning of a large body of information that a crowdsourced app could inform.

WHY TRAVELER?

After years of leading field studies, instructors like us who long to ignite a passion for place in our students and to see them develop ownership of their experiences may have become discouraged at the results of our labors. How can students get to the real meaning of place when they aren't even paying attention to some of the most basic details in the outings we organize for them? It is painful to construct the perfect walking tour and find no one remembers the work they have seen or can even decipher the notes they wrote during the exercise. That observations in the field are not remembered later is disturbing on its own. More so, students need these observational details to support higher-level thinking about the built environment. Observational skills tied to discussions in the field—taking photographs, making notes, constructing diagrams, and drawing sketches—are used to build our students' awareness of the issues of the contemporary city, an environment which all of our students must be familiar as emerging design professionals.

For disillusioned instructors, Traveler may offer some hope. By increasing our ability to take the trip with us once it is over, and making those experiences easier to reflect on and share with others, it creates opportunities for efficiency in preparing for a trip, in conducting the field study, and in the debriefing afterward. These observed benefits, coupled with the historically observed richness of field studies, means that mobile technologies like Traveler deserve further exploration, integration, evaluation and refinement for both educators and students alike.

As educators and software developers embedded in higher education, we also see that architecture field studies are only one aspect of a much larger challenge to use technologies in ways that help students make better sense of the world they inhabit. And we are ready to rise to that challenge. Students are now arriving to higher education with great comfort and reliance on their mobile devices. We aim to integrate, not ignore, this phenomenon and shape our pedagogy around effective experiences. We embrace the future of mobile media in this regard as new interfaces, devices, and connectivity are released into the market. We look forward to expanding Traveler for many other situations where better geographic reference can help produce insight. By continuing to develop and find interesting ways to use apps like Traveler, we may be able to help students heighten and improve their geographic awareness in the classroom and beyond. We are confident that digital journaling is a suitable companion to lesson plans and learning objectives within design education and all students of the built environment.

REFERENCES

Smith, P.D. (2012), *Cities: A Guidebook for the Urban Age*. Bloomsbury, New York and London.

Taylor, P. and S. Keeter. (2006) Millennials: *A portrait of generation next*. Pew Research Center, Washington, D.C. [online] Available at http://www.pewresearch.org/millennials/teen-internet-use-graphic/ [Accessed June 2, 2013].

Roper Public Affairs and Media. (2006) *Final Report: National Geographic-Roper public affairs 2006 geographic literacy study*. National Geographic-Roper, Washington, D.C. [online] Available at http://www.nationalgeographic.com/roper2006/pdf/FINALReport2006GeogLitsurvey.pdf [Accessed June 2, 2013], p. 6.

CHAPTER FIVE

MIT App Inventor: Democratizing Personal Mobile Computing

Shaileen Crawford Pokress
Director of Education, MIT App Inventor
MIT Center for Mobile Learning @ The Media Lab

MIT App Inventor is a blocks-based visual programming tool that allows anyone to design and build their own fully functional mobile apps. It was developed to provide transformative experiences to people who may not feel that they have much mastery over technology. App Inventor provides a low-floor, high-ceiling development environment that invites novices to engage in digital creation in personally meaningful and relevant ways. In short, it aims to democratize personal mobile computing.

Professor Hal Abelson of MIT developed App Inventor while on sabbatical at Google. He and a team of Google engineers launched the first version in 2009 as a project of Google Labs. Late in 2011, with a seed grant from Google, Abelson brought the project to MIT where it is now housed in the new Center for Mobile Learning (CML) at the Media Lab. CML is co-directed by Abelson together with Mitchel Resnick, Director of the MIT Media Lab's Lifelong Kindergarten group, the home of Scratch, and Eric Klopfer, Director of MIT's Scheller Teacher Education Program, home of StarLogo TNG.

HOW MIT APP INVENTOR WORKS

Building an app with App Inventor begins in a web browser where a graphical Designer provides a drag-and-drop interface for designing the user interface (UI) of the app, and also for specifying the functionalities that will be used in the app. For example, if the app developer wants to make a drawing canvas with a button to clear that canvas, they would drag out a Canvas component and a Button component, as shown in Figure 1. If the developer then decides that she wants the app's canvas to be cleared when the user shakes the phone, she would also add to the Designer an

Accelerometer component. This is a non-visible component that doesn't affect the UI of the app, but it is a piece of the app's functionality that has to be specified in the *Designer*.[1]

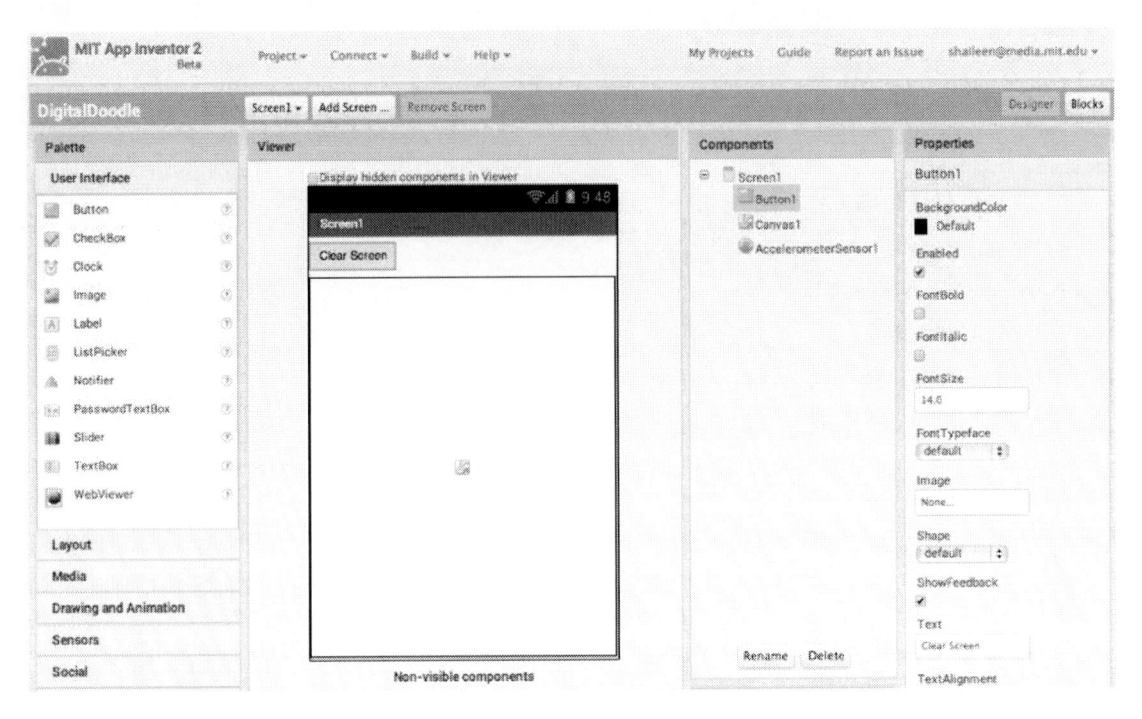

Figure 1. App Inventor Designer Window provides a staging area for choosing elements of the user interface and functional components of the app.

Once the app is laid out in the Designer window, the app developer continues into the Blocks Editor where the app's behavior is set through the logic of programming using intuitive blocks that snap together like puzzle pieces. Blocks languages have existed for many years and have been used extensively with novices. They can reduce the frustration caused by syntax errors while providing a positive experience with programming. This can breed motivation for novices to continue learning more about programming as a means for digital creativity instead of getting hung up on the little things.

App Inventor's programming blocks are organized in drawers, grouping blocks together to make things easier to find. For example, blocks for math and text manipulation are grouped in Math and Text drawers. Blocks for program control flow—like if-then-else statements—are in the Control drawer. Each component of the app has a corresponding drawer. So in the app example described in

---

[1] For more information on this app, including step-by-step instructions for how to build it, See MIT's Beginner App Tutorial: Digital Doodle at http://appinventor.mit.edu/explore/ai2/beginner-videos.html.

Figure 1, there are drawers corresponding to the components Canvas, Button, and Accelerometer. Figure 2 shows the contents of the Canvas component's drawer.

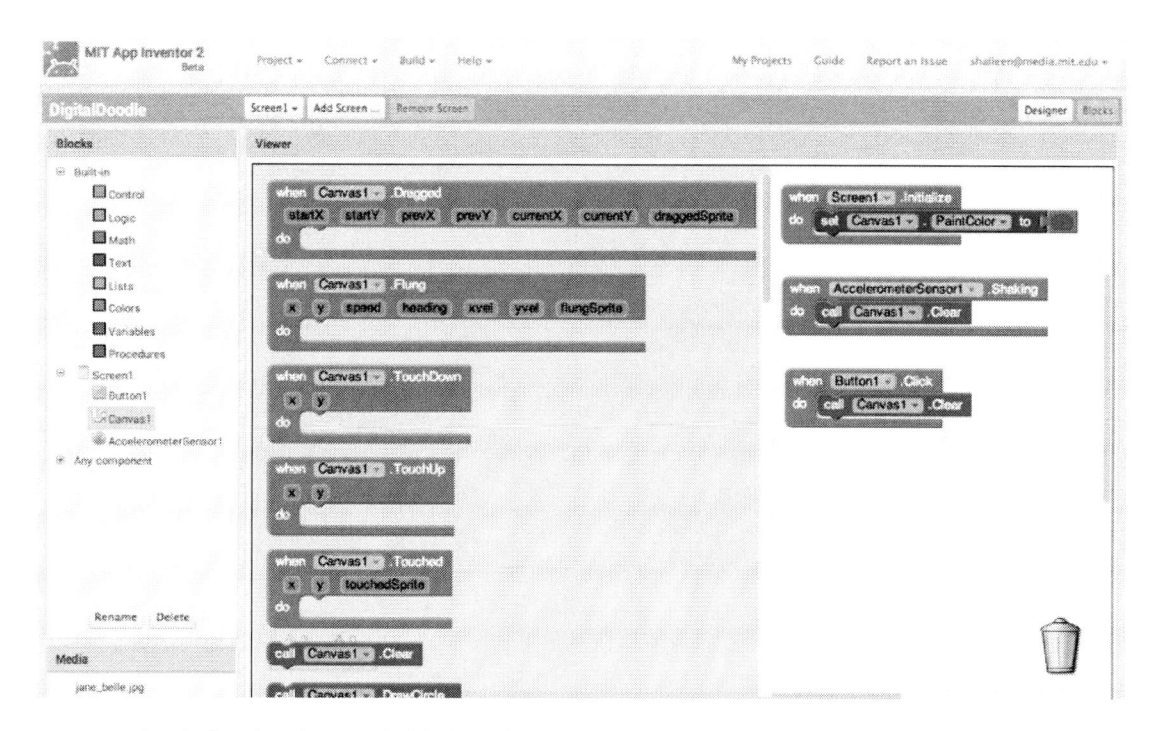

Figure 2. *The Blocks Editor* showing the blocks in the Canvas Drawer. In the work area to the right we see the app's program as it exists so far. Notice that the Canvas will be cleared when the Accelerometer reports that the phone is being shaken or when the Button is clicked.

One of the key aspects of App Inventor's development environment is that it supports live testing of the app as it is being built. This is especially important for beginning programmers in that it provides instant feedback to changes they make in their user interface and their program, as they make them. The power of this cannot be overstated. For example, a pair of high school students built their first app in less than an hour. Their app featured a ball that moves around the screen when the user flicks at it. Early on, the ball was getting stuck on the sides of the screen. Upon further investigation into the ball component's blocks, the girls discovered a "when Ball.EdgeReached" block and another block "call Ball.Bounce". After clicking these two blocks together in their program (as seen in Figure 3), they went back to their phone to fling the ball again This time time the ball bounced off the walls! This type of instant feedback is essential to lowering the frustration that plagues many other programming experiences for novices.

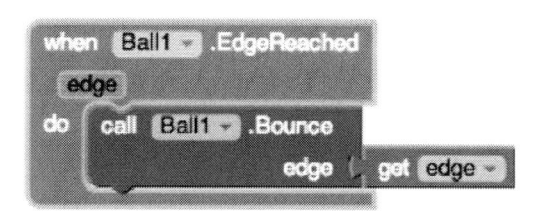

Figure 3. Blocks are readily available and understandable to novice programmers. App Inventor preserves the standard object-based programming constructs such as Object.Event (when Ball1.EdgeReached) and Object.Method (call Ball1.Bounce). Exposing some of the syntax of the underlying java program introduces novice developers to the language of computer science as they create.

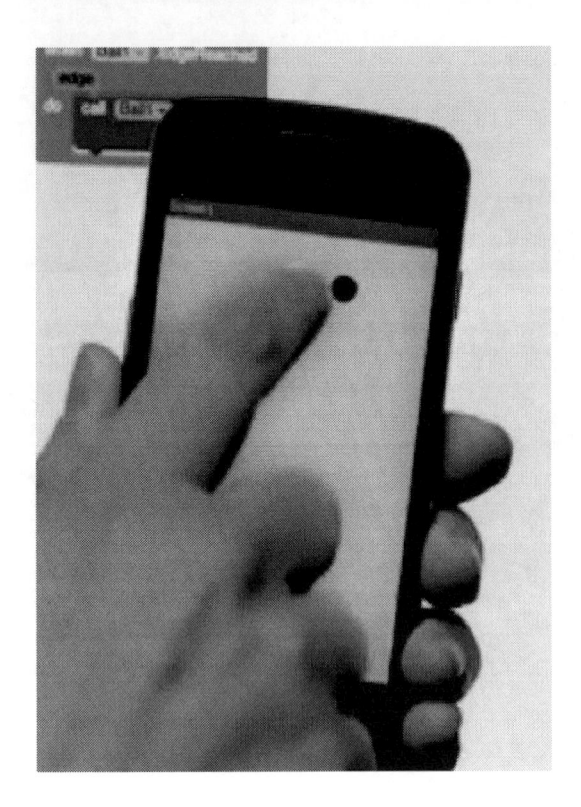

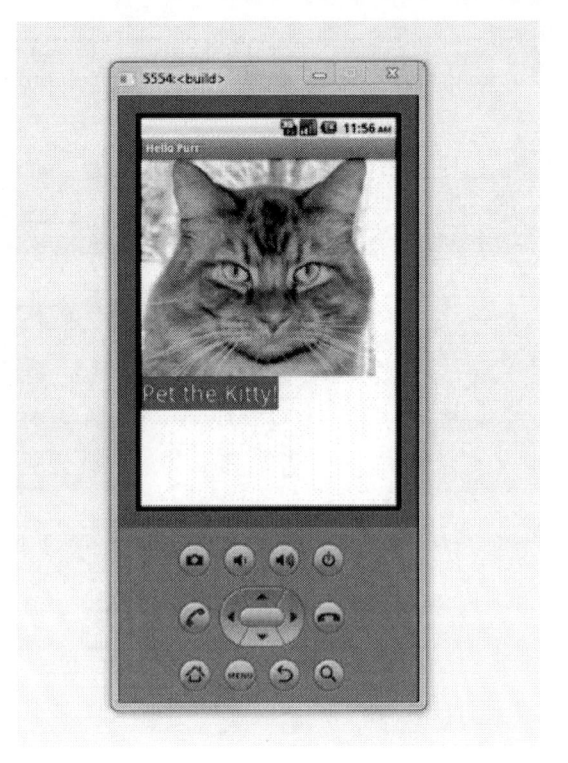

Figure 4. Left: An app shown live on a connected Android device using App Inventor's real-time testing capability. Right: A simulated device which can be used if the developer does not have an Android phone or tablet handy. This *Android Emulator* simulates many of the features of an actual phone.

HOW MIT APP INVENTOR IS USED

There are many great stories about App Inventor in the world, too many to share in the space here. Some of my favorites are the *Wild Hog* project in Alabama, the *Tag It!* app from Technovation girls in East Palo Alto, and the *Dhaka Bus* project from a student solving a major local infrastructure/transportation problem in India.[2] While App Inventor was developed primarily as an educational tool, it has been used by an array of individuals in scores of different settings. Our users generally fall into one or more of a few groups: students, teachers, hobbyists, and entrepreneurs.

Hobbyists tend to be the same type of people who build robots or play around with technology in other ways. They enjoy creating and playing with technology, and App Inventor provides them a way to do that with mobile devices. One of the delightful projects to come out of this community is the arduino-driven, bluetooth-controlled dancing Android doll.[3]

---

[2] More stories can be found at http://appinventor.mit.edu/explore/stories.html. There are also explanatory news entries and blog posts at http://appinventor.mit.edu/explore/news-events.html.

[3] For more information, see: http://appinventor.mit.edu/explore/stories/my-droid-robot-controlled-app-inventor.html.

Entrepreneurs are those who see App Inventor as a way to easily enter into the Android app market and make money without having to learn to program in Java. This group has mostly created games and utility apps for which people might pay. We are pleased to see App Inventor used in this way, as it goes hand in hand with our philosophy of opening doors to the world of computing to all. A nice example from the community of App Inventor entrepreneurs comes from a partner in Spain. unX is a free online platform that uses App Inventor as a way to help people who are underemployed in Spain to develop technical skills and to begin to think about ways to capitalize on those skills.[4]

Although we are happy to have others find uses for App Inventor, we consider teachers and students our primary audience. App Inventor is first and foremost an academic project. We focus our efforts in supporting educators in their use of App Inventor, and there are many exciting projects underway that engage students in app building, both within and outside of school walls. Technovation Challenge, by Iridescent Technology, is one the of the shining examples of an organization taking the free platform provided by MIT and using it to promote technical innovation and entrepreneurship among a group of people wouldn't otherwise have had an opportunity of this nature. Through Technovation, thousands of girls around the world have had empowering experiences with app-building and business skills. The results of the project in aggregate are outstanding and in many individual cases, life-changing.[5]

Computer Science Education in the United States is undergoing a major transformation with the impending release of a new Computer Science AP course, called Computer Science Principles (CSP). The College Board in partnership with the National Science Foundation has deputized several university teams to develop courses based on the new CSP framework. As part of this effort, Ralph Morelli of Trinity College in Hartford has been piloting a new high-school course Mobile Computer Science Principles entirely built around App Inventor. Initial reaction from teachers and students is very encouraging, and anecdotal evidence suggests that working with mobile devices, which are already familiar in students' technology-saturated world, is highly engaging and motivating.[6]

Over the five years since App Inventor's launch, many professional development courses for teachers have sprung up around our tool, both in likely and unlikely places. Several college faculty like Fred Martin at University of Massachusetts Lowell and Jeff Gray at the University of Alabama, with funding from Google's CS4HS program, annually host a three-day teacher workshop based on App Inventor, reaching hundreds of high school educators. During the summer of 2013, a new online course hosted by Jennifer Rosato and Chery Takkunen at the College of St. Scholastica spread App Inventor even further.[7]

---

[4] For more information, see: http://redunx.org.

[5] See chapter 14 for more on Technovation Challenge. -Eds

[6] For more information, see: http://mobile-csp.org/

[7] For more information, see: http://css.edu/cs4hs

In addition to these successful and far-reaching efforts, others have emerged. The MIT App Inventor education team has set up an extensive website which offers free resources and self-guided tutorials that help even the most inexperienced beginner get started building their own mobile apps. There is also an active user forum where developers, teachers, individual learners, and hobbyists exchange ideas and information.[8] The MIT team, with support from the Verizon Foundation, has played a key role in supporting regional and national winners of the Verizon Innovative App Challenge.[9] Now in its second year, the MIT team has enlisted a team of App Inventor expert teachers, known as the App Inventor Training Corps, to deliver in-person training to winning schools across the country. Last year the in-person training was the extent of the support offered. New for 2014 will be a 6-week online course that is facilitated by MIT education experts. The benefit of this online course will eventually reach well beyond the award winners of the App Challenge as MIT will make the course available for free online in Spring 2014.

LOOKING AHEAD: WHAT'S NEXT FOR MIT'S APP INVENTOR

The App Inventor team has intentionally kept the tool as open ended as possible so that the audience and the things they create can emerge organically. Unlike some authoring tools that are specifically for making games or programming a simulation, a simulation, App Inventor purposefully provides building blocks that can be arranged for virtually any purpose or goal. The tool itself is an access point to all of the features in a mobile device. The building blocks of an App Inventor program are components like the camera, GPS, accelerometer, texting, contact lists, Near Field Communication (NFC) sensors, Bluetooth, the internet, local and remote data storage, and more. App Inventor lets a user intuitively access all of the features in a mobile device so that they can create any combination of functionality into their app. App Inventor opens up the black box that many people perceive a computer to be.

In December 2013, the team at MIT unveiled months of hard work in the form of App Inventor 2, an entirely browser-based version of App Inventor. Formerly, the *Blocks Editor* part of the tool had to be run as a local java program on the user's computer. With App Inventor 2, the Blocks Editor was entirely rewritten based on Blockly[10]—a web-based block programming editor—so that it no longer requires a local java installation. This frees up users from having to struggle with administrator-level support for constantly evolving java software. It has also made the *Designer* to *Blocks Editor* transition much more intuitive for our users. Where they used to have to go between the web browser for the *Designer* and to the local java program for the *Blocks Editor,* the two are now side-by-side in a single browser window, making it much easier to navigate between them.

---

[8] For more information, see: http://appinventor.mit.edu

[9] For more information, see: http://appchallenge.tsaweb.org/

[10] Blockly is a Google project. For more information, see: https://developers.google.com/blockly/

Never satisfied with current accomplishments, the MIT App Inventor team has several projects on the horizon. In addition to constantly rolling out new components, such as the NFC component, the team is looking forward to one day offering an entirely Android-based solution where you can program in App Inventor on an Android tablet, eliminating the need for a traditional computer. While no launch date has been determined, this is the next major milestone for the project. In the meantime, MIT App Inventor continues to grow in popularity. Upon re-launch from MIT, App Inventor saw usage in the thousands. In February 2014 the number of unique users averaged 40,000 per week. People come from all over the world to use our tool to help them create.

App Inventor will continue to make it easy to for people to develop a type of digital literacy that many believe should be accessible to all, not just those with advanced technical knowledge. Installing Software Development Kits and programming in text-based programming languages are no longer prerequisites for app development. People everywhere, from all walks of life, can become empowered to create the solutions that they need or want in their daily lives.

CHAPTER SIX

ARIS: Augmented Reality for Interactive Storytelling

Christopher Holden

Several of the authors in this book use the Augmented Reality (AR) game design and storytelling platform ARIS in their work. Rather than have them explain the basics of the tool in each chapter, or send you off somewhere else (e.g. Holden et al., 2014) to read about ARIS just to make sense of our authors' use of it, we have chosen to describe the ins and out of this popular tool for creating augmented reality stories and games separately here. The editors have all used ARIS extensively, and—disclaimer—also have been involved with the ARIS project itself. Although we specifically sought submissions for this book from those not using ARIS, and the stories we share in the book are a clear indication that there are other games in town so to speak, we have come across a great number of people who have used ARIS to do some really interesting work. It is powerful, yet malleable and the price—free—is right.

This chapter should serve a conceptual as well as practical purpose. After all, the mobile landscape itself is changing quite rapidly. Details that felt practical as I write this for you will likely soon feel out of date as the world and software within it change. There is a lot of turnover among apps, platforms, and methods in mobile. It is unusual enough to see something like ARIS grow and stick around, and I wouldn't want the book to feel pointless if ARIS is gone or greatly changed by the time you read this.

So below, consider how the features and uses of this software do more than help you visualize the other ARIS experiments in this book or inspire your own use of ARIS this year. Details about ARIS here can inform in a concrete way perennial discussions about how a platform may function as a bridge between ideas and people. As other technologies come into play, we can look back at this time to see how ARIS looked to realize the concept of AR in a way that empowered regular people as explorers of new terrain, cutting across a lot of traditional boundaries like discipline, age, and individual educational settings in its creation and use. We can find, in this example, the questions that we need to find answers for in the software of the future.

The first lesson ARIS provides is the organic and collaborative nature of its development. Originally, it grew from a class game design by David Gagnon and Chris Blakesley in 2007, using a local art museum as a mobile game space. The following semester, Seann Dikkers joined them to develop a prototype design tool (that would become ARIS) in an independent study under Kurt Squire. Since then, ARIS has continued to evolve due to the attention and contributions of many more volunteers and programmers.[1] ARIS has gone through many iterations, seen new funders, team members, and has led to the creation of a Mobile Learning Lab (MLL) at UW-Madison and been used by thousands of people around the globe. Gagnon et al. are at the time of my writing, near the release of a much revised ARIS that should welcome even more people through an increased ease of use and reach.

The organic way ARIS has grown and continues to develop, and its life as free, open source software, is not something that makes sense within most institutions. It is also a little convoluted to describe briefly here. But I believe it is a major reason for its resilience and usefulness. ARIS has been free to become what it needs to be and the result is something a lot of people love, often for very different reasons.

In the sections below, first we give a basic overview of what ARIS is and how it works. Then we highlight some of the more popular kinds of experiences people create using ARIS. Finally we look at some of the many contexts in which ARIS creations find relevance. We describe each of these as separate categories, but they should be read more broadly as themes. Typical projects involving ARIS participate in many of these areas simultaneously to a greater or lesser degree.

DESIGN AND FEATURES OF ARIS

ARIS works by combining three pieces of software:

- Client - an iOS app to play games, take tours, collect data, etc.
- Editor - a web based, drag and drop authoring tool for making games and other experiences.
- Server - a database where the game contents are actually stored.
  The Client and Editor read from and write to the server to do what they do.

The server isn't very important for users to think about most of the time, but there are a couple of factoids of general interest. First, games do not need to be published as a separate step from being written. Working in the Editor updates the games' entries in the server which the Client can then read. For game authors, this minimizes the workflow of testing, debugging, and deploying. It also makes multiplayer games possible. The downside is that players need access to the internet to play. This complicates use, especially in scenarios without extensive WiFi and with WiFi only

---

[1] A more complete retelling of the history of ARIS up to 2010 can be found in David Gagnon's UW-Madison Master's Thesis (Gagnon, 2010). At the end of the chapter we mention a few further contributions to its development. For the last few years, Philip Dougherty has been the lead programmer of ARIS. The total list of contributors however is too numerous to list here.

devices (e.g. when school based teams go outdoors or leave campus); involving work in very remote locations without cellular data; and where WiFi service is present but authentication is problematic. At the same time, ARIS users have come up with creative solutions to these problems. Some use portable routers like MiFi's to provide internet connections to many devices simultaneously and paid for on prepaid plans, others negotiate with IT Departments to whitelist the arisgames.org domain on the local network. In practice, handled idiosyncratically, this complication of using ARIS, like the problem of getting devices in the right hands, turns out to be much more tractable than it would appear.

ARIS Objects

There are three basic objects to make games and stories using ARIS: plaques, items and characters. Each is a bit different.[2]

- *Plaques* are points of information. They can include text and media. They can also give out and take away items to and from players. The metaphor that gives *plaques* their name is an informational plaque next to a point of interest in the world; a statue in a public square may have a plaque telling visitors who the statue is of, when it was commissioned, who the sculptor was, etc.
- *Items* are the things in the virtual world. Players can pick them up, trade them with other players, drop them on the map, get them from *characters* or have them taken away. Players can have more than one of an item and when the last one is taken from a game map it is gone.
- *Characters* are virtual people. Players interact with them via multiple-choice style dialogue. They can exchange items with players in each bit of conversation.

Each of these three objects acts a bit differently and can be used for things other than their basic metaphors might suggest. All three objects can contain various forms of media (photos, images, and text) or reference other media through URLs, rendering webpages in an embedded web browser.

Locations in ARIS

One of ARIS's main functions is to coordinate media and place. Players access ARIS objects primarily through their locations. Originally, this was solely done with players' physical proximity to GPS coordinates: In the ARIS Editor, an author creates a location for an object by dragging it out to a place on a Google map to which the player would be directed. While within a certain distance from that point, a player has access to the content at that location.

---

[2] This description is basic and incomplete. It is accurate to guide an understanding of its use by our authors but not entirely so for the soon-to-be released update of ARIS you may soon be using.

More recently however, other methods for the ARIS Client "knowing location" have been developed, stretching the metaphor. An author can choose to have locations accessed via

- Quick Response (QR) code (e.g. an author places a QR code for a *character* on a museum wall and a player scans the code to interact with the *character*),
- alphanumeric string (instead of a QR code, a player enters information into the decoder in ARIS to interact with authored content),
- directly from another ARIS object (e.g. after a conversation with a *character*, the player's screen immediately and automatically displays a *plaque*), or
- by the player touching a location's icon on their on-screen map (i.e. Quick Travel).

Authors no longer need to directly place locations on the map to make them available for players. In addition to the above player-facing generalizations of location, instead of placing objects at locations, an author can specify parameters and intervals of time according to which these objects will regularly generate for players. This is called *spawning*. Together, these options in the ARIS Editor give authors flexibility in how they make use of location of game content in ARIS.

The ARIS Notebook

The ARIS Client, in addition to allowing the play of pre-authored AR games, has data collection features: the Notebook. Players can take photo, video, and text notes, and map, tag, and share them using the Notebook. The Notebook can interact with other parts of ARIS (e.g. a *character* shows up when you take a photo in a certain place) and players can communicate with each other about the notes they share using likes and comments.

Requirements

The glue that holds ARIS experiences together—what gives authors the ability to structure interaction beyond simply having a bunch of geolocative media present on a map—is *requirements*. *Requirements* drive the Interactive and the Story part of ARIS, and should be familiar as the basic if, then logical structures that glue together other computer programs. In ARIS, an author can for example ask for a player to have seen one of two possible *plaques* or to be carrying a blue key before gaining access to a character. This is also what allows individual bits of dialogue within *characters* to come together into interactive, branching conversations.

As we mention below, *requirements* in ARIS lean heavily in favor of a storytelling approach as opposed to helping to establish a virtual world. Most of them depend on the state or history of an individual player rather than the state of the virtual world or non-player objects within it. Besides the low level of graphical capabilities in ARIS, this is the area where is ARIS is least like typical game engines. Most other platforms have worlds and non-player characters whose internal states help determine outcomes in their games.

WHAT CAN YOU MAKE WITH ARIS?

Since ARIS is used in a lot of scenarios, by people with different goals in mind, using different methods, it is not straightforward to answer the obvious question "What is ARIS for?". We will mention some of the stories/games/tours/experiences that people have made, and how the creations fit into various purposes for their authors and players. Whether youth are playing ARIS games or making them, with adults or their peers, in school or on their own, one of the most exciting aspects of this project is considering some of the emergent mobile activity types encompassed by different ARIS projects. Below, we present examples of the major types of ARIS creations we've seen before, within the next section, describing the general types of scenarios we've seen ARIS used in.

Tours

We already discussed some of the possible benefits of MML tours in Practical Considerations (chapter 3). Here, we can describe more closely the choices a specific tool allows you. The concept of a tour is quite simple across media formats: Players travel to areas of significance and are presented with media on the mobile device (text, audio, images, video) providing information about what is at those locations. To make an ARIS tour, the basic authoring procedure described above suffices: simply create objects like *plaques*, upload media assets to them, and drag them to the map.

SIDEBAR: TOURS — MORE THAN MEETS THE EYE

As a kind of interactive content, Tours may not push the envelope in terms of what is possible with mobile. They are nonetheless an important example to remember. Because tours are simple to understand and familiar to pretty much everyone, the fact that ARIS makes the creation of geolocative or QR code based tours easy signifies an accessible on-ramp to creating with AR and mobile technology. There are four significant ways that people can be held back from agency with digital tools like these, and being able to put together a simple tour after an hour of training helps with all four.

The Conceptual framework of augmented reality. Newcomers ask "What is AR, how does it relate to my other interests, and how do I even think about a game-like thing that combines media, storytelling and physical place?" Tours fit many areas of content and are a relevant activity type for many situations. They show off the basic forms of interaction made possible by ARIS and readily suggest types of engagement that are just a bit deeper. After making their first tour with ARIS, a newcomer may ask "What if this location asked a question instead of simply presenting information? Could my tour branch into a non-linear story?"

Technical experience with the ARIS Editor. New tools, especially those built non-professionally on a shoestring budget, have a style of their own. New authors can make a tour as a way to trade the cognitive load of game authorship for time spent adjusting to the actual mechanics and vocabulary

(con't on next page)

Variations may include the use of contextual information (e.g. the player enters an address into the decoder) or QR codes (common in indoor spaces like museums where GPS doesn't help much). Information can be simple media or simulated text-based dialogue with *characters*.

When many people have the means to easily create them, we have found that many tours get made that otherwise would not. The democratization of authorship that is possible with tools like ARIS means that tours that were once only inside a single person's head or never published professionally because they addressed a small or marginal audience or a tour guide could not always be present can now see the light of day. Tours have been created to serve a wide variety of community needs, and even more often to provide unofficial tours to compete with the sanctioned ones in more popular locations. Just because tours are simple, and we have all been on deadly boring ones, does not mean they are not worthy of attention.

Scavenger Hunts

Like tours, Scavenger Hunts predate the widespread use of mobile technologies and have become an interesting target for mobile learning. ARIS is well suited for the creation of scavenger hunts because they are similar to tours but with an added element of gaminess. Scavenger hunts introduce competition and winning to the simple and often unmotivated basic tour. A tour focuses on the transmission of information while a scavenger hunt typically uses a place as a play space. Traditionally scavenger hunts have relied upon players collecting physical artifacts. In the mobile space this can be combined with collections of a more general variety, including snapshots, interviews, and virtual items. ARIS can be used to unlock certain content within a

SIDEBAR
(con't from previous page)

of the ARIS Editor. Just as building a tour may suggest deeper forms of interaction to a newcomer, letting a novice brush up against but not be overwhelmed by technical complexity exposes just enough of the editing environment to begin to make an author feel comfortable enough to click on some unfamiliar buttons and begin to dive deeper.

Access and suitability. The details of implementation also include actually obtaining any additional software or logins needed, as well as negotiating any licensing terms. ARIS is free and open-source in part to limit the difficulty of users at this juncture, but for open-source to mean actually usable, potential users need to be able to get all the pieces and see them running together to feel comfortable. Because tours are easy to get off the ground, rather extensive evaluation of ARIS can be quickly made by potential users.

Familiarity with the logistics of running mobile-based implementations. There are a lot of details between making a game as personal prototype and actually going on location with a say a group of students to use that game for a specific purpose. Again, it is better for newcomers to learn to manage the logistical details of devices, internet, and such without unnecessary complexity in the activity itself. Novice users are likely to be familiar with tours as well, and even with new hardware in their hands and new software to learn, the basic idea of getting to the next point and reading what's there is transparent. Teachers in particular can quickly assess their comfort and ability to add augmented reality gaming to their classrooms by trying a simple tour out early on.

scavenger hunt sequentially, making progression through the uncovering of a place possible. ARIS can also keep track of players' scores and other attributes through the use of *items*.

Interactive Stories

If there is a classic genre emerging within the nascent field of AR gaming for learning, it is the interactive story. Early examples like MingFong Jan's 2005 *Mad City Mystery*[3] have inspired many. Most of the ARIS experiences created by our authors who use ARIS as well as those that appeared in the previous MML book are interactive stories. There is something special to the idea of giving players not just a sequence of content to discover, but a role to play and a narrative that responds directly to their participation.

The basic idea of an interactive story is rather simple. Players are given roles to play and through these roles they interact with virtual and/or live characters and other parts of the world in which the narrative takes place. There is usually some motivating context like a mystery to solve. As the story unfolds through time and space, the outcomes depend on choices players make.

Users have many goals in mind when they use ARIS to make interactive stories, and they include a wide array of educational activities. At the same time, shared interest in them stems from a basic desire to create something rich and meaningful for others to fall into. To take presence in place, awareness and observation, and media on the device, and roll them into a context where content takes on meaning and has consequences, and where the player has a role to play in that situation aims directly at creating a truly immersive experience. Many scholars have described the power of situating content within meaningful contexts, or the agency to be gained by having a learner inhabit a role and extending participation beyond listening and responding.

A simple example to illustrate the concept and purpose of interactive AR stories as course curriculum is *Mentira*.[4] *Mentira* is a game for Spanish classes at the University of New Mexico in Albuquerque. The story unfolds much like a historical novel, where fact and fiction combine to set the context and social conditions for meaningful interaction in Spanish. While playing *Mentira*, learners must investigate clues and talk to various *characters* to prove they are not responsible for a murder in a local neighborhood. Players visit the local neighborhood where the story is set to collect additional clues and ultimately solve the mystery. *Mentira* feels like a natural fit to a Spanish class instead of technology that has been shoehorned in for its own sake because the goal of a Spanish class is to bring students into contact with Spanish in the world. It is a story told through the Spanish language and which takes place in a place where the language has been relevant for more than 300

---

[3] See (Squire & Jan, 2007) for a description of how role and story are imagined to be productive for engaging students in scientific inquiry.

[4] For more about Mentira see my and Julie Sykes' chapter in Mobile Media Learning: Amazing Uses of Mobile Devices for Learning (Holden & Sykes, 2012).

years. Instead of regurgitating vocabulary and grammar—the focus of much classroom instruction and almost all mobile games for language learning—in *Mentira* students use Spanish to understand and participate meaningfully in a situation.

Later in this book, there are several examples of interactive stories made with ARIS. Bressler has a multiplayer forensic mystery *School Scene Investigators* (chapter 7) similar to Jan's *Mad City Mystery*. Many of the creations detailed by Adam and Perales (chapter 10) start from the basic structure of an interactive story. And all the designs described in the Design Challenges section of the book are also interactive stories: May's *Quest for the Cities of Gold;* Dikkers, Rieder, and Soloman's *ParkQuest;* Blakesley and McIntosh's *Lift Off;* and Fisher and Dikkers' *Horror on the Ridges* (chapters 15 through 18).

One reason for the popularity of the interactive story genre among ARIS users is the universal nature of storytelling. We share ideas with each other in the form of stories. Regardless of the subject, audience, or setting, stories are the oldest and most used communicative strategy we have. Story connects people to ideas, and ideas to places. Time, intention, action, and reflection take form within stories. So when thinking about AR as a technology for uniting content and place through interaction, interactive narratives look like a natural format.

The interactive narrative is not only a preference of users, but also a central aspect of the original design of ARIS. The acronym ARIS stands for Augmented Reality for Interactive Storytelling. Many features were specifically designed to support the creation of interactive narratives distinctly as a certain type of game or experience. This preference is obvious when you look at what exactly ARIS makes it easy for authors to do:

- *Plaques, items,* and *characters* are author-centric. To a large extent, what the player does with them is read their contents.
- Multiple choice based dialogue with virtual *characters* is a heavily foregrounded feature.
- The requirement system allows future interactions to depend on logical consequences of the state and history of the player more than on the current state of the virtual world or its contents.

Although the lines between game genres, types, or even between games and other kinds of content can be rather fuzzy, generally a focus on storytelling means that ARIS is not so much a platform for action games, geometric puzzles, or interactive simulations. Our focus on interactive storytelling may take us away from some of the most popular areas of commercial mobile game design, but it allows us to reach out to very diverse audiences, help them to connect readily to what otherwise might be an uncomfortable space, and create games that have immediate relevance to their own subjects, places, and contexts.

Situated Documentaries

The situated documentary is another story-based AR genre, often an interactive story with the added notion that the story being lived through is tightly based upon actual events at a location. This concept was coined by James Mathews, who created *Dow Day* for his high school students, originally on MIT's Outdoor AR platform like Jan's *Mad City Mystery*. We later ported the basic story from this project to ARIS to be used as a concrete demonstration of AR storytelling (figure 1). In *Dow Day* players take on the role of a reporter in 1967, Madison, Wisconsin with the goal to interview virtual characters connected with student protests on campus regarding the Vietnam War. Historically, these protests culminated in a brutal conflict known as Dow Day. Participants in *Dow Day* view video and images surrounding this event in the media's authentic locations, situating them within the event.

Generally, authors of situated documentaries want to know whether and how combining physical location and documentary materials can result in compelling, immersive storytelling of real-life events. A key mechanic is being able to physically situate this historical media in relevant physical locations. In *Dow Day*, the use is similar to what one finds in the popular *Then & Now* photo books, where a contemporary photograph accompanies a historical one taken from the same place and in the same direction. The familiarity of the modern landscape helps us get into the historical context, noting similarities and differences. In a situated documentary, players are not given a contemporary photo to establish context. Instead, they are physically present where the original events took place and their senses provide the contrasting reference while the mobile device provides the details of the historical setting. Adam and Perales describe some of their and their students' creations as documentary (chapter 10), and Owen Gottlieb also uses the term refer to his ARIS game, *Jewish Time Jump*.[5]

Figure 1. A screenshot from the ARIS port of Mathews' *Dow Day*. An archival photo is used to illustrate and situate the story in the game.

---

[5] *Jewish Time Jump* was a finalist for a G4C award at the 2013 Games for Change Festival.

One may question whether an interactive story can ever really be considered a documentary. Because we imagine giving the player a role to play and decisions to make, the result is necessarily ahistorical, at least in part. However, many authors will make player roles generic—i.e. the reporter you play in Dow Day is not an actual reporter and your actions do not affect the outcome of the protests—invented for the story rather than actual historical figures in an effort to lighten the disturbance. In practice, designs like Dow Day retain a documentary feel that is distinctly different from historical fiction like *Mentira*. Watching authors face this and other boundaries demonstrates the vitality involved with this creative act. In AR storytelling, fiction and non-fiction are clearly not opposites, but the foundation for broad experimentation. The intent to help others get inside past historical events may indeed be enacted most efficiently by pretending to be someone who never lived at all.

Data Collection Activities

ARIS can also be used to set up data collection activities, typically through use of the Notebook. Data collection activities turn authorship around by giving the players the primary responsibility for telling a story. By carefully selecting the data to be collected, an engaging game mechanic can be created, compelling players to fill the game world with content that then can become fodder for further investigations.

Possible content areas for data collection through the ARIS Notebook include anything from citizen science to community ethnography. An early entry in this genre, *Digital Graffiti Gallery*, is a curation activity developed by University of New Mexico undergraduate Ivan Kenarov in my *Local Games in ABQ* class. Players document graffiti on the UNM campus (figure 2). As the real graffiti is removed by cleaning crews, it remains in place in ARIS and can be revisited in the future. This collection activity serves to preserve a lasting, locative record of this ephemeral art form. Later in this book, Frandy has his students use the ARIS Notebook to practice ethnography (chapter 8), and Graza and Rosenblum's students use it to record observations of a neighborhood in East Austin (chapter 9).

Figure 2. Alyssa Concha plays *Digital Graffiti Gallery* by photographing graffiti.

Data collection activities have become popular with ARIS because they require less effort at upfront production and also perhaps because they give players a larger role to play, themes we mentioned in the previous chapter. To make a data collection activity, a teacher pretty much only needs to come up with an idea and a name. A couple words and checkboxes in the ARIS Editor and they are ready to go. In contrast to a tour, which takes about an hour to learn to make and at least ten times that to find and prepare the content for the tour, a data collection activity takes five minutes of training to author and just as little time to set up from scratch. The structure of the inquiry can be largely provided by the existing social environment and the technology serves to house and share the collection among all the players. And those players, instead of simply working through a path set out for them by the author, become the primary producers of content. By placing students' actions in the foreground, a data collection approach can quickly produce a context of productive inquiry among a group.

Geolocational Games

Despite our frequent use of the term games in talking about ARIS, a reader could be forgiven for not seeing how the above categories and examples above sound much like games at all. While I think the term itself is slippery[6] and justifying it here is not really to the point, there are some features and uses of ARIS that do feel a bit more gamey. *Items*, because they can be collected and referenced in quantity, have been used to create scores, scenarios of scarcity and completeness, and even crafting schema. The other major ARIS element that lends itself to gaminess is *spawning*. The ability for authors to *spawn* locations according to parameters rather than directly placing them on the map can be used to create familiar scenarios to many action-based games, the difference here being a human body traversing space instead of an avatar. Together, these features can be used by authors to explore the space of geolocational games directly.

Currently the most popular geolocational game made in ARIS is *Rupee Collector*. Virtual rupees (Zelda, not India; technically *plaques* that hand out *items*) spawn on the map around a player and last there a short duration. If the player can run to them and pick them up before they disappear, they receive points that depend on the color of the rupee. Another item in the player's inventory links to a webpage that references the statistics for the game. It is a leaderboard and players can compare their scores to all other players of *Rupee Collector* in the world. Although this game was made for its own sake, there is much interest in this kind of game mechanic for those coming to ARIS from the world of exergames. It seems possible that a fun geolocational game could be good exercise for its players.

---

[6] Wittgenstein famously used the word game to describe the difficulty with definitions generally in his *Philosophical Investigations*.

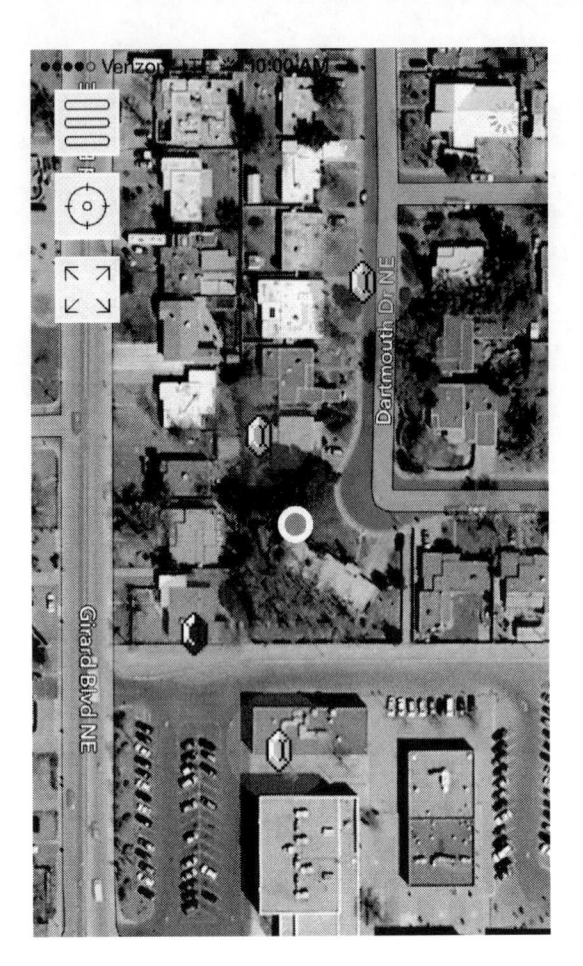

Figure 3. A screenshot from the ARIS game *Rupee Collector*. Gems spawn on the player's map and must be collected before they disappear or other players grab them.

WHO USES ARIS AND WHAT FOR?

In the previous section, I described the *kinds of things* one might create using ARIS. In this section I'd like to describe the motivations of that use as an almost orthogonal concept. To begin, ARIS is loosely but consistently linked with use in educational environments. Its design does not directly seek to address functionality schools are interested in for managing their learners—there's no quiz template or student progress reports, no official distinction about who should be using ARIS and how—but it is certainly designed with learning in mind more than entertainment and the vast majority of users seem to be interested in this aspect of its use. There is a great variety in where and how ARIS is put to educational purposes too. There seems to be no natural limit to the content areas that are applicable. ARIS is used in schools, museums, after school programs, experiments for academic research, and community organizations. Players and authors range from middle schoolers to retired professors. In this section, we describe some of the more popular settings and uses for ARIS games.

AR Games as Curriculum

Garza and Rosenblum (Chapter 9) present their work in developing an AR game (close to a data collection scavenger hunt) for students in a design course. This, *Mad City Mystery*, *Dow Day*, and *Mentira* are examples of this once standard imagining of the use of AR for learning.[7] The basic method is to find an existing curricular area and design and implement an AR game within it. The play of the AR game can help connect content to context, find ways to include content and practices unfortunately absent from the classroom. Sometimes an AR game can be used to actually invert the values expressed by instruction taking a focus on textbook content and changing it to the local context.

---

[7] Most of the experiments run and written about by Klopfer and Squire for example use AR in this vein. See (Klopfer, 2008), (Klopfer & Squire, 2008), (Squire et al., 2007).

Place can make content come alive. *Mentira* again can be a helpful example to understand the general concept. Students learn Spanish in a classroom and don't often access the language outside that classroom. Yet the language is worth learning because it is used so widely. Especially in places like Albuquerque, NM, the Spanish language is deeply wrapped up with the place and the people. Scarcity of opportunity to use the language is an artifact of learning it within a classroom. If you can bring students into the lived world of Spanish, you might be able to help them find meaning in their practice. This is very similar thinking to the long-standing practice of study-abroad.

Typical implementations also are characterized by features and concepts stemming from research into games and learning. An example of something a researcher or instructor might seek to gain by implementing a game in a curriculum is for students to see failure as a productive opportunity for learning rather than an admonishment of their abilities. In most curricular situations, failure, say on tests, mostly is used to tell students that they are not doing well enough. In games, failure is an essential part of progress. You learn to beat games by falling down pits, getting killed, simply losing, over and over again until you are better (or give up). By making a game that is played by part of a curriculum, planners hope to infect students with a more productive attitude towards failure.

Museum Exhibits and More: Indoor, Semi-formal Uses

More and more people have been using ARIS indoors to add structure and content to installations like museum exhibits. Since GPS does not work well indoors, these games usually work through the use of QR codes. Just as tours give authors a chance to tell the story of a place, ARIS games that sit atop museum exhibits can take the artifacts and dates and weave them into an actual story, providing extra meaning and context.

Examples are far ranging. The Minnesota Historical Society has produced *Play the Past*, the biggest ARIS game ever in terms of players and production effort. It is a combination exhibition space and ARIS game. Players play as early white settlers in Minnesota. 100,000 people are planned to play this game over the next 10 years.[8] At the other end, an undergraduate student made a game for her local history museum last summer. May's *Quest for the Cities of Gold* (chapter 15) layers a story over an existing exhibit to help the museum try to reach a younger audience. In both cases, the basic intent is to use ARIS to create a story that links the artifacts in the museum to one another, the contexts in which they take on meaning, and pull players into those worlds.

---

[8] *Play the Past* won a 2014 Muse Award (Bronze) and an International Serious Games Award (Gold) for its design. Its early development is chronicled by Seann Dikkers in the previous volume of *Mobile Media Learning* (2012).

Student Design Studios

Probably the most common use of ARIS in classrooms and after school environments is to create opportunities for students to make games, an instance of student MML design as suggested in the previous chapter. Sometimes this is done generically, as is common with other technical design tools like Scratch, accompanied by similar rationales for such use fitting into existing educational paradigms.[9] Possibly more unique to ARIS however, are the student design studios organized around producing games that speak to a specific context of inquiry. Mathews (2010) described using mobile game design as a lens for doing community research and action and has inspired many to follow his lead, including the editors and some authors of this book.[10] Within these environments, AR game creation can be used as a way to interrogate the values, methods, and content of a discipline—i.e. if you learn a lot of content while playing a game, you would stand to learn even more by making a game. AR game design is considered as an example area for learning lessons from the act and practice of design; making ARIS games can be a way to learn about working with others to make something complex.

Not only are the learning opportunities presented by design deep and multifaceted, they can also be authentic. Within the nascent area of AR design, even inexperienced youth can come up with designs that can go beyond the classroom and take on life in the world. There are so many avenues of exploration and so many open questions that it is not hard to find new areas to contribute to. Finally, design studios, as with the data collection activities, do not take much preparation to enact. Certainly facilitating design studios successfully is no easy task, but for those who wish to take on the challenge, facilitation doesn't imply close preparation; the necessities are more along the lines of existing interpersonal skills than prior media production or acquiring new technical skills.

Design-Based Research

Not every ARIS game made for use in the classroom has the classroom as its main theater. Instead many games are designed primarily as instruments of research. In its early life, ARIS was thought of first as a tool to support design-based research experiments. Following Anne Brown (1992) and others, design-based educational research is characterized by the concept of making something to be used within an existing learning context rather than setting up a laboratory setting specifically for the testing of a theory. Usually accompanying this basic intent to study learning in situ, are preferences for including participants as co-researchers, iteration, and a desire to read beyond the immediate situation in analyzing the study. There is also a hope that the instrument developed is not just diagnostic for research but can play some meaningful role in the learning context after

---

[9] See for example (Resnick, 2008) to see a description of patterns of activity emerging from informal Scratch use as useful for encouraging computational literacy.

[10] Frandy also describes a student design studio in his folklore course, and May's work in chapter 15 began in a class of mine modeled after Mathews'.

the study is over or be scaled for use in other contexts. Although the lines between action and research are often fuzzy with design based research, Bressler's work (chapter 7), fits this paradigm neatly, and the artistic experiments taken on by Adams, Perales, and their students (chapter 10) share some features as well.

Contributions to Community Resources, Art, and Entertainment

ARIS is also used to develop AR games, tours, and data collection activities to be used generally by a community as a resource. We see this with Dikkers and his team in their development of *ParkQuest* (chapter 16) and Wagler and Mathews' development of *Up River* (Wagler & Mathews, 2012). There are millions of possible such designs, otherwise forever undeveloped for want of resources. Sometimes the design experiences organized for youth have a community resource as a specifically designated form of output for student work. Other times ARIS is picked up outside any formal context and used to make something some community needs. May's game fits this context.

Artists interested in examining the possibilities of combining mobile media and place have likewise made use of ARIS (e.g Adams and Perales). Though they involve their students in the design of ARIS games, they see the format itself not as a tool for learning, but a tool to be learned so they can use it to explore the possibilities of mobile cinema. Finally, ARIS has been used totally informally, without any serious intent of any kind. Scavenger hunts have been made for the birthday parties of young children. *Rupee Collector* and other titles of mine have been made just for fun. Fisher and Dikkers' *Horror on the Ridges* (chapter 18) looks to make an AR horror game succeed first as entertainment, with learning applications left for a later stage. The lasting fun with ARIS for me is that it draws attention from such diverse centers.

ARIS IS MORE THAN A TOOL

What makes ARIS feel really powerful to me is the way in which it has become more than just a tool. The collective actions and conversations among those who use it have made it into something alive in a sense that is descriptive of the kinds of deep change to teaching and learning I suggested might be possible in the second chapter of this book. ARIS is characterized, among other qualities, by:

- Multiple possible uses. ARIS is not derived from or towards a particular discipline, topic, or skill set. People who use it bring their learning contexts with them and an incredible diversity of activity is the result.

- Diverse, non-hierarchical models of participation and multiple portals through which people become involved. No one is in charge of how you're supposed to use ARIS. You might make games, teach others to do so, use the code to make a different AR engine, or simply underwrite the cost of development.

- Many forms of expertise around and with ARIS can be independently developed. Those who have developed expertise in their work with ARIS can emerge as guides for others to follow, and this is across many possible contexts: within a school, across the internet to other ARIS users, and through academic research for example.

In describing ARIS above, it was impossible to do so other than through the concrete and diverse uses people across many educational contexts are putting ARIS to; the technical structures of ARIS really have little meaning outside the kinds of creations being produced and the situations from which users are coming. They are a big part of what ARIS has actually come to be, inseparable from the software itself. Indeed, the meaning and uses of ARIS were not designed in advance by its creators but instead have emerged and evolved through the actions and inventiveness of its users. The whole is more than the sum of its parts.

Finally, we should recognize how users contribute to ARIS itself. There are too many examples to mention but a few should help convey this idea. I fit the well-known paradigm of the evangelist early adopter. I came to the platform as a simple user in 2009 before you could actually download the ARIS Client from the iOS App Store, but have ended up helping to design the tool, largely wrote the documentation (http://manual.arisgames.org), am responsible for much of the content on the project's homepage, and the most active member of a discussion forum for ARIS users. Oh, and I'm writing this chapter about ARIS right now. ARIS has also had investors, groups like Engage, The MacArthur Foundation, The New Learning Institute, and The Library of Congress: Teaching with Primary Sources Program who saw some potential in these ideas and funded them, and others like the Minnesota Historical Society who have funded ARIS and used it to develop the rather large *Play the Past* game/exhibit mentioned above. Owen Gottlieb through ConverJent has managed to fill both of these roles in his work to produce *Jewish Time Jump*. The support and use of ARIS by a few key people and groups has provided resources and concepts that have trickled back down to all users. On a less obvious level, each person who makes an ARIS game and uses it or tells someone else about it expands what has been previously done with the platform.

The diversity of work hinted at above and displayed by our authors is the outcome of a distributed conversation among many people experimenting and sharing. Seeing ARIS in this way prevents us from pigeonholing our efforts or the ideas of our users. We begin to understand how to think about tools like ARIS from a humanistic rather than instrumentalist point of view. We see ARIS as a community and not just a piece of software.

REFERENCES

Brown, A. L. (1992). Design experiments: Theoretical and methodological challenges in creating complex interventions in classroom settings. *The journal of the learning sciences, 2*(2), 141-178.

Dikkers, S. (2012). History in our hands: mobile media in museum adventures. In *Mobile Media Learning* (pp. 171-184). ETC Press.

Gagnon, D. (2010). ARIS: An open source platform for developing mobile learning experiences. *Unpublished Master's thesis.* Available at arisgames.org.

Holden, C., Gagnon, D., Litts, B., & Smith, G. (2013). ARIS: An open-source platform for widespread mobile augmented reality experimentation. In M. Mendes (Ed), *Technology platform innovations and forthcoming trends in ubiquitous learning.* IGI Global.

Holden, C., & Sykes, J. (2012). Mentira: prototyping language-based locative gameplay. In *Mobile Media Learning* (pp. 111-130). ETC Press.

Klopfer, E. (2008). Augmented learning: Research and design of mobile educational games. MIT Press.

Klopfer, E., & Squire, K. (2008). Environmental Detectives—the development of an augmented reality platform for environmental simulations. Educational Technology Research and Development, 56(2), 203-228.

Mathews, J. M. (2010). Using a studio-based pedagogy to engage students in the design of mobile-based media. *English Teaching: Practice & Critique, 9*(1).

Resnick, M. (2008). Sowing the Seeds for a More Creative Society. *Learning & Leading with Technology, 35*(4), 18-22.

Squire, K., & Jan, M. (2007). Mad City Mystery: Developing scientific argumentation skills with a place-based augmented reality game on handheld computers. *Journal of Science Education and Technology, 16*(1), 5-29.

Squire, K., Jan, M., Mathews, J., Wagler, M., Martin, J., DeVane, B., & Holden, C. (2007). Wherever you go, there you are: Place-based augmented reality games for learning. The educational design and use of simulation computer games, 265-296.

Wagler, M., & Mathews, J. (2012). Up river: place, ethnography, and design in the st. louis river estuary. In *Mobile Media Learning* (pp. 39-60). ETC Press.

SECTION THREE

Connecting to Classrooms

7.   School Scene Investigators:
     A Collaborative AR Game for Middle School Science Inquiry
8.   Building a Student-Centered Classroom with AR
9.   Introducing a Neighborhood
10. Experimenting with Locative Media Games and Storytelling in Fine Arts

---

This section collects stories from teachers, researchers, technologists, and artists using Mobile Media within classroom or school environments. The transformation of formal learning environments using MML presents unique challenges and constraints. These authors see their use of MML as a way to address shortcomings of method and pedagogy in their instructional situations, from elementary school science to folklore and art in higher ed. Most of the authors are also the classroom instructors in these settings, while Bressler is an education researcher using a class within a school as the test group for her design-based research, and Rosenblum's role in their project is technically as IT instructional support. This section, along with the field study classes in Traveler (chapter 4) illustrate some of the possibilities of transforming an existing curricular space with MML. They describe several strategies to make MML—complex as it may seem— within familiar constraints of time, expertise, materials, and curricular goals.

CHAPTER SEVEN

School Scene Investigators: A Collaborative AR Game for Middle School Science Inquiry

Denise M. Bressler, PhD
Stevens Institute of Technology

Did you ever think that you could engage and excite students by sending them to the Principal's office?

Imagine you are a middle school student. Your iPhone pops up with an alert. "Go see the Principal right now!" You head down the corridors, down the stairs, and arrive at the front office to find a quick-response code (QR code) with the word PRINCIPAL next to it. You scan it. A picture of your Principal appears on the screen with the text, "Hello." You click to keep reading the onscreen conversation. The Principal says:

> I just came into my office and found my drawer broken into. I had the answer keys in there to the test everyone is taking! You're always causing trouble and I think you did it. Confess!

This is the beginning of *School Scene Investigators: The Case of the Stolen Score Sheets*—a forensic science mystery game played on iOS devices in a school environment. Students collect forensic evidence to prove their innocence and determine who really stole the answer sheets. As they move around the school, they encounter QR codes that they scan to access game-related information (see Figure 1). In some instances, they converse with a virtual character. At other times, scanning a code means discovering evidence to keep in their virtual inventory. Throughout the game, players are exposed to some basic elements of forensic science, like analyzing fingerprints, hair samples, and other trace evidence. They also work through other problems like interpreting a coded message on a slip of paper and determining whether characters have ulterior motives.

In making this game, my goals were to 1) design a game that supported collaborative problem solving; 2) create a game design that other educators could easily replicate and implement; and 3) make a game that was a fun, learning experience for the students. In this chapter, I share my game development process revealing what design aspects were important to me and how they were integrated into the game. Then, I explain what happened during gameplay by sharing observations of what the groups said and did. Next, I summarize my thoughts on what worked well and what needs to be improved. Ultimately, I end with my thoughts on the power of well-designed learning games.

Figure 1. Student scanning QR code.

BUILDING THE GAME

AR games hold promise to support active learning scenarios such as collaborative problem solving. Popular culture has had a recent obsession with forensic science television shows that follow multi-functional teams working together to solve mysteries. To me, there seemed a natural synergy between the affordances of AR games and the group dynamics of the popularized version of forensic teams. Since forensic science is also popular with science teachers, and had the potential to appeal to both boys and girls, it was a sensible choice for a middle school science mystery game. Additionally, no other mobile AR games focused on forensic science, especially not within the context of the students' own school.

To create a portable game that other educators could use, I wanted a technology that is relatively cheap and simple to implement in as many schools as possible. Most mobile augmented reality games take advantage of place-based information, which requires the player to use a GPS-enabled device. Since mobile devices with GPS are expensive and require cellular plans, I decided to use printable QR codes, school wi-fi access, and the free ARIS editor. Since ARIS only runs on iOS, usable devices included wifi-enabled models with cameras: the iPod Touch and iPad as well as iPhones, both with and without cellular plans.

Lastly, I thought it would intrigue students to see their school environment from a different viewpoint. In this case, their school would become the crime scene for a theft. I also thought it would add to the personal feel if the school's Principal was the game's Principal; he agreed and allowed me to use his picture in the game. Using the school as a personal context made the game not only enjoyable but also easier to implement since there was no need for chaperones, permission slips, or busing. Usually AR games are set outside in places relevant to their story lines, so minimizing attendant bureaucracy of field trips is a benefit of school-based AR games.

GAME DESIGN

There is research showing that collaborative problem solving could be achieved through a jigsaw technique (Dunleavy, Dede, & Mitchell, 2009). Recognizing this led me to two important design decisions:

- No player would have all the information needed to solve the mystery.
- Not all players would have quests, or tasks within the game, at the same time.

This research also indicates that jigsawing could be achieved by organizing players into roles. For the player, the role functions as an in-game identity. For the jigsaw technique, each role has different abilities and is given a different part of the puzzle to solve. All the roles come together to form a collaborative team.

Another concept I found helpful for creating my game is the theory of Flow. Flow is a positive psychological state that people experience when they are totally consumed by an activity. Rules of Play by Katie Salen and Eric Zimmerman (2004)[1] explains the connection between game design and the components of Flow as defined by Csikszentmihalyi (1990)[2]. Specifically, they suggest giving players clear goals, a sense of control, unambiguous feedback, and a challenging activity to help them achieve Flow while playing. To do this, I added four additional prerequisites to my game design:

- Reliance on the quests feature to guide players through the game with clear goals,
- A non-linear game so players had control over the order of game elements,
- A win state so players received feedback on successfully completing the game, and
- A decryption challenge which needed to be solved to unlock the final phase of the game

---

[1] A great reference for game design detailed enough to provide extra insight to those with a foundation of knowledge and broad enough to give newbies a chance to get their feet wet.

[2] As an athlete and intellectual, I have certainly experienced feelings of Flow for a long time; Csikszentmihalyi gave me the words to understand this complicated feeling in a tangible way.

GAME OVERVIEW
Introduction

Before students started the game, I provided players with a brief tutorial. Since it was a mystery, I did not want to reveal too many specifics of the plot line. Furthermore, I trusted that the students would be able to figure out the technology together. The tutorial included the following software features along with these brief details (see Table 1 for screenshots):

Table 1. Screenshots from *School Scene Investigators*.

Sample Quest Screen	Sample Inventory Item	Decoder

- *Quests provided in-game tasks.* Students viewed their active quests by using the tab at the bottom of the screen. They were told to pay attention to the quests because they tell you where to go and what to do. Not every player had a quest at the same time.
- *Inventory stored virtual items.* Students viewed their inventory items by selecting the tab at the bottom of the screen. They were told that when you select an item on the list you will see a picture. To read more about the item, select "Detail." Items appear and disappear from your inventory throughout the game.
- *Decoder enabled players to interact with game elements.* Students used the decoder tab to scan QR codes. There is one point in the game when they also needed to type numbers; to do this, they used the text field at the top of the screen.

Once the software tutorial concluded, I confirmed that all players knew basic iPhone navigation techniques such as pinching to zoom and swiping up and down to scroll. Finally, I explained that every player needed to scan every code and that players had to stay together as a group.

Storyline

In *School Scene Investigators,* the first thing a player does is pick a role. A Player can be the social networker, techie, science whiz, or photographer. Based on their role, each player collects a unique piece of evidence from the crime scene as well as each suspect. Briefly, each player becomes an "expert" in a specific strand of evidence, such as blood, hair, fingerprints, or shoe prints (see Table 2). The mystery cannot be solved without all players communicating correctly to the group about their collected evidence, with the exception of the photographer. To allow flexibility, the photographer's role was made non-integral so that groups of three or four could successfully complete the game.

SIDEBAR: GETTING YOUR OWN GAME GOING

For those who might enjoy building a similar project, I'd like to offer a few pointers:

- *Do your homework.* Find other games that you like and model your game after your favorites.

- *Find an engaging topic or story.* A compelling narrative is a great place to start thinking about your characters, locations, and inventory items.

- *Run your ideas past your target audience.* I had nieces and nephews who gave feedback on my early ideas. Their input was priceless!

Table 2. Description of roles and assignment of game information to each role.

Role	Description	Crime scene evidence	Evidence from suspects
Social networker	Good with people and knows everybody's business at school	Hair sample from drawer	Collects hair samples
Techie	Good at solving puzzles and has cool phone apps	Pen (with fingerprint)	Scans suspects fingerprints with an "app"
Science whiz	Conducts experiments at home with household supplies	Blood sample from drawer	Collects blood samples
Photographer	Carries a camera and takes pictures of everything	Picture of shoe print	Collects pictures of suspects' shoes

The narrative of the game is partly inspired by the time frame scheduled for implementation of this study: a two-week period in March when students take the state standardized test every morning for 3 hours. The game fits into the empty afternoons and the testing serves as the instigator of the plot. When students are called into the Principal's office, they are accused of having stolen the answers. Players' initial goal is to prove their collective innocence.

After the initial accusation, the Principal agrees to let the players explore his office...the primary crime scene. Students open the door, spot the next code, and scan it. Players then read a description of the scene:

> You have entered the Principal's office. In his desk, you see a drawer with a busted lock. This is the drawer where the answer sheets must have been stolen from. In the drawer, you find a strand of hair, blood, and a pen. On the floor under the drawer, you also find a shoe print. You decide to divide up the evidence.

Players each take a piece of evidence depending on their role. For example, if you are the photographer, you take a picture of the shoe print left at the crime scene. The storyline takes you to the gym next where you meet John and take a picture of his shoes. The game continues to guide you around the school to meet and interact with other virtual characters, collecting more evidence along with way. Over the course of solving the mystery, the photographer ends up with a set of shoe prints from possible suspects that can then be compared to the print left at the crime scene. (See Table 3 for collected images). This is only one clue about the thief, teams need to consider all other trace evidence in order to prove their innocence.

Table 3. Crime scene shoe print and relevant evidence.

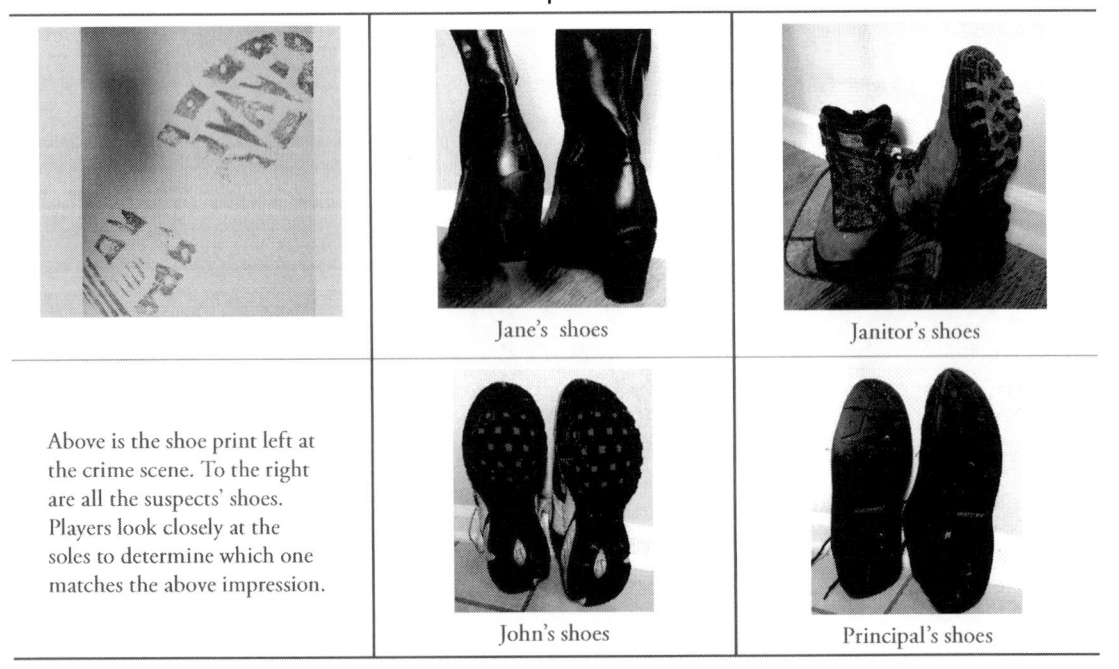

(shoe print image)	Jane's shoes	Janitor's shoes
Above is the shoe print left at the crime scene. To the right are all the suspects' shoes. Players look closely at the soles to determine which one matches the above impression.	John's shoes	Principal's shoes

The final step in the game has players analyze all the evidence they have collected. Each player has several pieces of evidence to analyze by assessing their similarities and differences. Most of the evidence indicts one of the suspects, but there is some room for additional interpretation. Ultimately, the group reports back to the Principal with an allegation of who really stole the answer sheets.

GAME ON! RUNNING THE RESEARCH TRIALS

Students were recruited through science teachers who were willing to let students miss a class period to participate. A total of 68 students volunteered to participate in the study. There were 19 groups of students representing eighth grade students (47.1%), seventh grade (29.4%), and sixth grade (23.5%). Most groups were mixed gender (n=14); however there were three boy-only and two girl-only groups. Since I wanted to observe every group play through the game, groups played one at a time. I followed every group trying to remain in the background as I took field notes. I paid particular attention to their collaboration.

Collaboration seemed to build over the course of the game. In the beginning, players would stand alone reading with minimal discussion amongst the group (see Table 4). They quickly realized that not everyone had a quest and they started questioning each other by saying "I didn't get anything... Who has a quest?" or "What's your quest?" After reading the information provided at a location, I observed them asking questions, for example: "What did you get as a sample from the office?" Early in the game, I also saw players helping each other learn to scan codes and to use the software.

As the game progressed, players seemed to interact more by looking at each other's phones, sharing information verbally, and even sitting or standing closer together (see Table 4). After visiting the first or second suspect, players realized that each suspect was saying different things to each player as well as giving different items to each player. Students started directly interacting with each other to fill in gaps in their knowledge asking other group members, "What did you get?" or even showing fellow teammates their phones and saying, "Look what I got." As play continued, students started talking out loud as they tried to make sense of the evidence, and fellow players might confirm or deny their thoughts. For example, one student said, "Maybe it was the Principal" and his teammate responded, "No. No. Wouldn't make any sense. Look at his hair sample."

Table 4. Progression of physical proximity of players.

Beginning of game	Middle of game	End of game

In the middle of the game, players had to decode the janitor's locker combination; it was the first and only time that a correct answer was required in order to continue in the game. Many teams struggled with the task; in fact, despite several attempts, some groups could not get into the locker and decided to complete other unfinished quests and come back later. Often, students worked through a trial and error process with different team members offering suggestions for what the decrypted code might be. Students could have let their difficulties defeat them, but they always persevered and it paid off. With shouts of "Oh yes!" and "I love this game!" players were often thrilled to decipher the code and unlock the locker. Since this challenging task was located mid game, students had experienced enough gaming enjoyment to know that it was worth persevering. Plus, they were getting close to figuring out the identity of the thief and breaking into the locket would probably reveal another clue!

At the end of the game, a great deal of discussion and interaction occurred as students tried to determine the real thief (see Table 4). Once the players had collected all the possible evidence, most groups sorted through the details together. Here's a sample conversation amongst a three player group as they start to narrow down the possible suspects:

> "Well then. We have to discuss evidence."
>
> "What do we have?"
>
> "Pen… blood…fingerprints."
>
> "So, it's the Principal. The janitor. Or the cat" [laughter]
>
> "Oh yeah. The janitor. Let's check his hair."
>
> "Janitor AB positive and Principal AB positive. And the blood from drawer is like that."

As groups began to narrow down the suspect list, students also referenced some of the content knowledge that they learned during gameplay. Here are sample comments from a group that showcased their adoption of specific terminology (arch, loops, and whorls) to describe fingerprints:

> "That looks like an arch."
>
> "This kind of looks like it, look at the loops and whorls."
>
> Player A: "See if it matches." Player B: "That's not an arch."

Time and time again, players were trying to make sense of the information they were given by talking to each other; all of these interactions occurred naturally and were not prompted by direct instructions in the game. However, after visiting all game locations, all players received a quest that prompted them to discuss all the evidence with their teammates. Some groups immediately sat down and analyzed all the data thoroughly before reporting back to the Principal to make their final allegation. However, other teams did not follow the instructions. Some groups went to the Principal's office first, and then when the game asked for their answer, they discussed the data and came to consensus before entering the answer. There were even some groups that did not come to consensus before selecting an answer. So while the game scaffolded collaborative problem solving using the jigsaw technique, the game design did not require students to discuss the information. Many students naturally and willingly discussed their evidence, but not everyone did, and those who did not had greater difficulties identifying the correct thief.

After groups finished gameplay, I sat and talked with them for a few minutes hoping to delve into the most and least enjoyable aspects of the game as well as what they learned, if anything. Focus group discussions revealed that students felt they learned how to work well as a team. Many students were truly surprised by how well they worked together. A number of students said they normally argue with each other in class, yet they actually worked well together during the game. Others indicated they were not necessarily friends but they got along fine. In one extreme case, two boys admitted to being arch enemies yet they both agreed they did a good job together during the game. In fact, the group interactions between these arch enemies were some of the best of any group in the sample. Since I had specifically built the game to support collaborative problem solving, it was encouraging to hear that the students learned about teamwork.

BRINGING IT ALL TOGETHER
Things That Worked Well

Looking back at my goals for the project, there was a lot that worked well.

Collaborative problem solving. One of the goals of the project was to design a game that promoted collaborative problem solving. By dividing up the quests and giving each player a strand of evidence to follow, the game design seems to have supported collaborative problem solving and minimized the hogs and logs problem that sometimes occurs in collaborative groups. The student who might be inclined to take control of the situation (the hog) could not direct the group unless he or she had a quest. In a similar vein, the student who might be easily overpowered in a group (the log) had a voice and responsibility because each player followed a unique line of evidence.

Additionally, I think the game afforded students the opportunity to synthesize data in a way distinct from traditional classroom based activities. Unlike a worksheet activity, the students were not sitting in science class alone trying to answer questions out of context, rather they were moving about the school experiencing content in context. One player, noticing the difference in mode, referred to their actions in the game as "actually experimenting." Every analysis problem, such as which shoe made the shoe print, gave the group deeper insight into who the thief might be. Many players seemed invested in solving the game problems; the scientific thinking they did in the game was not only different from their usual school experience but also deeply engaging.

Create a portable game. Another goal for the project was to create a game that others could replicate and implement. Even though the game has not yet been used elsewhere, given the hope of making this game portable to other school environments, it was nice to see the technology work well. It was not perfect, but it worked really, really well. Students got bumped out of the game here and there, or stuck on a screen, but it was never enough to be frustrating. The secret was stable software, reliable wireless internet, and the use of QR codes. Using QR codes instead of GPS meant that students did not have to rely on an imprecise signal to move them through the game and other educators need only to print out the codes to implement this game at their schools. If you are interested in setting up the game at your school, information is available at the end of this chapter.

Create a fun, learning experience. The final goal for the project was to make a game that was a fun, learning experience. Student enjoyment was witnessed during gameplay; some players clearly articulated their enjoyment by exclaiming "This is fun stuff!" or "I love this game!" and even "This was awesome!" For some players, enjoyment seemed to stem from being proud of their achievements. In one instance, an apprehensive girl successfully scanned the first QR code and announced, "Oh! I did it!" In another example, one boy selected the correct thief and then proclaimed, "I am the BEAST!"

Ultimately, I believe that the players had an enjoyable experience because it was outside school norms, it was novel, and it incorporated strong game design principles. First, it was outside school norms because students were actively breaking school rules to participate in my research. Students were in the hallways during class doing a list of unauthorized behaviors, such as running, talking, and using mobile phones; it was exciting for students to transgress such familiar boundaries. Second, the human brain loves novelty and the experience was unlike anything they had ever done before. Specifically, it was unlike any prior school experience and, although players had some familiarity with smartphones and QR codes, no one had ever played a collaborative mobile AR game. Lastly, I believe the game benefited from directly incorporating knowledge of Flow and jigsaw-based collaboration into the design principles. The game design met the prerequisites of promoting Flow, which led to a positive psychological effect for participants, and dispersed information to individual players which led to communication and often collaboration amongst participants.

Areas for Improvement

Even though a lot went well in this first iteration, there were some rough edges and challenges that have yet to be addressed.

Collaborative problem solving. Groups played one at a time so there is no way for me to confirm that it effectively supports collaborative problem solving during a full class implementation. Before teachers can use this game as a complete class activity, there are several issues that need to be addressed. First, QR codes are in static locations and can only be scanned by one player at a time; therefore, there is potential for bottlenecks. In this study, students did not mind waiting for the 2 or 3 other group members to scan the code; however, they might have been frustrated if there was a bottleneck of 20 students! Second, with other groups playing simultaneously, groups more apt to freeload might follow the stronger teams instead of figuring out the information themselves. Lastly, competition might increase, and groups might rush through to finish first rather than take their time to read through the information and solve the problem correctly.

There are several design decisions that could be incorporated to enable full classes to play simultaneously. First, more QR codes could be generated to create different codes depending on player role. In other words, when players arrive at the new location, they might see a set of 4 labeled codes and they scan the one that correlates to their role. Second, the early part of the game could offer more choices in hopes of spreading out the students to different locations throughout the school creating less overlap at the same locations. Finally, different versions of the game could be created so that each character is moved to a different location. For example, in Game A, John is at the gym and Jane is at the library whereas in Game B John could be at the guidance office and Jane could be in the music room. If groups are playing in different areas of the school, this might reduce the likelihood of teams following or competing with each other.

Create a portable game. Fortunately and unfortunately, the entire game takes place in the hallways and students are expected to talk to each other. Certainly, this is part of the fun. Yet, since the game does not fit the mold of school it may be difficult for others to implement. Field observations revealed that students talking and running in the halls can disrupt classes that are in session. In fact, during the early part of the two-week research trial, almost every group was stopped and reprimanded by teachers for running in the halls, talking in the halls, or simply being in the halls during the class period. The Principal quickly remedied the problem by sending a school-wide memo to briefly explain the research project and ask for their patience and understanding. However, this disruption problem will persist in other schools given the convention of school buildings and class periods. Rather than be discouraged by this, I am inclined to consider this as a small way to challenge the often stifling norms of school.

Create a fun, learning experience. Students had fun, but it is unclear what they learned. The game did not have content learning goals; but rather, it was a puzzle to be solved. The game gave players all the pieces they needed to solve the puzzle. I assumed that I had laid out the information so clearly that almost every group would make the correct accusation. Unexpectedly, only 60% of the players guessed the thief correctly on the first try. One of two scenarios is probably responsible:

1. Groups did not employ problem solving skills and used trial and error instead.
2. The game was challenging and, despite employing their problem solving skills, some groups could not successfully complete the challenge.

The first scenario was observed on occasion; groups did not make a final decision together but rather instructed different group members to select different thieves and see which player got the right answer. Ironically, it showed teamwork but was not demonstrative of the intended way to solve the problem. This distributed trial and error technique did not require students to synthesize the data collaboratively and thus students did not engage in higher-order thinking skills, namely the scientific practice of arguing with evidence. Luckily, the game design allowed students to revisit their evidence and make another guess if their first answer was incorrect.

The second scenario was observed as well. Several teams narrowed the thief down to two suspects but could not conclude who did it; groups retained the Principal as a suspect because his shoe print was at the scene as well as the real thief for whom all the fingerprint, blood, and hair evidence matched. In the game design, the Principal's shoe print is at the crime scene because it is his office; the shoe print is a red herring intended to mislead the players, since the Principal is not the thief. This design decision was intended to reflect real life, showing that you have to make the best case you can because the evidence is not always perfect. But students were confused when the answer was not immediately clear from the simplest reading of the available evidence.

Ultimately, there is still more room for students to learn how to collaborate and solve problems together. Students were not used to this new manner of working together and relying on each other. Therefore, not every group solved the puzzle correctly. But collaboration is a necessary life skill. So even though all students did not get the right answer, they seemed to leave the game with a heightened sense of teamwork and an impression of what it felt like to collaborate well with others. If the players had a thought-provoking journey rather than arriving at the intended destination, that's fine by me.

CONCLUDING REMARKS

As Jane McGonigal (2011) proclaims…we are our best selves when we are playing games[3]; I definitely saw students become the best version of themselves. As they struggled to overcome obstacles together, they become empowered. Working on their own was not something they were used to: players explained that the teacher usually tells them what to do and "you didn't help… you weren't the teacher… you didn't tell us every step." According to my field observations, it did not take long for them to start embracing their new freedom and control over their learning. Afterwards, players realized what the experience offered them: "It teaches you how to do things on your own." One of the best examples of empowerment was a group of girls who said they felt like Charlie's Angels afterwards. They even broke into the theme song from the movie: "I'm a survivor. I'm not gonna give up…" as they were walking back to their classroom after the game concluded. Empowerment arose as their in-game identities helped them to find kinship with a well-known crime fighting group of powerful women from popular culture.

Creating good games is a great way to empower students to learn. I saw students persevering in the face of challenge and learning to work together to solve a problem. The game experience also resonated deeply with players. After gameplay, one boy mentioned that, "If I could go back in time, I would. To this day. So, I could do this again." One of the female players stated that, "if every single class was like this, everyday, I would want to come [to school] like for the rest of my life." In playing *School Scene Investigators: The Case of the Stolen Score Sheets,* students became empowered and successfully completed challenging tasks; I am convinced that well-designed games make powerful learning environments.

---

[3] McGonigal and her magnificent book fundamentally shifted my view of games in an enjoyable, rational, and entirely visionary way.

REFERENCES

Csikszentmihalyi, M. (1990). *Flow: The psychology of optimal experience:* New York: Harper and Row.

Dunleavy, M., Dede, C., & Mitchell, R. (2009). Affordances and limitations of immersive participatory augmented reality simulations for teaching and learning. *Journal of Science Education and Technology, 18*(1), 7–22.

McGonigal, J. (2011). *Reality is broken: Why games make us better and how they can change the world.* New York: The Penguin Press.

Salen, K., & Zimmerman, E. (2004). *Rules of play: Game design fundamentals.* Cambridge, MA: The MIT Press.

Appendix

If you would like to implement the game at our own school, please email the author Denise Bressler (dmbressler at gmail dot com) for the instructions and printable QR codes. The game is freely available in the ARIS application.

CHAPTER EIGHT

Building a Student-Centered Classroom with AR

Tim Frandy
University of Wisconsin-Madison

Service learning, team-based projects, flipped classrooms, and high impact learning have come to dominate the discourse of innovative pedagogies in higher education in recent years. Unfortunately, in an era of difficult budgets, increasing class sizes, and canonization of knowledge through standardized assessment, teachers face many difficulties implementing these new pedagogies in today's classrooms. With the ideal classroom far removed from today's political realities, online and mobile technologies offer recourse for educators to teach more effectively for increasing numbers of students. This was my own goal, in integrating Augmented Reality Interactive Storytelling (ARIS) into the course Introduction to Folklore between 2011 and 2013. I developed two separate uses of augmented reality technologies for the course. The first involved having students use augmented reality on a mobile device for the purpose of ethnographic data collection, research sharing, and subsequent analysis. The second involved student curation of their own ethnographic fieldwork into a narrative-driven, place-based game for a mobile device. In this book chapter, I will relate my motives for integrating these two projects into the classroom, explore the successes and shortcomings of each project, and examine some of the needs folklorists and other humanists have for mobile technologies in the coming years.

TECHNOLOGY AND CURRICULUM DESIGN FOR DEEP LEARNING

Folklore is, succinctly defined, as the study of everyday life and culture. A disciplinary cousin to cultural anthropology and ethnology, folklore is rooted in ethnographic fieldwork and the documenting of cultural practices, traditions, arts and crafts, oral narratives, and much more. Folklore has a rich history of collaborations with communities to create public projects—like exhibitions, archives, films, radio programming, cultural tours, festivals, social networks—that address a community need or advocate for the community's interests.

In the classroom, we folklorists often ask our students to conduct fieldwork, to work in the local community, and to curate their research for a public audience. Folklore educators need to cultivate a wide set of skills with their students. Not only must students write and research well, but they must also learn the art of the ethnographic interview. They must learn to take compelling photographs and video, conduct digital editing, and create digital products for a general audience. Teaching such a wide array of skills to students poses great challenges to folklore educators. As I designed my course, I wondered what role emergent and mobile technologies could play in teaching students the difficult process of how to conduct fieldwork.

The challenge I faced was that many available educational technologies were seemingly designed to fit the top-down pedagogies of lecture-hall classrooms. However, students tend to learn the complex skills of photography and interviewing best through practice, through their own failures and successes, and not through traditional lecture-based instruction. Innovative pedagogies (e.g. service-learning, high-impact learning, team-based capstones, flipped classrooms, student-centered learning, etc.) often seem at odds with the de facto approach of educational technologies. Conventional online course management systems have proven very useful for sharing text-based information and multimedia, but student interaction is conducted primarily through instructor-initiated message boards (an online tool predating the emergence of social media) and chaotic or rigidly structured large-group chats. Trying to encourage students to participate in meaningful and thoughtful discussion online is a challenge in its own right. In my own experience, student participation in online fora is more dependent on graded participation than on the desire to critically engage with the course content.

My interest lies in building a student-centered classroom where students want to engage with the materials of their own accord. To do so, I aspired to use new technologies to simulate the small-classroom environment in which student-driven pedagogies have a track record of success. In my own classroom, I aim to not merely transmit information, but also to teach critical thinking, effective argumentation, and historical construction of the present. These skills are best acquired through close mentorship, through interaction in small groups, and through a classroom that acts as a learning-community. With conventional online teaching tools catered toward information transmission, I hoped I could make use of mobile technologies in a way better suited to simulating the small-classroom environment—conducive to my pedagogical goals—inside a large classroom.

USING AUGMENTED REALITY TO TEACH ETHNOGRAPHIC DOCUMENTATION

Facing the challenge of familiarizing students with what good ethnographic fieldwork looks like—and unable to take the time to personally mentor eighty students in their interviews, photography, and videography—I developed a mobile game using ARIS in which students could collect, discuss, and critique the fieldwork of their peers. The game was played early in the semester, to give students an introduction to conducting fieldwork, with the idea that abundant mistakes would allow for many teachable moments. As students played the augmented reality game on their mobile devices, they were asked to upload video, audio, and photography into the gamespace. This fieldwork would relate to student culture at the University of Wisconsin-Madison, a community with which all students would have some degree of familiarity. Viewable by other players, students populated the gamespace with their fieldwork, and students could "like" and comment on the fieldwork of other players. Finally, after the two-week documentation project was completed, I asked students to write a reflective essay about the fieldwork within the game. Students reflected on their own and their peers' documentation, focusing specifically on which examples succeeded (and failed) and why.

The plot of this ARIS game was simple. Two Teaching Assistants and I were written as in-game characters who asked students to go out into the field, and to document one place, one example of material culture, and one oral narrative that was important to student folklife in Madison. I included a handful of examples of already completed activities in the game in advance of its release to further demonstrate our expectation. Using ARIS' Notebook feature, students could directly upload this media collected using their mobile devices' cameras and microphones. Each of these Notes would be mapped accordingly within the gamespace in the location they were documented. Over the span of two weeks in the field, students recorded street musicians and political protesters, collected stories about the stresses of "move-in day" in the residence halls, documented places of work and play, and chronicled the murals in campus elevators created by art students. Many of these examples were excellent. On the other side of the spectrum, some students used scripted and rehearsed stories, selected stock images of places, or chose to document places that were somewhat uninspired. The varied quality was the expected result for the project, and was essential for the reflection essay which followed.

Following the period of documentation, students were asked to re-enter the game, to review the fieldwork of their peers, and write a reflection essay that 1) analyzes how students view and represent student culture in Madison as detailed in this game; and 2) evaluates what makes certain fieldwork successful in content and presentation, and what makes the less-successful fieldwork fall flat. Because students could easily differentiate amongst the quality of the Notes, the reflection essay helped tangibly illustrate how fieldwork succeeds in presentation and why it sometimes struggles. As students reviewed the game in preparation for writing their essays, comments and "likes" helped elevate certain Notes into prominence. Students themselves came to relative consensus over the quality of the Notes, which put students collectively at the center of the learning process, while saving me hours of mentorship time.

The early exposure to a large selection of student-created ethnographic fieldwork proved to be a great success for the students. Having gotten their hands dirty with interviews, photography, and videography, students developed a good intuition of developing fieldwork for production within the first month of the semester. In previous semesters, students acquired these fieldwork skills much more slowly, pushing essential learning toward the end of the semester as their semester projects came due. In turn, this jeopardized student grades, as simple and commonplace fieldwork mistakes were left unaddressed until the end of the term. Using the mobile game, however, allowed a student-driven peer evaluation process to cultivate these skills early in the semester. By the end of the term, students were outperforming my expectations.

Perhaps similar results could have been obtained through the use of online fora or courseware. But mobile technologies allow for a streamlined user experience from camera to archive, thereby eliminating cumbersome file compatibility and upload troubles. Further, the mapping of ethnographic data—a basic feature of the ARIS Notebook—creates a convenient and intuitive system for students to interact with an abundance of stored information. Peer evaluation would have been considerably less pleasant if students were, for instance, required to review a list of uploaded documents and images in a cloud-based service.

Yet, in my opinion, the greatest reason for student success is that the use of an experimental and unproven augmented reality mobile game helped cultivate a sense of community and teamwork within the class. By being forthright with my uncertain expectations about the game, I undermined my own authority in the classroom. The mobile game did not conform to the tried and true expectations that students have acclimated to with their other educational technologies. Even the challenge of trying something new and risky with a course allowed students to warm to the project with a sense of adventure and wide-open expectations. Students learned to work together to overcome obstacles, to seek out learning within the assignment, and to work collaboratively with their instructors to make sure the assignment's expectations were met. With the game as a fabricated common obstacle and challenge for us all, students and instructors were cast onto the same team. This sense of camaraderie endured throughout the semester, and allowed students to fully participate in a learning community of their own design. This sense of community helped break down barriers to learning that are common in large lecture-hall environments. The mobile game circumvented the information-transfer model of education and the instructor-student hierarchy, instead putting student-driven content and peer-evaluation at the center of the learning process.

Although many educational technologies are most frequently used for the mass dissemination of information, there is little reason why these technologies cannot be purposed for the use of innovative small-classroom pedagogies in large lecture-hall environments. Technologies like social media and mobile technologies are still untouched arenas in most university classrooms. These technologies have great potential to create a co-constructed virtual and situated interactive learning environment. The potential for an interactive augmented reality gamespace to serve as the basis for small-group work and peer feedback is virtually limitless.

FROM EXPLORATION TO CURATION: STUDENT DEVELOPED ARIS GAMES

Although conducting quality ethnographic fieldwork is a major concern for folklorists, curating it for a public audience is of equal importance. Representing living people to a public audience is a challenging process, which depends largely on conscious choices of the ethnographer. Yet learning to ethically represent living research subjects is an essential objective of student learning in an Introduction to Folklore course. Conventional term papers live within the safe zone of student and instructor, where the ethical responsibility of students is minimized; in term papers, students can generally represent their informants in any light, without fear of repercussions from their informants or their communities. Public projects require students to deliberate over a host of ethical concerns, an essential topic of study for anyone engaged in human subjects research. Given the need to cultivate technological literacy within students, and given the ease of accessibility associated with digital media, UW-Madison folklorists again turned to mobile technologies to teach students curation and presentation skills.

In 2011, I sat on a team of UW folklorists with Ruth Olson, Thomas DuBois, and Casey Schmitt to redesign our Introduction to Folklore course. At the heart of this redesign was a set of semester-long team-based digital projects. The projects would be digitally published, and be based on the students' own research interests. The course's theoretical content would subsequently emerge from student-driven fieldwork. We arranged students into four-person teams to develop these projects based on their own unique ethnographic fieldwork and library research. Students could opt to present their project publicly as a WordPress site, as a digital documentary, or through an ARIS game—the focus of this section.

Mobile technologies like ARIS are exciting tools for ethnographers. Folklorists often take interest in the relationships between a spaces and people, looking at the stories, objects, and experiences that create a sense of place out of mere space. Augmented reality is an outstanding vehicle for offering contextual information which illuminates what a place means to its local community. Particularly, since folklorists frequently work in marginalized and peripheral communities, the tools of augmented reality help narrate alternative histories and discourses which are otherwise invisible to the outside eye. Many ethnographic ARIS games have been designed as walking tours where players learn about a community by experiencing historical events, interacting with historical objects, and by communicating with virtual characters who tell about their own experiences. At their most effective, these games can tether compelling historic events to a contemporary place.

As a form of digital representation, ARIS offers an innovative means for ethnographers to represent a diversity of voices inside a single narrative. Folklorists have long contended tradition, identity, history, and events consist of a network of negotiated meanings which is often disagreed upon within seemingly stable communities. Over the past four decades folklorists have attempted to represent communities not as a singular entity, but rather as an amalgam of disparate yet cohabiting voices. Although the task of representing a panoply of voices can be challenging for both author and reader in traditional written essays, mobile games like ARIS are natural vehicles for representing diverse and divergent interests of a community. For instance, in the ARIS game *Wisconsin Uprising*—designed by Carrie Roy, Thomas DuBois, and myself—the 2011 protests at the Wisconsin State Capitol were documented from a variety of occupational, personal, and political perspectives. Each character brings his or her own agenda and personality into a larger discourse that the game presents about the thematic topic.

Since we began teaching Introduction to Folklore with mobile games in 2011, approximately one quarter of our students opted into designing mobile games for their final projects. These games assumed a wide variety of topics and thematic content, although most were centered around student life in Madison. Several games, for example, focused on Halloween in Madison. One, called *Freakfest Folklore* explored changes to Halloween in Madison after the city officially began sponsoring the event, following years of unruliness. Another game attempted to explore how one's gender and costume choices affected what one's experience was like on Halloween night. Others focused, in varied ways, on political activists, food cart owners, ethnic restaurants, and on the UW marching band.

Most students followed the narrative blueprints of earlier ethnographic games as they designed their own game, where a player is cast in the game as a newcomer to an event, only to be educated by a series of knowledgeable guides and mentors. For instance, in *Mifflin Street Block Party* the player is invited to the annual Mifflin Street Block Party only to meet characters who inform the player about the history of the neighborhood and the origin of the notorious block party as an anti-war protest during the Vietnam War. The students who designed the game combined the sights, sounds, and formal and informal rules of the block party with interviews they conducted with the party's original activist organizers. A similar example, *Bucky 101,* was an ambitious student project that detailed the life of a student who becomes a Big 10 mascot. The game begins with auditioning, rites of passages, important milestones, and ends with the Bucky alum mentoring a new generation of newcomers.

Some projects engaged more theoretical questions in folklore through the narrative plot of their game. *Luck of the Irish* details what St. Patrick's Day means to different people, showing the contemporary holiday is a composite of the experiences of different people: whether the holiday involves wearing green and drinking green beer, whether it involves marching in a parade, whether it is a time for Irish American families to reflect on their own family and ethnic heritage, or whether it is a time for bartenders at the local Irish pub who have to work extra shifts. In *The Cafes of Madison*, the player is put on a quest that crafts a nuanced argument about how local coffeehouses differ from their corporate counterparts. The player visits three coffeehouses, each of which serve as a place for community to come together for purposes other than coffee (whether for political gatherings, for a local music venue, or for the sale of local art). As reflections of their own neighborhood and builders of community, these cafes serve much more than coffee and scones. Through this game, the student designers probed the issue of folk culture and commercial culture, trying to understand how they differ, and how that figures into contemporary hostilities over corporate coffee.

However, not all students chose to create a guided-game. *Food Cart Trail*—based on the classic *Oregon Trail*—allotted the player a budget to operate an empanada food cart in Madison. With this budget, the player needed to purchase appropriate amounts of foodstuffs and cleaning products for the cart. While operating the cart, customers requested different kinds of food and beverages, and if the player ran out of the requested empanada, the player needed to offer appropriate responses (a free drink as an apology, for instance) to ensure follow up business. Randomly, a health inspector would arrive, and if the owner hadn't purchased enough cleaning supplies, the cart owner would be warned and then fined. If the player could successfully operate the food cart for one week without going out of business, the player would win the game. This game immersed the player into the occasionally frustrating world of operating a small business, and proved its point in illustrating the complexities of working life that exist on the inside of the food cart.

At least within the narrative-based games, the instructors and Teaching Assistants who integrated ARIS into the classroom quickly came to agree that students learned more by creating mobile games than actually playing them. While the playing of a game could educate about an event or a concept, it was the design of the game that forced students to raise deep questions about curation of ethnographic materials and about ethical presentation of fieldwork. Like any media for expression, ARIS faces certain limitations. Screen size prohibits long blocks of text; images are limited in resolution, and excess video slows interactive game-play; the game editor makes the construction of complex, branching narratives difficult; and dialogue needs to be succinct for effective presentation. Yet these limitations of the platform forced students to think actively about making editorial choices in representing their ethnographic work, in a manner not dissimilar to crafting museum exhibitions. Whereas websites and term papers allow for a greater abundance of information, the realization of a genre's own limitations helps create an awareness of the editorial process that occurs with any and all acts of curation and presentation. With player attention to text, images, and media lasting for seconds or perhaps a minute, all materials must be presented in ways that allow for the player to be satisfied with the game experience. Experienced folklorists contend that curation figures into every genre of ethnographic representation, but certain genres (like essays) have become so familiar to us that we often fail to see our own editorial choices. Working with mobile media helps students recognize their own hand in shaping the fieldwork materials into a polished and highly edited product.

The other great challenge students faced was the ethical challenge of transforming fieldwork into the games. In scholarship, folklorists highly value long and unbroken quotes, an abundance of contextual information, and full portraits of human subjects as complex and dynamic individuals. Mobile gaming, however, is a genre defined by succinctness. Folklorists must therefore venture into the uncomfortable territory of fictionalization and generalization of their informants. In an ethnographic book or journal article, folklorists certainly would not be permitted to invent a character, to attribute a quote to a real person who never spoke those words, or to fuse two real people into one fictitious character. Yet folklorists clearly filter information, and ethnographers have a long history of censoring or casually omitting unsavory elements from publication in order to cast their informants in positive lights. Designers of games faced difficult decisions about how to present their informants in their mobile games. Some invented characters based on their interviews; some used real people as characters in their games but heavily edited dialogue while still using snippets of quotes from their interviews. Wrestling with these ethical questions heightened student awareness of representing human subjects while using more conventional media.

CONCLUSIONS

Our two uses of ARIS in the Introduction to Folklore classroom show how mobile technologies and augmented reality can be used to create student-centered pedagogies in traditionally lecture-hall environments. Mobile games offer students opportunities to engage with each other in ways that are reminiscent of small-classroom settings. They can be an outstanding platform for community-engaged research projects, helping students better understand the process of composition, editing, and curation by forcing them to work with challenging new media for their ethnographic presentation. And augmented reality can serve as a matrix for data exchange, peer-evaluation, and a student-centered classroom, which allows teachers to install small-classroom pedagogies into larger classroom environments. However, both projects leave much room for improvement. Mobile games designed in our courses are not frequently played after a semester is at its end for the purpose of community advocacy, and our use of a mobile game to share fieldwork resulted in an unsatisfying, uncurated final product. Yet in spite of these shortcomings, these two small projects offer some optimism for educators that new technologies can be used to advance better pedagogies and build a better classroom.

CHAPTER NINE

Introducing a Neighborhood: Mobile as a Springboard for Exploration

Kim Garza and Jason Rosenblum

Have you ever wanted to challenge students to go beyond the superficial in their course work? We have. As collaborators, Garza, a graphic design educator, and Rosenblum, a digital media educator with a background in educational technology and games research, began to re-envision the opening assignment for Garza's Graphic Design III course at St. Edward's University. Student work from a previous iteration didn't meet the course's learning objectives. Garza identified some of the issues inherent in the curriculum, and Rosenblum helped envision a new introductory approach that used mobile to solve curricular problems creatively. As a result, we designed a mobile application using the ARIS game platform to help students learn about the complexities of a local neighborhood in Austin, Texas. Immersive experiences, like those mobile offers, can help students learn about and tackle complex problems in authentic ways.

THE COURSE

Graphic Design III challenges students to explore issues of urban growth and respond as creative, yet critical designers. In the Junior-level studio course, students learn to define their own work within a given set of constraints and continue to develop their design skills through two projects. The main constraint is a definition of place—the coursework is centered on an old, but rapidly changing, neighborhood in East Austin along East Cesar Chavez Street. Students focus their projects on a narrow strip of the neighborhood three blocks high by twenty-four blocks wide on the east side of Interstate 35, which historically has been a racial and economic dividing line in Austin. Predominately Hispanic, the designated area contains a diverse mix of small businesses, government services, churches, schools and residences.

The projects should leverage the students' on-the-ground experiences in the neighborhood: visual research in a place where the growing pains from population shifts, property value increases and loss of cultural heritage are evident. For the first project, students create a website or short film to explore a facet of or to dissect an issue from the neighborhood. The second project requires students to edit/write, design, and bind a book that further examines a student-defined theme related to the neighborhood. Most of our students have never ventured far from the St. Edward's campus, located in a trendy part of South Austin, and they find themselves challenged by their experiences in this different setting.

THE CURRICULAR CHALLENGE: HOW DO YOU INTRODUCE A NEIGHBORHOOD?

The main student objective—to generate design work based on a neighborhood—requires first that students experience an unfamiliar place in order to discover its complexities. A previous iteration of the course did not support this goal due to at least two weaknesses: Garza focused on the design outcome rather than the experience, and no formal introduction to the neighborhood took place. The opening assignment required students to go to East Cesar Chavez, take 85+ photographs and sort them into categories such as color, architecture, daily life, etc. As a result, students treated the assignment solely as a way to gain imagery for the semester's design projects, not as an opportunity to think critically about the place. While Garza encouraged students to explore the neighborhood further, few went back for additional visits. Instead, students developed their projects based on their limited experiences, resulting in concepts that were flat and superficial: "the colors are so cool," "gentrification is bad," "yay for Mexican culture," etc. Upon reflection, Garza realized that the single visit only engaged students in one mode of experiencing a place and more were necessary for students to produce discerning, place-relevant design. The course and neighborhood needed better introductions.

THE NEW SET-UP: THREE EXERCISES

Semester-long projects need a strong foundation for the resulting work to be of any depth. To this end, Garza redesigned the introductory portion of the course. Instead of one required visit to the neighborhood, the next Graphic Design III students would go to the neighborhood three times in the first two weeks of class. Each visit would be assigned as an out-of-class exercise. The first visit would be a walking tour of a representative few blocks to serve as a safe entry point into an unfamiliar neighborhood. The second visit would be what's known as a dérive—an exploration of an urban landscape that allows room for chance encounters, engagement of all the senses and discoveries off the beaten path. In this dérive, students would wander the neighborhood in small groups for three to four hours and share a story from their experience in response. The third visit would find students behind their cameras taking photographs that they would use in designing the subsequent projects. In addition to the exercises, Garza planned to hold four class sessions in the neighborhood: two would be to eat together at local establishments while discussing assigned readings, and two would be in public spaces to critique student projects. Garza believed that immersion in the neighborhood could lead to more thoughtful reflections of the spaces they visited.

THE WALKING TOUR: GOING MOBILE

New curriculum, even at a small scale, requires careful consideration of its implementation. In this case, Garza wanted to shape the introductory exercises so that students could engage the neighborhood quickly. The second two exercises would be easy to create and assign: students could be sent out with a bit of background and some simple instructions. But the walking tour would require additional planning.

The walking tour posed challenges in determining where, when and how it should be delivered. Where was the best entry point into the neighborhood? The walking tour needed to be easily accessible, safe and typical to ease students into the experience of the place. When would the tour happen? It needed to be between the first and second class sessions, two days apart, for the introductory exercises to leave enough room for the design-specific instruction around the projects. Adding a field trip for a guided tour the first week of classes did not seem realistic, so the walking tour needed to be completed asynchronously. How would the tour be delivered? One option would be to create a printed map that detailed all of the locations of interest and text highlighting the details and themes. However, students could easily feign completion of the tour unless they were required to bring an artifact back from the tour. A better option would be to use a mobile device that could deliver location-based information and allow students to capture and share data from the neighborhood. To Garza, the first option seemed static, boring and ignorant of mobile technology's potential; the second, dynamic and exciting, but overwhelming to implement. Before jumping in, the mobile option needed to be checked for its ability to support the curriculum.

To make sure the technology would serve the learning objectives, Garza went to Rosenblum, who at the time conducted research and development of instructional technology for St. Edward's, to get another perspective on mobile's fit for the walking tour. We discussed the tour, its place in the curriculum and whether mobile would deliver on the objectives and provide an engaging experience for the students. We agreed that an approach using mobile technology made sense. Through analyzing past student work, Garza recognized that the previous curriculum favored the design-specific objectives and left the research and critical thinking objectives more to chance. The new introductory exercises could allow more focus on awareness and analysis of the neighborhood.

Mobile learning can support critical thinking and student engagement in several ways. First, a mobile tour can provide students with relevant information or prompts in a content-relevant location as a way to situate learning. Location-specific content can focus students on particular issues, asking them to pay more attention to detail in the spaces they occupy. Second, a mobile tour can leverage students' ability to record observations on the spot and share them with one another, building a collective dialogue to enhance the experience of a place. In addition, a mobile tour can encourage student engagement as students discover new things about a neighborhood while walking along the path. The unknown can drive interest in paying attention and looking for what might be next. A mobile tour requires students to use their devices' cameras, keyboards and microphones to actively participate in the tour, as opposed to passively reading a map. Once the technology proved consistent with the objectives, the resources required to develop and implement the mobile tour needed to be pulled together.

THE DEVELOPMENT: PUTTING IT TOGETHER

Introducing cutting-edge technology into the curriculum requires resources: people with appropriate skill sets, the right tools and dedicated time. After our discussion, we decided to form an ad hoc team of professor and technologist to implement the project, calling on Rosenblum's colleagues in Instructional Technology to help with the work. As a small team, we split up duties according to our strengths and availability. Our discussions then turned to which tools we would use to develop and deliver the mobile walking tour. Rosenblum recommended the ARIS mobile game platform for its ability to deliver on our needs; its simple interface and clear logic would allow us to quickly develop, test and publish the walking tour. Garza had not considered the introductory exercise as a game before, but others' use of the ARIS platform to make interactive, place-based games suggested new possibilities for student engagement beyond what a walking tour could offer. In addition, the ARIS platform allowed for the game to be created in an online editor and to be played in the free ARIS iOS app, meaning that we could develop and run this walking tour without spending money on software. The third essential resource, time, needed to be allotted to various portions of the project. With only one month until the start of the semester, we decided to use a lightweight, rapid prototyping approach to design the app. This flexible approach allowed us to effectively manage our time identifying the type of game, writing the narrative, developing the logic and testing the game. Our choice of tools and design approach, combined with frequent check-ins and all-around positive attitudes towards the project, helped us to smoothly work together as an ad hoc team. We discovered that with the right people and a solid design plan, a new technology-based curriculum can be pulled off with limited resources.

With the resources in place, many questions about the game's particulars—mechanics, narrative and visuals—still needed to be answered. What kind of a game did we want? Once the idea of making a game was on the table, we excitedly envisioned a grand interactive mystery caper in the neighborhood. We quickly realized this was much more than we could put together in the time available and settled for creating a much more manageable virtual scavenger hunt. Rosenblum recommended that we organize the scavenger hunt in ARIS using a quest-based approach so that individual locations could be programmed to deliver notifications and important content. Rosenblum sketched the basic architecture for the tour within the app and trained the design team on how to build in ARIS. Together we developed a prototype design in less than two weeks, much more quickly than anticipated.

We then turned to a more specific focus on the content of the tour. What quests would be picked for the scavenger hunt? Since the entire neighborhood would be too large to cover on foot, we mapped out an easy-access part of the neighborhood for our game's boundaries. Garza determined the pairings of locations and quests by walking the area many times and filtering decisions through the lens of neighborhood issues and the activities that mobile enabled. For instance, standing at the corner of San Marcos and East 2nd, Garza looked back towards the city—the skyline is visible but access is completely blocked by I-35, a raised highway—and decided to call attention to boundaries through the use of the camera (Figure 2 and Table 1, #3). Garza wrote a narrative to engage students in thoughtful activities, which Rosenblum, together with the design team, then embedded in the game (Table 1). What would the game look like? ARIS allows the developer to upload custom visuals into a game, and Garza wanted to take full advantage of this feature. After all, the game would be played by graphic design students. Garza took photographs to use on game plaques. And Rosenblum's current student worker, who happened to be one of Garza's former students, designed all of the game icons and the logo. While working out details, we followed the plan but were willing to adjust accordingly when new opportunities presented themselves.

Technical glitches will happen while developing technology-based curricula. The more variables that exist in a project, the more time it will require to test and iterate in order to minimize potential glitches. We used multiple technologies—mobile devices, cellular networks, open-source beta software (ARIS) and GPS—any of which could go wrong and render the game unusable to students. Near the end of development, Garza, Rosenblum and several student workers did three rounds of testing, where we played the scavenger hunt out in the neighborhood. We encountered differences in game performance depending on cell provider and iOS version, challenges reading our screens in harsh sunlight, user confusion based on complexities in the original narrative, faults in the programming logic and ARIS server errors. Some errors, such as lag due to cell phone connectivity were not immediately solvable. However, for other errors we attempted to isolate and debug problems on the spot. This process first entailed walking the neighborhood between key quest points to discover problems in the logic that prevent notifications from appearing properly. With a laptop and access to a WiFi signal, we fixed some of the logic problems and retested immediately. For the things we didn't tweak on location, we reconvened on campus to solve and adjusted the logic prior to the next round of testing. The game became more stable with each iteration, and we successfully completed all the quests on the last round of testing. *Explore East Cesar Chavez* was ready.

THE DETAILS OF THE GAME

The scavenger hunt *Explore East Cesar Chavez* runs on the ARIS app on iOS devices (Figure 1). The game covers a one-by-two block section of the East Cesar Chavez neighborhood a few blocks east of I-35 and contains nine quests that map to a specific location (Table 1). Some quests are informational and others require players to engage with the environment through taking photos, recording sounds or posting notes to the game's map. Each quest touches on various aspects of a community—commerce, neighbors, governance, boundaries, pollution, history, etc.—and offers a prompt for further consideration. Players need to complete each quest in order to unlock the related journal prompt and the next quest in the sequence (Figure 2). Players earn a completion badge upon finishing all of the quests. The journaling component exists independently from the game.

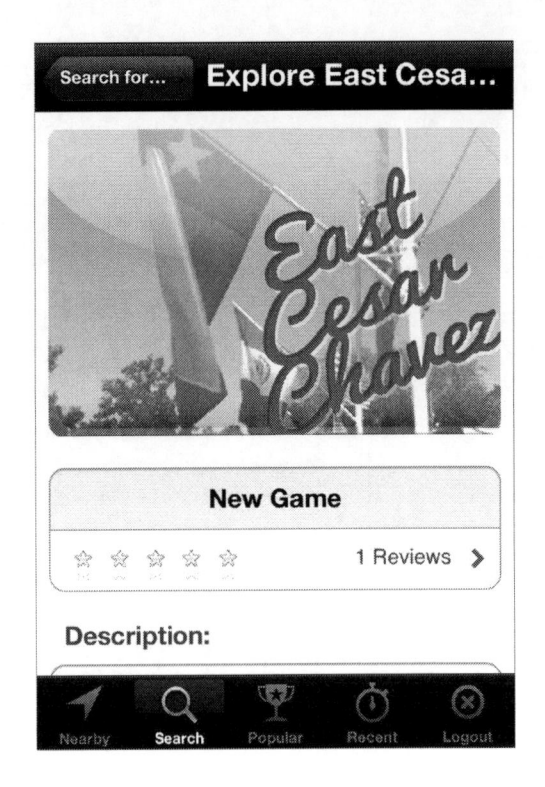

Figure 1. Introductory screen of the game inside of the ARIS app.

Figure 2: A progression of screens within Quest 3 (left to right): active quest instructions, taking a photo of downtown, uploading the note and completed quest prompt.

114

Table 1: *Explore East Cesar Chavez* quests and journal prompts.

Map Icon	#	Quest	Journal Prompt
	1	You will walk two blocks in the East Cesar Chavez neighborhood to begin looking closely and thinking critically about what defines a place. Check your inventory for the instructions on how to complete the tour.	What preconceived notions did you have of East Austin before the walking tour?
D	2	Go to the SW corner of San Marcos and Cesar Chavez where Domy Books is located. Read the plaque. *Plaque*: Domy carries an eclectic selection of books on art, literature and culture in addition to housing a small gallery and two other small businesses on its property.	How do small businesses survive?
+	3	Cross Cesar Chavez and walk north along San Marcos. At San Marcos and E 2nd St, look towards downtown. In the notebook, select the camera icon; take a photo of downtown; select "use" to upload the photo; and title the note.	What is the nature of a boundary?
+	4	Walk away from downtown (west/right) down E 2nd St. As you walk the next block, to Medina, record the sounds of the neighborhood. In the notebook, select the recorder icon; begin recording; save; and title the note.	How do residents cope with noise, light and sound pollution in their neighborhood?
⚱	5	Go to the SW corner of E 2nd St and Medina where the First Mexican Baptist Church is located. Read the plaque. Plaque: Primera Iglesia Bautiso began in 1899 and moved into this building in 1959. It is one of the largest Latin American Baptist congregations in the state.	What is the role of a church or community of faith in a neighborhood?
+	6	Continue walking away from downtown (east) down E 2nd St. Choose a residence along the north or south side of the street to make notes about: Is the house renovated, original, new? Is the yard landscaped, wild, barren? What type of fence? What type of driveway? What is on the front porch? Be sure to consult the map to make sure that the residence doesn't already have a note attached to it. In the notebook, select the clipboard icon; type your notes; save; title the note; and add the note to the map with the location tool.	Can you judge a neighbor by the outside of his/her property?
🎨	7	Turn south/right on Waller and go to the NE corner of Waller and Cesar Chavez where Long Motors is located. Read the plaque. *Plaque*: !Si Se Puede! is one of many murals in the neighborhood. Long Motors, a used car dealership, has five Austin locations and proudly supports the Hispanic community.	Who is Cesar Chavez? Does the street that bears his name give identity to the surrounding neighborhood?

Table 1: *Explore East Cesar Chavez* quests and journal prompts.

	8	Stay on the north side of Cesar Chavez and walk back toward downtown (west/right). Choose a business along the north or south side of the street to make notes about: Does the business cater to the neighborhood or is it simply occupying space? What clues did you use to make your judgment? Be sure to consult the map to make sure that the business doesn't already have a note attached to it. In the notebook, select the clipboard icon; type your notes; save; title the note; and add the note to the map with the location tool.	What are different ways businesses can engage in a community?
	9	Continue walking toward downtown (west) to the NE corner of Cesar Chavez and San Marcos where the bus stop is located. Read the plaque. *Plaque*: Cesar Chavez is a main thoroughfare into downtown. The bus stop is often crowded well beyond its one bench and canopy.	Where do the 17 and 21 buses go, and how often do they come? How does access to public transportation shape a community?

Designing the game allowed for customized content that supported the learning objectives. Beside considerations about the place and the device, Garza wrote content that directly addressed the dissatisfaction with students' previously shallow ideas. The quests and prompts opened students' eyes to relevant community issues. In the past, students connected to the neighborhood's churches as buildings to be photographed for architectural details. But the inquiry stopped at the photo. In the mobile scavenger hunt, Quest 5 asked students to think about the church as a participant in community building, not just as architecture (Table 1, #5). Previously, students had never stopped to ask "Who is Cesar Chavez?" even though the street, neighborhood and prominent murals bear his name and likeness. Quest 7 brought the question forward (Table 1, #7). Garza created the quests with the intention that students make a connection that they could explore more critically in subsequent projects.

FINAL LOGISTICS

Even after the planning and development of a mobile game, a number of student-related logistics—transportation, devices, network connection and support—need to be considered before running the game. Prior to the semester, Garza emailed the eleven Graphic Design III students to find out if any alternative plans would need to be made. The first logistic to be solved was transportation. Because our game required students to be in the neighborhood, Garza asked if those who owned cars would be willing to carpool. With enough affirmative answers, everyone would have a ride; the backup plan of public transportation did not need to be explored further. The next logistic took into consideration if everyone had an iOS device. Since the ARIS app, which runs *Explore East Cesar Chavez*, is only available for iOS devices, Garza asked if students owned an iPhone, iPad or iPod Touch. Not everyone did, and Garza arranged for these students to check out iPod Touches from the lab. The third logistic involved managing the reliability of the network connection, which varied based on the student's device. The students borrowing iPod Touches would not have access to a built-in data plan for internet access while in the neighborhood, a requirement for ARIS to function. To solve the connection issue, Instructional Technology ordered a MiFi router—hardware that uses a cellular connection to provide WiFi access for up to five devices—on the school's mobile account and paid for one month of data. Students could checkout and pair the MiFi router with their iPod Touches during the game. The final logistic was handling support for students while playing the game. In response to the technical challenges during testing, Garza decided to add a printed map that highlighted the locations featured in the game and provided shorthand instructions for navigating the game's interface (Figure 3). Albeit an ironic choice in light of the early decision to go mobile, the map gave students a broad overview of the tour and documentation of technical details yet kept the details a mystery until revealed in the game. As we handled the student logistics, practical resourcefulness proved essential to keeping the game on track.

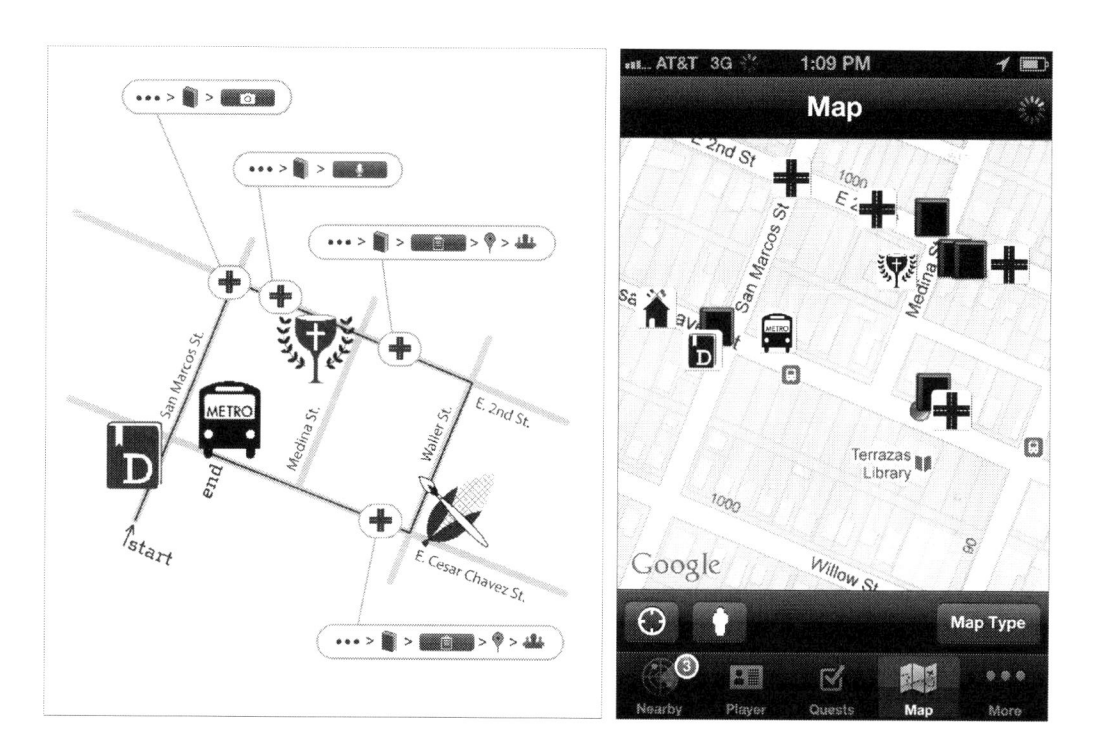

Figure 3. The printed map (left) used the same graphics as the map within the game (right).

Students needed an overview of the technology prior to playing the game. During the first class, Garza had students load the ARIS app on their iOS devices, whether personal or borrowed, and log into the app for the first time. Garza briefed them on the components of the game, told them where to park, gave them the printed map and sent them out to play, hoping that we had considered everything they needed for a successful experience.

PLAYING THE GAME: DISASTER!

The scavenger hunt did not go according to plan. Most students went in small groups and experienced a range of similar issues that we uncovered—and thought we had resolved—in our testing and subsequent iterations. The groups had divergent experiences, and occasionally students within groups hit problems at different points in the game.

Three students were not be able to play at all. The first group sent frantic emails to Garza from the neighborhood; they couldn't load the game. *Explore East Cesar Chavez* was not visible to the students because of a single missed checkbox in the ARIS editor to make the game show up when searched for (Garza later pushed the game live, but not in time for these three). They walked around the neighborhood with the printed map as a reference, not knowing the specifics of the quests but keeping their eyes and ears open.

The second group loaded the game and got started, but these three students were impeded by issues with their cellular data service. Two of them got stuck at different points in the game—at the photo upload and audio recording upload respectively. Because the game didn't see they had collected media, the subsequent quests never unlocked, which effectively ended the game for these two students. They tagged along with their third group member for the rest of the game. One student who went alone couldn't upload a photo and finished the walk without the context of the quests and completion prompts.

The third group had issues as well. One student was stopped by glitches in the ARIS app. This student made it further than those with provider issues. But one plaque never appeared on the map despite the student having completed previous quests and being within GPS range of it. One student used the software incorrectly. The other student in the third group did not follow the proper sequence of upload instructions. Because of the user error, this student was unable to unlock the additional quests. The third group abandoned the game and continued to walk the neighborhood from the printed map.

Three students managed to complete the entire game; five if you count group members tagging along after their games failed. One student in the second group was able to avoid connection and user errors. This student shared the device with other group members; all finished the game from one login account. Two other students went independently to play the game, and both completed all of the quests.

Out of eleven students, only five students got to the end of the game, but on three devices—not quite how we imagined things going, especially after all of the testing and iterations. From the description above, it would appear the technology got in the way of the neighborhood introduction.

THE DEBRIEF: ALL IS NOT LOST

When trying out technology-based approaches in the curriculum, an honest conversation about students' experiences can provide useful insight into what actually happened. From the student emails and online time stamps of user interactions, Garza could tell that the game had not gone according to plan and thus began the next class with a debrief about the scavenger hunt. The students who finished the scavenger hunt told about what they did to complete the various quests. The students who ran into issues shared the details of when and where things went wrong and how they tried to recover. They also told about their reliance on the map after being shut out of the game; students were thankful they could visit other important spots even if they didn't know the specific quests to complete. The narratives and feedback that students provided helped Garza pinpoint the connectivity issues, technical glitches and user errors that thwarted the game. Knowing what happened was one piece of the puzzle.

Students perceptions of their experiences can lead to deeper conversations about the use of technology in mediating spaces. Though the mobile scavenger hunt was simply the method for introducing the neighborhood, the technology itself made a significant impact on the learning experience. Garza wanted to explore where the intent and reality separated and aligned. Several students, mostly those who didn't finish the game, expressed concern over how much time that they were staring at their mobile device to read the quests, check the app's map or troubleshoot; they felt the use of the device distanced them from the neighborhood and garnered stares from residents. These students finished the route with the printed map that provided them enough information to know the points of interest, but not the details or the activities required in the game. They contended that a map was easier to use and could easily be altered to convey the same information. Conversely a number of students, those who got further through or completed the game, argued that using the device was more normal than using a printed map, especially given the ubiquity of smart phones. These students claimed that using a mobile device called attention to details they would have walked past, especially when the device vibrated in range of new plaques or user-generated notes. They expressed enjoyment in the immediate feedback of a "quest completed" upon uploading a photo or pinning a note to the map. This guided action, use of the device's inherent tools and on the spot reflection combined to create what they felt was a unique experience of the neighborhood. Garza pointed out some additional benefits of the mobile platform: the ability to share a dialogue around specific locations and to capture student quest data for review. After much back and forth, the original naysayers readily admitted that mobile delivery of location-specific content would be amazing, but only if the platform could provide a seamless experience. The conversation allowed students to recognize the benefits and drawbacks of mobile technology.

A debrief can also reveal what students think they learned from an experience. Garza wanted to know if *Explore East Cesare Chavez* had met any objectives—student engagement and critical thinking—after its seeming failure. In the conversation, students confirmed that the mobile scavenger hunt, novel for any class assignment, helped them quickly engage with the neighborhood in a way that was fun, safe and directed. The mystery of not knowing what to expect next motivated them to participate. And the shy students expressed that the planned structure and partner format gave them confidence to go to a new place. Regardless of completion rates, the mobile approach offered engagement for everyone. Students who finished got even more engagement in the neighborhood when uploading photos, recordings and notes to the map. On the other hand, the critical thinking objective needed more time to emerge. No clear evidence existed to determine which students—those who completed the mobile scavenger hunt versus those who didn't—could provide more insightful words about the neighborhood. Students shared particular moments when they realized something about the neighborhood in the midst of a quest. The students who didn't finish talked about paying particular attention to details at the places marked on the printed map even though they weren't sure of the exact quest. Both sets of students could identify some of the neighborhood's issues in their own words based on their experiences combined with the journal prompts. This is a reminder that we must look to the outcomes to determine if the benefits of the mobile introduction outweighed the technical difficulties.

THE OUTCOMES: EMERGING SUCCESS

Evidence of met learning objectives can surface slowly in students' work. Garza paced the projects across the semester in a way that would allow the first experience in the neighborhood, *Explore East Cesar Chavez*, to be a foundation upon which to build. The debrief served as one marker; the journal prompts, another. The subsequent two projects, the website or short film and the book, would ultimately determine if the revised introduction to the neighborhood enhanced students' critical thinking.

Reflective writing can help students critically process their experience. After playing the mobile scavenger hunt, students wrote responses to their choice of two journal prompts from the game. Garza set up a Blackboard course blog for students to share their writing. For those who didn't finish the game or no longer had access to the ARIS app, Garza included a list of journal prompts. Their responses were idiosyncratic and insightful. Already students were forming an informed voice about the neighborhood, something rare in previous semesters' projects. The majority of students wrote about their preconceived notions of the neighborhood—unsafe, poor, dodgy, nothing to offer—and how they had been surprised by friendly residents and hip businesses. *Explore East Cesar Chavez* had given them a safe entry into the neighborhood. Several students responded to the prompt about boundaries (Table 1, #3); they had never stopped to think about the role I-35 played in dividing the city. The simple act of taking a photograph of downtown during the game and writing about the image made the connection evident. Students had taken photographs before based on what looked good in the viewfinder; they hadn't stopped to ask what the photographs might mean about the neighborhood. Between the pairing of quests and prompts, the mobile scavenger hunt had delivered on getting students to provide thoughtful reflections.

The mobile scavenger hunt provided direct inspiration for further student exploration. A number of students used the journal prompts as a starting point for their own projects. One student project involved the design of a build-your-own East Austin business interactive game, which emerged from the small business prompt (Table 1, #8). Another project resulted in a book that featured illustrations of houses paired with crowd-sourced stories about the neighborhood homes—a project that was inspired by the "judge a neighbor" prompt (Table 1, #6). Yet another project resulted in a video exploration about the neighborhood's bikeability. The final video, created with a helmet-mounted steady-cam, began as a result of reflecting on the transportation prompt (Table 1, #9). Students delved deeper into the neighborhood issues raised in the game.

Not every project linked directly to the mobile scavenger hunt, but each still exhibited a thoughtful approach to experiences in the neighborhood. Some projects exhibited a strong authorial voice—a retelling of Hispanic folk tales set in the neighborhood, using the neighborhood as a backdrop for a children's adventure story and exploring how plant species serve as a metaphor for community dynamics. Even the students who based their design projects off of the more visual aspects of the neighborhood moved beyond the superficial. The visually inspired projects included a book that explored the history of graffiti, a short film analysis of a business based solely on its signs, and a practical guide for choosing color palettes based on the neighborhood's colors. Compared with the prior year, the projects displayed more critical and creative thinking about the place. The new introduction to the neighborhood had, despite significant difficulties in the moment, satisfied our curricular challenge in the end.

LESSONS LEARNED

The students met the learning objectives for the semester, but we also learned many lessons through our work on the mobile scavenger hunt. *Explore East Cesar Chavez* was an exciting first pilot of the ARIS game platform at St. Edward's University. We would be remiss without reflecting on our experience and offering some recommendations for other mobile learning designers to consider for their future projects.

During the development of a mobile-based curriculum, we recommend the following:

- **Lead with the learning objectives.** Look at how student learning can be supported by the affordances of mobile and then choose the platform for development. Our decision to go with a mobile game in ARIS came well into the curriculum design process. The combination of quests and prompts in specific locations aided student engagement and critical thinking.
- **Collaborate with a diverse team.** Our core team included a faculty member and an instructional technologist. Garza brought the knowledge of the curriculum and neighborhood; Rosenblum added in the knowledge and experience with game-based learning and mobile technology using the ARIS platform. The mobile scavenger hunt was shaped by the collaboration.

- **Be creative with resources.** To add to our core team, we asked student workers to help out. We followed a bring your own device (BYOD) model, and for those without iPhones, we used the school's iPod Touches and MiFi card for students. Our actual expenses were $50 for data.

- **Use an iterative process.** Plan the design, make a prototype, test it on location and revise based on what didn't work. Without this process, our project would have been a complete bust! Imagine if we would have given the app to students without ever testing. Garza would have been blindsided, and students would have walked away with nothing but frustration. The revisions made the game (partially) playable in our time frame, and a flexible attitude let us see beyond our initial disappointment with the technical issues that arose.

When your mobile-based curriculum is ready for student implementation, consider the following:

- **Have a backup plan.** For us, this meant designing the printed map as a supplement to the scavenger hunt. Setting student expectations or giving tips on app troubleshooting could also go a long way towards a successful student experience.

- **Do a trial run in class.** Garza did not do this, got burned, and now heartily recommends students at least load the game in class to gain a basic familiarity. User error would have been greatly reduced by spending a few minutes using the app together before relying on it alone in the neighborhood.

- **Offer technical support while in use.** Again, not something we did, but an absolute must given the high level of user error, ARIS's then alpha-version glitches and spotty mobile provider service. Know that email support won't be immediate enough, as the first group of Garza's students found out.

- **Go with the flow.** It doesn't have to be perfect the first time. Garza turned what looked like a disaster into a great teaching moment with the debriefing conversation.

Most importantly, find the space—physical and curricular—where mobile integration makes sense and where your students can be engaged in immersive, authentic learning. While *Explore East Cesar Chavez* was not the only introduction to the neighborhood the students had, the game made a lasting impact on the semester. The tone was set, and students continued to observe and draw their own connections in subsequent design projects. Getting students out of the classroom and exploring a neighborhood can be an incredibly rich learning experience. Add curricular integration of a mobile device—where relevant information can be delivered at a particular location and by which students can connect, comment and create with each other and their community—and the experience becomes transformative. Mobile can be a springboard.

CHAPTER TEN

Experimenting with Locative Media Games and Storytelling in Fine Arts

Fred Adam

Veronica Perales

Translated from Spanish by Amie Belmont

As teachers of art, we prepare our students to be artists in the 21st century while defining, along the way, what that might mean. This work takes place largely within our courses at the Fine Arts Department at the University of Murcia in Spain. Our courses make use of place, mobile technology, and the language of games to engage our students in new artistic modes. Some may see technology as something that distracts people from art, but artists are playing a key role in understanding, in a emotional and creative way, the potential for mobile technology in society. Specifically, this chapter describes our explorations with two significant affordances of the medium: (1) Geolocation—the ability to link place and media, and (2) distributed authorship—the common ability of many people to contribute to the creation of a single artifact or to remix existing content to fit their needs. We provide examples of student projects that model these affordances and demonstrate a merging of art and technology in order to begin to understand possibilities for art that intersects cinema, hypermedia, mobile, games, and public space.

Much of our work builds on the concept of expanded cinema, as defined by Gene Youngblood in the early 1970s. He proposed the term to express his understanding that the traditional way of making cinema and its separation of the audience from the creator was over. Today, with this same understanding we use mobile technology and games, as well as other formats and genres, as means to ask students to approach broad themes of importance to the future of art and society. To expand cinema, we combine typical media formats, production, and performance. Additionally, we especially seek to take advantage of new formats like mobile games and the unique senses and aspects of the world—like public space, smell, sound, and/or energy—that these new media open up. We aim to create cinematic moments in the first person and first place across a variety of digital and analog formats.

It is important to clarify that the projects we mention here are not finished creations. We are interested in the process of opening minds to new ways of thinking about art with digital media and mobile. We consider these designs as ephemeral moments of creativity. They stay alive in the minds of students during their long and hard journey to the world of corporations and markets.

PREPARING STUDENTS FOR HYPERMEDIA AND TRANSMEDIA

During their first years in the degree program, our Fine Art students generally receive an education that enables them to create short films. They learn how to prepare a storyboard, shoot footage, edit, and post-produce video making use of programs, such as Adobe Premiere and After Effects. This gives them a solid foundation in what it takes to later propose and create their own experimental media. We also familiarize our students with hypermedia and transmedia techniques framed in the scope of locative media. As their projects progress, we want them to understand the very large umbrella of audiovisual practices, sometimes mixed into a single narrative, what Robert Pratten calls "Transmedia Portmanteau approach".

Transmedia means that we're interested in multimedia (artifacts in many formats) and hypermedia, but also about stories that are simultaneously told across a variety of media[1]. Besides its current relevance, working in transmedia gives students who are less comfortable with modern technologies a chance to participate alongside their peers; we can organize heterogeneous working groups with students using traditional or analog media formats, and students using hypermedia, social networks and so on.

The creation of transmedia is complex; it especially needs good coordination between its parts. As Isidro Moreno says in *Creatividad y discursos hipermedia* (2012), the reader today wants also to be author (p. 39), so we need thinking in a complex but also open and dynamic way. To help our students to accomplish this, we ask them to create a puzzle where the different media are each needed to complete the whole. The puzzle format allows them to more easily grasp the notion of transmedia as something separate from multimedia: each piece of the puzzle is unique and complementary as a part of the whole. In the conception of transmedia projects, it is necessary to work with the narrative, taking into consideration the tools linked to each part—one part may be a character or a determined event.

When students begin to create in this realm, the first phase of each project is creating a storyboard (Figure 1). From a pedagogical view, storyboarding provides space for introducing and discussing questions that affect the works' final interpretation. The plan is more important than a mere map to enable execution in production. It also represents the conceptual framework that unites the pieces—it is analysis, a systematic study of the relations between the components.

---

[1] See for example Nicolas Bourriaud's modern concept of the radicant (2009).

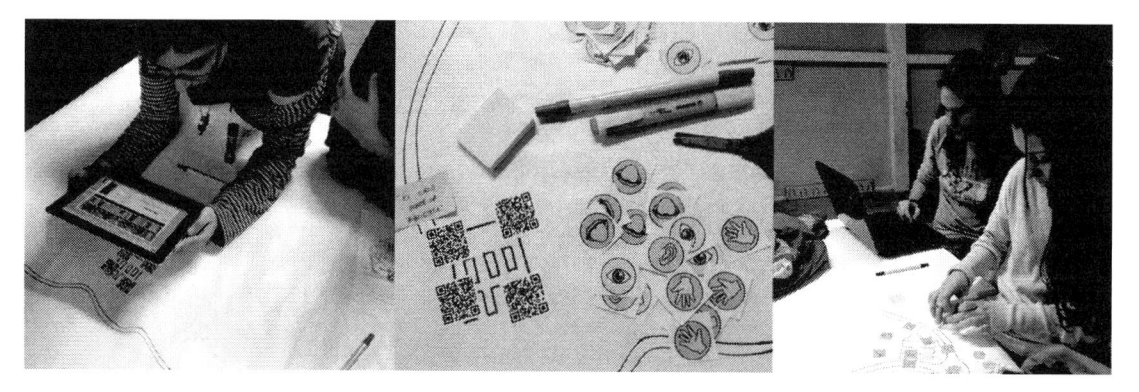

Figure 1: A storyboarding session for the production of a transmedia project.

The students' storyboards are therefore not just written scripts with x number of pages as is typical when planning linear narratives. A plan may contain a written script, but also include documents that operate as descriptors or legends for the other elements, often visually arranged like a map. The script should indicate, from each part of the work:

- Localization,
- Timing,
- Characters or personalities,
- Ideas referenced but not present (such as memories), and
- Determinants and possibilities within the content (we might think of how "choose your own adventure" books work).

Storyboarding begins with drawing on large sheets of paper a geographical map with the important information from the project. The groups, about three to six people, also create a shared blog that generates Smartphone-compatible web-pages. We show them how to use QR codes and overlay them on maps. This permits us to rapidly visualize the media without going outside and also gives us an idea of what the experience would be outdoors. We use mind-mapping techniques in order to visualize the branching of the projects prior to creating with more complex tools like ARIS (mentioned below). MindMeister (www.mindmeister.com) in particular allows us to generate shared-use diagrams that are really adapted to this purpose facilitating the interactive work. We also have techniques designed to help our students think about using multiple forms of perception as part of the storyboarding process. We use paper icons to represent sensory or perceptive organs and this helps students understand the degree to which senses like smell and touch are generally omitted from their initial designs.

As production progresses, it can be easy to lose sight of the major objectives of the design, to get lost in the details. This map helps students to remember that the individual bits of media they are creating are intended to play a pragmatic and functional role in the whole.

Practice with transmedia is an important perspective on the values and forms that art can involve. In the next three sections, we discuss areas of inquiry motivated by the possibilities of transmedia in a connected world that we and our students have worked in. There are three areas where versatile digital tools, in our case mostly ARIS, play a big role in making our ideas reality. The first of these is the creation of geolocative games, a particularly natural way to begin thinking about art that traverses formats and physical space.

GAMES IN PUBLIC SPACES: REIMAGINING AUDIENCE AND ACTIVITY

Certainly, game design is not a common practice for all Fine Arts schools. Most artistic production is focused on the creation of more traditionally acknowledged formats of art. Paintings and sculptures form part of the market of Art and galleries, mobile games are artifacts that may be created and packaged or used, but they're not part of this market. From the Social Art movement of the 1970's, attention was given within the art world to the process as part of creation in addition to the product. If we can now teach game design in an Art school, it is because the past has paved the way for us to see art as more than what is hanging in galleries.

We spend a lot of time talking with our students about how our work may be ludic or draw inspiration from games and how that might be different from many perspectives on games and learning. We believe it's important to see the creation of a game as more than a vehicle to deliver (and trivialize) content. A game, when used, should be a fundamental aspect of the work and not just a simple vector for content. Regarding learning designed in games, the game structure and play itself should become a key part of that learning. This contrasts with how the field of Serious Games or typical modes of gamification treat gameplay as a mode of content delivery. So when we adopt a game authoring platform like ARIS, it is with the notion of exploring the game-ness of what we can create.

Despite our strong involvement with game design and production, our students do not immediately jump into it. Our students in particular can be intimidated by game authoring platforms that require programming expertise. Instead, we wanted to quickly focus students on understanding what we can do as artists and building games and stories in the public space. This is why we have principally used ARIS for our development work (and combined ARIS with other locative frameworks like Notours—http://www.notours.org—for the creation of soundscapes). Software like this makes it possible to create interesting products quickly and simply without the time or expertise usually involved in software development. Even with easy-to-use creation tools, to achieve the best results, students approach the creation of content only after they study the possibilities inherent in these spaces and are trained to imagine the diversity of results—artistic actions, fiction, documentary, and games.

When students finally begin to design their games, they try to create something that lives at the intersection of what the device can provide and a series of actions—often performance—in public spaces. In this direction, we have been inspired by many other previous works, including

- PacManhattan: a version of the classic game PacMan, played out by real people on the streets of Manhattan instead of on a screen (http://pacmanhattan.com).
- Gigaputt: an iOS app that converts the streets of any city into a virtual golf course (http://www.giganticmechanic.com/project/gigaputt/).

Games like these have the capacity to help us play with and begin to understand the convergence of physical and virtual realities. Some of our work aims to explore this idea further, either by using mobile devices to turn the world into a setting for a game, or a space for performance. As Jesper Juul has said, "to play (a videogame) is therefore to interact with real rules while imagining a fictional world" (2005, p.1).

Example 1: Microcosmos Explorer
Our first prototype for game set in public space is titled Microcosmos Explorer.

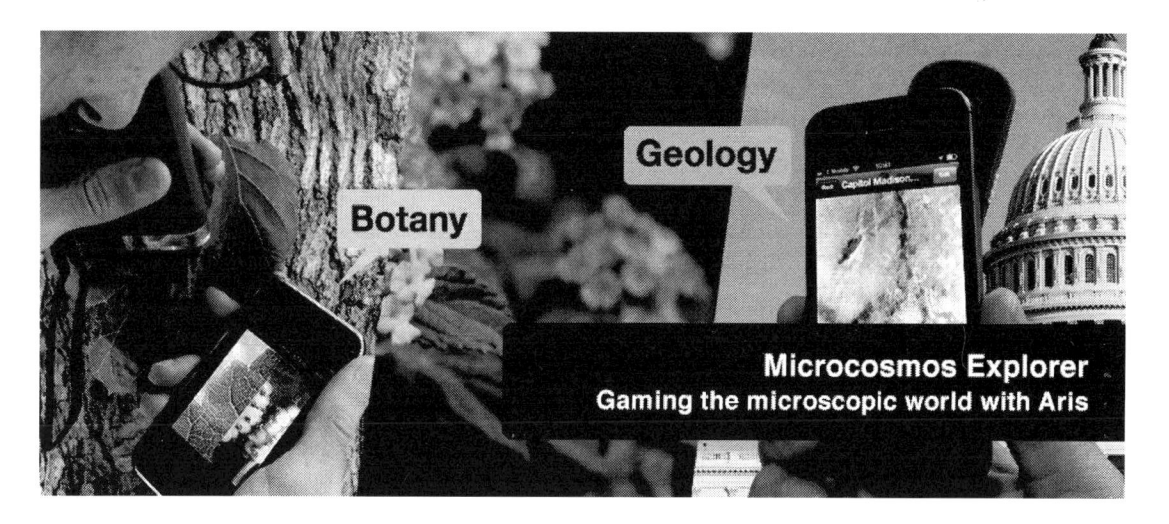

Figure 2: *Microcosmos Explorer* (2011), http://arisgames.org/featured/microcosmos-explorer/.

Microcosmos Explorer (Figures 2 & 3) was designed to be a mobile learning app for botany fans. We take advantage of a complex of themed gardens that can be situated on our campus and we present content through a game of clues. The narrative guide is given by a fictional character based on a historical figure from the 19th century, a botanist named Gastón Bonnier who inspired the creation of the Lousteau Museum at the campus. The principal mechanism of the game is based on the search for seeds that Gaston has lost and to plant them virtually in corresponding places according to the characteristics of the gardens. The players can see different views or photographic macro images of the plants that they can find with the help of a portable microscope for cell phones and then plant in the appropriate garden. Smart phones, in this case equipped with microscopes, are converted in assistive agents for the senses, implementing players' perceptions of the environment, stimulating their senses.

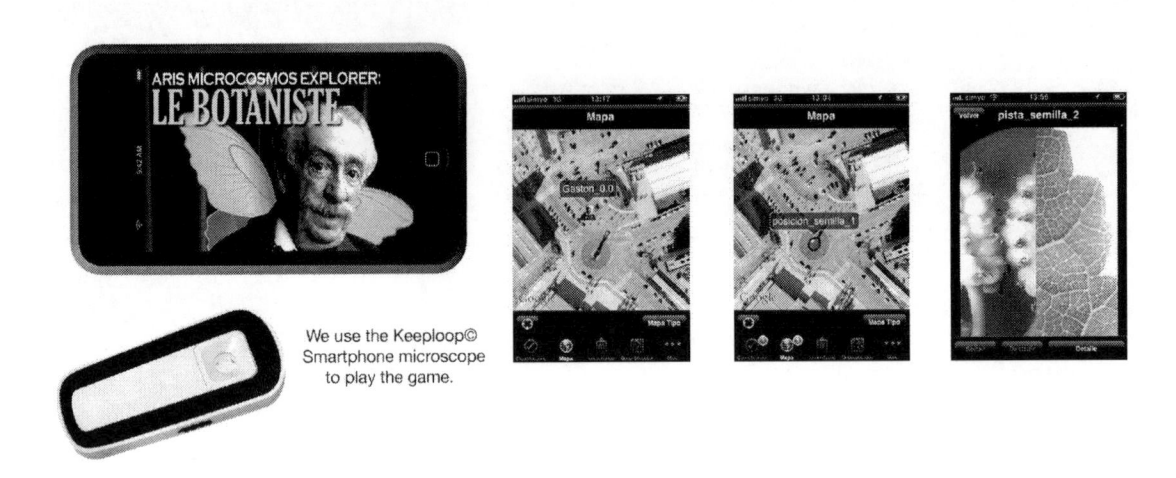

Figure 3: Screenshots of *Microcosmos Explorer* (2011), http://arisgames.org/featured/microcosmos-explorer/.

On one hand, Microcosmos Explorer is a fun exercise for Biology students and those from related fields that puts their knowledge of Botany to the test. Exploration of the microcosm is possible and even desirable for the enhanced knowledge of our environment. On the other hand, this game generates collaboration between Botany and Art, two rather distinct disciplines. It is an example of how the creation of content in mobile learning can be a good opportunity to generate interdisciplinary collaborations and favors the rise of innovative pedagogical practices.

Example 2: Being la Baubin

In 2012 a group of students finished a prototype of a social game—**Being la Babuin** (Figure 4). This game is based on the idea of connecting actions or interventions in public space with online performances. The objective of the first part of the game consists of situating the player by creating a determined context for him or her. Specifically, it is about being a new kind of primate in the world of humans—another species—and getting a new point of view of the world. The main intent is to challenge our ingrained anthropocentric ways of seeing the world. For this purpose, the player is asked to find a primate mask, previously hidden in a plastic tube, that he or she will carry throughout the experience. Suddenly, the players find themselves in a particular situation, like a crowded auditorium, that becomes the background for their actions or performances as this primate. Who could cross a library with hundreds of students with their head covered by a mask of a monkey without generating a interactions with the people around?

The game thus provokes a fracture with the established social rules, and the player tends to draw the attention of those that find themselves nearby. The mask, and the anonymity that the mask provides, offer the player certain liberty to put his creativity into play; he is not a witness, but rather an actor in a story in which he takes part. The narrative is not really pre-established here, but just contextualized with a general mission to achieve. Being in a specific place at a certain time is the only requirement, then the interaction with the people appears naturally and yet has been created.

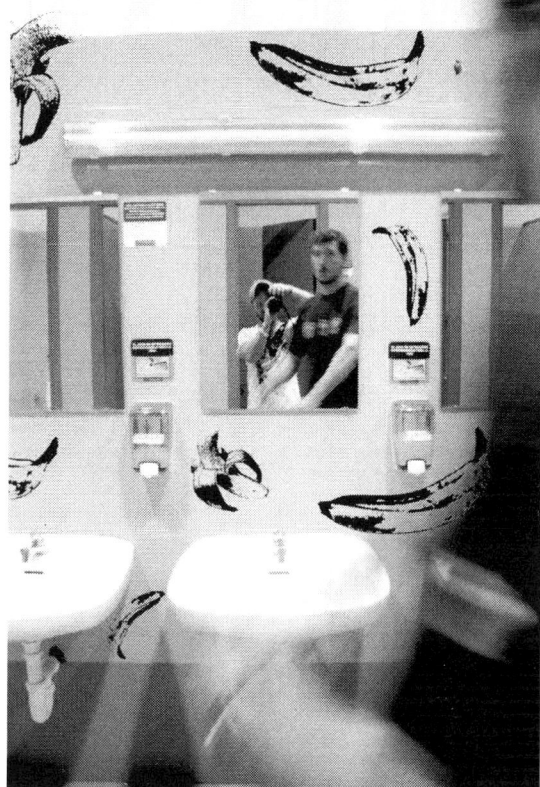

Figure 4: *Being la Babuin* (2012), (http://beinglababuin5videoycine.blogspot.com.es/).

Being la Babuin pushes the limits of gaming rather far into the social fabric of urban space. The action in the game symbolizes the desire to "act" (to enter in action) felt by the generation born in the 1990s who confront the sudden violence of the economic crisis in Spain, where more half of the young population was unemployed. To produce artistic action, the creators of this game have intervened in the street landscape without degrading it.

Another interesting way in which this project became really more of a process than a defined story—a conspiracy among many players and authors—is how participants included signs or footprints from supposed actors in the fiction, specifically, traces from other primates from the same family or from incompatible families (lemurs). The story the students created began somewhere but is probably never ending. Players used the ARIS notebook to share these invented details with others who were not present at the time but came later, creating another location of importance for the game. If ARIS integrated with social networks, then this impact could have been even greater.

The authors of *Being la Baubin* also involved people from the physical spaces in which the fiction takes place, workers in said public spaces. For example, they involved a custodian from the Main Library from the Espinardo Campus who gave certain information to those who asked him a key question. These temporary actors were active agents in the progress of the ever-changing plot. Taken together, this game became a concrete activist strategy that allowed its players to interact with their environment in new ways.

FICTION IN URBAN SPACE—REIMAGINING CINEMA IN THE OPEN WORLD

As one of our goals is to help our students become practiced in the ways of cinema, many of our experiments are not really games, even when we use processes and tools familiar to game design in their production. However, teaching students "cinema" only from a conventional point of view (the movie theater) is not a very strategic option given the opportunities in the job market. It is difficult to find an opening in European cinematographic industry and it is even more unlikely that our students would be likely to end up working in Hollywood. These unattainable goals seem to be the direction art schools point their students to. Existing industry and formats are not the only setting for cinema in the 21st century, so we ask students to experiment within the developing tradition of expanded cinema, where our objective is to make the students perceive that it is possible to break standards of traditional cinema and think of innovative models of audiovisual creation outdoors and connected to the Internet and other forms of hypermedia.

As the French social thinker Gilles Lipovetsky put it in the book *Global Screen*, "We are in an era of the multiplication of screens, in a world-screen in which the cinema is no more than one among many" (2009, p. 28). It is necessary to define alternative channels for cinema, open new perspectives that strongly tie cinematographic experience and social networks, and make use of new digital foundations of skills like reading for visualization. In looking to train our students with expanded cinema, we often seek to situate cinema in physical space in non-traditional ways. ARIS is still very useful here, even though we are not using it to make "games", as other tools that can give our students easy access to re-situating media in relation to the audience.

Reviewing the history of cinema—its methods of reading, production, and postproduction—can be a fantastic source of content for linking cinema to physical spaces. In other words, by paying attention to how some movies invent new possibilities conceptually of what can happen in a physical space, we can find clues for how to create cinema that goes one step further and makes those conceptual ideas part of a fiction that is directly embedded in reality. A good example is how we sought to reinterpret an aspect of Wim Winder's film, *Wings of Desire* (1987). The film uses a group of angels who listen attentively to the internal voices of those living within the city and through this the viewer discovers their intimate thoughts; the viewer hears a multitude of otherwise inaudible voices while the story ambles through Berlin.

In class, we debated possible strategies to take the film experience to the public through a real on-foot tour (Figure 5). We looked for ways to make the voices heard as the viewer—not the camera—navigates physical space, and asked our students to explore how they might repurpose and reimagine the angel's abilities from the movie. To resolve this exercise proposed in class, we asked our students to create original content and at the same time recycle audiovisual material from movies, deconstructing image and sound in order to recreate elements that can be adapted to both the smartphone formatting and to the requirements of the storyboard. The movie is understood as a mine from which each plan can be analyzed and modified.

To implement these ideas we needed to extend the possibilities of ARIS by creating the soundtrack of the spatial narrative. We used the tool NoTours (created by the Spanish art collective Escoitar, http://www.escoitar.org), a mobile authoring platform which allows us to place audio clips in physical space in very complex configurations. By overlaying and staggering different sounds, you can create a rich and diverse soundscape for someone to walk through. From our point of view, it is the perfect audio tool for pairing with ARIS.

Figure 5: Students experimenting with ARIS and NoTours.

Our work with the concept of realizing disembodied voices in space also displays how we approach mobile game creation. Before authoring the full combination of audiovisual media, we had students thinking of this project as exclusively sound-based, creating a one-channel soundscape that does not require interaction through the screen on the user's device. The user can then amble in tranquility with his headphones and an Android device in his pocket, a less complex target for our students to initially aim for. After this stage is complete, we use it as a background against which we accomplish further design, using ARIS to layer a narrative and actors over the initial soundscape.

Our basic research into the combination of geolocated audio and augmented reality game design also encouraged us to reconstruct a scene from the Jean Renoir's *La Bête Humaine* (1938) at the campus Les Tarongers at The University of Valencia. We analyzed elements from the urban streetscape to give significance to the integration of cinematographic fragments and renew their meaning in the context in which they are placed. *La Bête Humaine* is a classic, speaking about the deep and tragic feelings of low class workers, and we looked for a way to bring that feeling alive for the audience. In the center of the campus, there is an old locomotive we chose to use as an anchor our recreation of scenes. In a certain way the locomotive is keeping the memory of the movie alive; historical elements in the public space become charged from their inclusion and reference in movies, documentaries, and books. Each place can be a door for rediscovering the traces of the past.

We can imagine an amazing collection of creations nurtured by the cinematographic production of the last century, interactive geolocalized applications accessible through mobile devices to give new opportunity to productions that have become forgotten or lost some meaning. It is a clear opportunity to assess our cinematographic heritage and to open new readings of the historic places selected for its positioning.

DOCUMENTARY IN URBAN SPACE — REIMAGINING REALITY

Another aspect of our work is in relation to the genre of documentary filmmaking. The basic affordance of mobile game design for documentary purposes is to situate past narratives in relevant places through the use of media on the mobile device. In the majority of cases, this consists of a superimposition of multimedia information (digital and/or analog) in the physical space and can be interpreted in some way as augmented or enhanced reality. We use environmental resources to reinforce the sense of dialogue between physical space and virtual space that makes life feel real. One common example is to use physical space to stage the viewing of historical photos and film from relevant physical points of view, say the point of view from which the original photo was taken.

Art on Campus (El Arte en el Campus) is a documentary made by our students and is an example of the mode of creation described above (Figure 6). They looked for sculptures and painted murals on campus with the objective of creating a guided visit that would better allow for the understanding of the artistic harmony of the place. They searched for connections between the works on campus and their historical referents. For example, there is a sculpture in one of the roundabouts, a car split into two flowerpots, Symbiosis, that was connected to the work *Split House* (1973) by Gordon Matta-Clark. This deep analysis by art students focused on public sculptures was then produced into an ARIS-based cultural tour of the campus. ARIS allows students to do more than mention the histories represented here—to actually create an imaginary dialogue with artists represented in the works such as Frida Kahlo and Salvador Dalí.

Figure 6: *El Arte en el Campus* (2012), http://geolocalizacionum.blogspot.com.es/

Femenino y Plural (Feminine and Plural) was one of the most outstanding projects from 2012–2013, and is a good example of how transmedia documentary design can come together (Figure 7). The project makes the audience participants in the adventures of a female character who discovers she is the heir of the Beguinas, feminine medieval spiritual and secular communities that existed independently from the ecclesiastical hierarchy and from men. This begins a documentary-based fiction, as the fictitious main character (Beguina) encounters real information and characters. The work was inspired from an interesting entry in the blog *Sociedad* in the Spanish newspaper *El País* that covered the recent death in Belgium of the last Beguina. *Femenino y Plural* articulates this story through three principal and complementary parts: an ARIS game, a comic we find physically in our own tour of the city of Murcia, and a blog.

Figure 7: Femenino y Plural (2013), http://enfemeninoyplural.blogspot.com.es/

Femenino y Plural is also an example of how the students at Bellas Artes can produce transmedia narratives that transmit content with social purposes (in this case, values of equality especially). Our use of ARIS in the experience is constitutive; it conditions their way of thinking and plants the story. It opens an enormous field of possibilities for the creation that rouses and motivates them.

Together, these strategies help make evident the artistic and educational potential that the spatial contextualization of information has. It is by tying the resources around us to narratives that they can take on life for others. But there is an additional sense in which physically experiencing a documentary can take on value. Like our other educational uses of this medium, we look for the learning to happen through the creation of the content. We encourage students to work in two modes, straight documentary and fiction. This can be seen as a question of "angle"—we can be the cameraman or the public. We can enter into the fiction or escape from it depending on our relative position to the mediascape.

It is important to understand this opportunity offers a variety of points of view that crosses the line between fiction and documentary, and opens a dialog between the creator and the spectator. We can do exactly this with locative storytelling because we are moving around in the space. We have students do this because, in the words of Henry Jenkins, "it becomes increasingly critical to help students acquire skills in understanding multiple perspectives, respecting and even embracing diversity of views, understanding a variety of social norms, and negotiating between conflicting opinions" (2009, p. 100).

CONCLUSION

The technologies that permit the access and exchange of information tied to geographic positioning have modified our ways of thinking and constructing narratives; this is unquestionable. We are all potential consumers of these technologies and potential receptors for the discourses they produce. If we desire to possess the capacity for initiating and proposing lines of dialogue (in a broad sense), beyond responding in participating in those already created—often by powerful organizations—we have to be part of its use. Knowledge of these mechanisms is fundamental in order to understand the potential of the technology and the capacity for action that the user has in the system in which he or she is integrated. The principal objective of these experiences is to create, with adequate tools and formats, within the technological actuality in which live, shaping students for new forms of writing and narrative, forms which can be important in a near professional future. But, the control of these technologies, or at least the comprehension of their functions, beyond the professional sphere is a social question. From the point of view of artistic activism, the technology continuously opens spaces that can (and should) be occupied by public voices.

The audiovisual work we do at the Department of Fine Arts is more than individual oeuvres within a single genre or format; it is converted, expanded, and articulated with the real world and virtual reality. The integration of social networks and spatial narration permits the transcendence of experience, establishing new relationships between information, communication, and place. We are helping our students to help define new forms of fiction, or reality, or documentary, or game, or perhaps, all at the same time. The creation is liberated from the static screens: the movie theatre, television, or computer screen, to flourish in a type of experience that requires time but whose duration is not predefined. This mutation requires we dismiss those usual presupposed closed spaces where we expect to encounter stories and look to raise questions capable of stimulating new or forgotten forms of perceiving such as smell and touch. Advanced tools, like ARIS and NoTours, for the creation of prototypes that involve geolocation and interactivity permit students to confront the challenge of innovating with their creations; that, is to nourish their potential for success in the professional sphere for the creation of audiovisual and multimedia informed by these new ideas.

Our objective is to prepare our students for the challenges of the 21st century—a society with new modes of access to audiovisual media. They must learn to articulate information and physical space as has never been done before. We need to create future experts with artistic perspectives capable of accomplishing and transcending audiovisual creation, addressing new forms of experience and perception through new formats such as hypermedia and transmedia, and exploring alternative forms from a creative point of view. Providing these future creators with the tools and knowledge necessary to experiment is fundamental; it is sowing the adaptation of their forms and discourses to the changing society in which they have to integrate.

If you want more details about the above projects, we invite you to check the website http://www.um.es/arisgames/. The website "Hypermedia and Transmedia Creation Lab" displays some class projects and other information related to pedagogy that further reveals our methodology.

REFERENCES

Bourriaud, N. (2009). *Radicante*. Buenos Aires: Adriana Hidalgo Editora.

Jenkins, H. (P.I.)(2009). *Confronting the Challenges of Participatory Culture Media Education for the 21st Century*. The John D. and Catherine Foundation Reports on Digital Media and Learning. Massachusetts: MIT Press.

Juul, J (2005). *Half-Real. Videogames between Real Rules and Fictional Worlds.* Massachusetts: MIT Press.

Lipovetsky, G ; Serroy, J. (2009). *La Pantalla Global. Cultura mediática y cine en la era hipermoderna.* Barcelona: Editorial Anagrama.

Moreno, I. (2012): Narrativa Hipermedia y Transmedia. In Perales, V. (Ed.), *Creatividad y Discursos Hipermedia* (pp. 21–40). Murcia: Editum.

SECTION FOUR

Connecting to Communities

11. "To Have Fun and Display Our Awesomeness": Mobile Game Design and *The Meaning of Life*
12. Project Exploration's Environmental Adventurers: Amplifying Urban Youth Agency, Identity and Capacity with Mobile Technology
13. Civic Engagement and Geo-Locative Media: Youth Create a Game to Discuss Political Issues
14. Technovation Challenge: Introducing Innovation and Mobile App Development to Girls Around the World

---

This section collects stories from teachers, researchers, technologists, and artists using Mobile Media largely in informal learning environments like summer and after school programs. These authors see their use of MML as a way to integrate passion, coming into the world, and accessing professional skills and habits of mind. The first three chapters describe small youth programs while Technovation Challenge is a franchise, a small program that has grown tremendously since 2010, implemented independently across the world. Some of the goals of youth programming tie very closely in with curricular goals, but others look to have a broader and more personal impact on the people they serve. These chapters give a concrete sense that MML is comfortable in helping educators do both at the same time.

CHAPTER ELEVEN

"To Have Fun and Display Our Awesomeness": Mobile Game Design and *The Meaning of Life*

Bob Coulter

Litzsinger Road Ecology Center, Missouri Botanical Garden

In *The Meaning of Life*, Monty Python presents an inspired spoof of schools and learning. As the scene opens, students are on their own in the classroom but hard at work, with one student carefully peeking out the door looking for the teacher. As the teacher approaches, the students quickly put away their work and begin the usual mischief you might expect while the teacher is out of the room. Like any good satire, the inversion of self-directed interest and compulsory education at the heart of the vignette raises provocative questions. How do traditional school expectations interfere with our natural curiosity and desire to learn? Conversely, what are kids capable of in a more supportive setting?

To explore these issues, the Missouri Botanical Garden has been running game design camps for the past few years using MIT's mobile augmented reality software (first with MITAR and now with TaleBlazer—see Figure 1).[1] While our larger program goal as an ecology center is to leverage the affordances of a variety of different games and simulations to engage school groups with the environment, any school experience is by nature compulsory and thus somewhat constraining. We have found that the more open-ended, totally elective game design camps put kids in their "native space," freeing them to show what they can do.

---

[1] As we finished putting this book together, MIT made Taleblazer available to the general public. Sign up at http://taleblazer.org. -Eds

Figure 1. The Taleblazer web-based authoring interface.

So how do these camps work? By design, the game camps are intended to be driven by kids' interests rather than having them simply complete a set of lessons toward a pre-determined outcome. We want them to be active in setting and modifying their goals for their project, drawing as needed on the expertise of the camp staff and their peers as the work progresses. As you can imagine in this more collaborative, studio-like environment, a good bit of sharing ensues, with particularly compelling ideas starting with one kid and over time appearing in other projects. Still, a little orientation and scaffolding helps kids get started. Since mobile augmented reality gaming is such a fundamentally different paradigm for most kids, we start by getting them outside playing a demonstration game. Typically this introductory experience embeds several key game mechanics (such as navigating outdoors with the handheld, making choices, "picking up" items offered within the game, and managing your inventory). Later that first morning, we transition from playing to designing, inviting the campers to personalize the game they just played by renaming characters and adding their pictures to the game they just played. Within a couple of hours we have gone from a cool game to *their* cool game. Moving from player to creator has a profound impact in terms of supporting their personal and intellectual development.

While the changes kids make at this stage to the game they just played are modest, it's an essential first step toward design work. They can readily see how their game play experiences were created, and in the process come to understand how the block-based programming environment in TaleBlazer lets on-screen events get expressed in code. From there, they begin thinking about how to make their goals come to life on screen. To support this development, we challenge the kids first to make a simple navigation game and then to enhance it iteratively with increasing levels of complexity and challenge as their design skills grow. Over the course of the week, the camp becomes a mix of mini-lessons for all of the campers, 1-1 tutorials to address specific issues, a good bit of peer collaboration, and a lot of fun playing, testing, and revising games.

A skeptic might counter with the point that yes, the kids had fun designing a game, but so what? Did they actually learn anything, or were they just playing? To answer that question, we need to be clear about what we mean by learning. While most schools in the United States focus an inordinate amount of time on testable growth in a narrow spectrum of academic learning, we're trying to promote a more holistic view of education. By design, the camps (and the other programs we offer) integrate cognitive and non-cognitive skills that are essential elements in successful living. To gain a better understanding of how game design camps can achieve this broader goal, let's consider four dimensions of character development (Shields, 2011):

- *Moral character* generally refers to how people interact with each other. Issues of kindness, consideration, and empathy are key here. What does it mean to be a good person, and to see the value in others?

- *Civic character* moves past the individual to describe ways in which people show their commitment to their community: Are they committed to improving the quality of life for others? Are they seeking to improve the local environment?

- *Performance character* describes how people approach tasks: Do they work hard and persevere in their efforts? Are they focused on doing their best, or just getting by?

- *Intellectual character* describes ways in which people approach information and ideas: Do they keep an open mind and weigh evidence? Are they willing to reconsider previously held beliefs in light of new information?

SIDEBAR: PROS OF CREATING HANDHELD GAMES

Ross Stauder

I got into designing games because Bob invited me to sign up for a Star Logo game camp three years ago. I've really enjoyed that and done some more game designs on my own. The second year I came back to the camp and along with Bob there were two people from MIT and they did TaleBlazer with us. What I really like about making handheld games with TaleBlazer is that you can have fun playing outside. The games are fun and easy to make. I like making them because it's a lot different than making other kinds of computer games. The format in TaleBlazer is mostly setting up a story in sequential order, whereas in my Star Logo games I set the blocks and let it go. My first effort to make a game was at design camp.

One important thing to think about in TaleBlazer is giving good directions, because people need to know how to navigate when they are outdoors. Another important thing is making sure that everything is in sequential order. Otherwise the player will get messed up and go to things in the wrong order. Also, be sure the characters have some useful information or interaction to make the game interesting and exciting. In my game you had to fight the monsters and when you killed them they would drop something. As a player you would have to bring it to someone as proof you slayed him and then he or she would reward you. Your game should also include puzzles to solve to make the game harder.

(con't on next page)

We have found over the years that design projects have a lot of potential to build *moral character*. While many games are criticised in the popular press for promoting violence through conquest and killing, in our experience the kids do a good job of segregating a violent game environment from their personal lives. Phrased differently, most kids do a good job of being a warrior in-game while remaining kind and helpful in real life. In fact, we usually see much more positive, pro-social interaction in our game design camps than we do in working with school groups. Removed from the artificial competition of school grading, our young designers are remarkably willing to share their ideas and techniques. Like many gift cultures where recognition accrues to the most generous members in the community, the personal rewards in a game design environment are not attached to having the best grades. Rather, there is a benefit in being recognized as a capable contributor. The feeling of accomplishment a young designer feels when his peers appreciate something creative or innovative in his game—and perhaps even go on to adapt it for use in their own game—is much more meaningful than simply getting a top grade. As one of the campers put it in the title quote for this chapter, kids want to "Have fun and display our awesomeness." For our tween-age designers, building a feeling of personal capacity is critical. A collaborative design studio environment that recognizes personal excellence, an ethic of sharing, and an appreciation of the gifts and talents of each member is a great place to nurture that growth.

SIDEBAR
(con't from previous page)

For example, in my game your path was different depending on which class you chose. Each class had locks, and to open them you had to solve questions using information you received earlier in the game.

Being able to work with others at the camp and get feedback was especially helpful, because everyone finds different things fun and that's why games turn out better when you work together. In my first game idea, the objective I came up with sounded cool but my friend pointed out that it wasn't. I realized that it wasn't my best idea needed work still, and after revision and more brainstorming, our game overall turned out better. Making handheld games is a lot different than school because it requires smarter thinking and trial and error x 17. In school you don't get a second trial because when it's done it's done and that's your grade.

TaleBlazer was overall a great experience for me. I'm looking forward to more game design projects this summer. This time the games will be even more challenging and interesting since they will require harder thinking and more puzzles.

Civic character has been less of a focus in the mobile game camps than it has in other design projects we've led, such as helping kids in an after-school program create StarLogo TNG simulations that embed ecosystem dynamics (Coulter, 2014). But, the potential in the mobile space is there. We expect to capitalize on it in a new initiative we are starting where young designers will develop mobile games to engage visitors to the Missouri Botanical Garden with local and global food issues and other environmental concerns. These new design projects will give kids an opportunity to learn about critical science issues and engage the community in a meaningful way. In terms of civic character development, the kids will be learning about their community as they offer a service to it. Beyond the design process, we're also exploring in this new project how civic engagement in a game context may lead to virtuous behavior in the real world: Does being a protagonist on behalf of the environment in-game spur you on to taking action back home? We know kids can make choices not to bring their violent game persona into the real world. Can they choose to bring a virtuous one to life to benefit their community?

Moving ahead, *performance character* is where we see some of the most important benefits of game design camps. Running counter to the school model of "tested, graded, and done" outcomes, the design studio model for our camps is based on persistence and continuous improvement within the week we are together and beyond. When kids participate in more than one camp, we have seen growing craftsmanship in designing engaging game environments. While a first-time participant might develop a game that relies on simple point-to-point navigation to achieve a goal, a veteran designer will embed complex, consequential choices for the player and show greater sophistication in how they leverage the design tools to create the game play they want. Imagine the difference between simply having to get your food once to survive and a more complex game play where you have to manage and monitor your character's energy level throughout the game.

Regardless of the designer's level of experience, there is always a sequence of making a trial version, testing it out, making improvements, and testing the next iteration. Inevitably some aspects of the game design don't work as well as they might, and fixes are in order. As Ross—a frequent participant in our game camps—notes in the sidebar, game design "is a lot different than school because it requires smarter thinking and trial and error x 17." While in a graded school assignment "good enough" might be sufficient, the internal motivation to make a game you're proud of, and the external hope to "display our awesomeness" motivates persistent effort toward improvement. Eventually, working with the camp staff and their peers, most challenges get resolved which leads to a real feeling of accomplishment. In one camp, we had a normally quite reserved student get up and dance a jig every time he had a breakthrough. Persistence pays off, especially in an environment that provides authentic motivation.

A fourth dimension of character development to consider is the extent to which a good game design promotes *intellectual character*. Instead of memorizing facts and rote procedures, mobile game players need to think on their feet as they navigate clues, weigh evidence, and make consequential choices (Gresalfi et al, 2009). Doing this well requires keeping an open mind and a willingness to reconsider positions based on emerging issues. Designers have an even greater challenge, as they chart out complex paths "behind the scenes" with multiple contingencies. For example, *The Nights of Lore* developed by three middle school students had an upgrade path players could earn that went from having a wooden sword to steel and perhaps even on to 'mirthil.' These swords of course, were not to be confused with other weapons in the game, such as the elvish blades that other characters might have. Depending on what you as the player have done before within the game, you might have achieved a level of success that allows you to pick up a powerful (and highly desired) monobow, but only if you have defeated the baby trolls. While the specifics just described may not make complete sense if you are not immersed in the game environment, the important point is the level of complexity underlying the design. Listening in on the planning meetings reveals an astounding level of thinking among the kids as contingencies are laid out, checked for conflicts, and set at levels that are just challenging enough to be motivating (but not too hard).

While some mistakenly think that game play hinders developing basic skills, my experience has been that kids actually develop and maintain robust skills through their efforts to design and play games. For example, I've seen kids spend much more time looking for just the right word for their game than they ever will for a writing assignment they don't value. For example, one game's design plan had a player's role changed throughout the document from perpetrator to the much more evocative role of 'infiltrator.' Despite the negative stereotypes, it's clear to anyone who works with kids on meaningful projects that the texting generation can still write well when they need to.

So, four dimensions of character, each nurtured in a game design environment. None of these examples are meant to suggest that games and game design are somehow a Holy Grail for learning. Rather, they provide one of many possible means for supporting kids in taking on a deeper and more meaningful engagement with the world they are a part of. As we become increasingly aware of how learning and growth is a 24/7/365 process, we need to be mindful of how the full scope of kids' experiences feeds their development. More so than highly regimented school programs, game design camps can provide opportunities to develop character attributes that can be applied across the life span. Here, the cognitive academic skills that schools have an almost exclusive focus on come to life through larger applications that are personally meaningful to the kids. Complementing the academic focus, the non-cognitive skills such as maintaining good interpersonal relations, building civic commitment, showing persistence, and living a life of the mind are a natural part of the work and not an artificial add-on. Kids learn what they live with. By combining joy and purpose—or if you prefer, by "having fun and displaying awesomeness"—kids can find the meaning of life.

REFERENCES

Coulter, B. (2014). *No more robots: Developing kids' character, competence, and sense of place*. New York: Peter Lang.

Gresalfi, M., Barab, S., Siyahhan, S., and Christensen, T. (2009). Virtual worlds, conceptual understanding, and me: designing for consequential engagement. *On the Horizon 17*(1), pp. 21-34.

Shields, D. (2011). Character as the aim of education. *Phi Delta Kappan, 92*(8), pp. 48-53.

ACKNOWLEDGEMENTS

Thanks to Josh Sheldon and Lisa Stump at MIT for co-leading this game design camp and for ongoing technical support.

This work was supported in part by National Science Foundation under grants #0639638, #0833663, and #1223407 All opinions expressed here are those of the authors and not necessarily of the National Science Foundation.

CHAPTER TWELVE

Project Exploration's Environmental Adventurers: Amplifying Urban Youth Agency, Identity and Capacity with Mobile Technology

Jameela Jafri, Gabrielle H. Lyon, Stephanie Madziar, & Rebecca Tonietto

---

Project Exploration's week-long summer Environmental Adventurers program immersed eleven Chicago Public School middle and high school students into the world of urban bees and biodiversity research. We employed a place-based approach to ground learning experiences and exploration within uniquely urban spaces. Students used mobile technology to explore the environment, document native bees, and engage in authentic fieldwork research and data analysis. Students maximized the potential of the technology in ways that forced program leaders to rethink the potential of mobile technology as an amplifier rather than simply an enabler.

BACKGROUND:
MOBILE TECHNOLOGY IN A RELATIONSHIP-BASED PROGRAM

Project Exploration is an organization dedicated to making science accessible to young people through personalized experiences with science and scientists. Since our inception in 1999, we have built relationships with more than 1500 middle and high school minority youth. We focus on recruiting students who are not academically successful, but who are curious and open-minded. We work on getting to know students for who they are, what they like and are curious about, and what they can do in science. Our program reflects what we most care about: creating access and equity in science for young people who historically have been overlooked by meaningful science education. Project Exploration uses structured ways of co-creating curriculum with youth: reading and writing together and sharing our work with the public in culminating events. Most importantly, once you're in, you're in: facilitators focus on fostering and supporting long-term relationships with students and most participants stay actively involved with Project Exploration for a minimum of two years; many participate for more than five.

In the summer of 2012, we set out for the first time to include mobile technology as a major part of what we do with youth. In Environmental Adventurers—a week-long summer program—Chicago Public School middle and high school students would use mobile technology to explore the environment, document native bees, and engage in authentic fieldwork research and data analysis[1]. When we decided to use mobile technology as part of Environmental Adventurers, we knew this tool would not change our core practices. We would be student-centered; youth would work alongside scientists to do meaningful work; students' interests would shape their research projects; we would read and write together; we would host a culminating showcase for the community; and because Project Exploration's program is relationship-based, we knew that when the summer program concluded we would work to support students to stay involved with science, and we would continue to stay involved on their lives. What we did not know was what the students would teach us about the power of mobile technology to amplify the experience.

WHY ENVIRONMENTAL STUDIES IN AN URBAN SETTING MATTERS

Environmental science has long been considered a valuable way to engage young people in their local habitats. Programs for urban youth are often designed to take students into natural spaces, away from the city. There is certainly value in introducing young people to new environments away from their homes. But, when natural science programming is conducted away from cities, it can suggest to students that urban environments do not harbor natural spaces, and that scientific research on ecology and the environment only takes place away from urban communities. This is particularly problematic for urban young people of color who are typically underrepresented in the sciences.

In the summer of 2012, to develop a youth-centered environmental science program for Chicago middle and high school students, we grounded scientific fieldwork in local issues with the goal of facilitating a program through which youth could build a scientific identity in themselves *and* their city. As a result, we intentionally incorporated several of Chicago's active learning spaces as places where environmental research can be conducted—local museums, universities, parks, and urban green spaces—by collaborating with key partners, such as the Chicago Park District and the Shedd Aquarium.

Youth-Centered, Science Driven

The youth named the program *Environmental Adventurers*, a title that articulates the identity-building and active engagement they were seeking. With input and design parameters from youth, staff next engaged environmental scientists to help distill a set of locally based research questions

---

[1] A short video about Environmental Adventurers within the context of Project Exploration's science programming was produced in 2012 by Free Spirit Media: http://www.youtube.com/watch?v=7UfI1slaBkk.

we could meaningfully investigate with students during a summer program. After direction from the youth, we identified a scientist with content expertise in the topic of environmental science to assist us in planning the program.

In particular, we decided to study bees due to a long-term relationship with a graduate student in bee ecology at Northwestern University, Rebecca (Becky) Tonietto, whom we asked to serve as the scientist in residence. Becky had already done considerable outreach as a guest scientist for Project Exploration's gender-specific middle school program (Lyon & Jafri, 2010). Through this previous outreach work, Becky knew young people will quickly move beyond the initial fear of bees and become immersed in questions as they hone their observation skills and begin to look closely at the bees. Moreover, native bees were perfect animals to study to study for this program because they illuminate localized ecological and environmental issues and lend themselves to conversations about local flora and fauna, food production, and pollination.

Technology as an Enabler

To support youth in developing identities as scientists engaged in research, we knew it was critical for them to become familiar with the tools of the practice. Biologists and ecologists are increasingly using mobile technologies as data collection and data sharing instruments, as well as traditional technologies like water-resistant journals. We paid particular attention to enabling our Environmental Adventurers to use authentic, traditional and cutting-edge technologies alongside research scientists. The journals were simple to plan for. When we sat down with Becky to map out the program goals and content, we provided each participant with high-quality water-resistant journal for documenting location, bees collected, notes, maps, and drawings similar to those Becky had long used (see Figure 1).

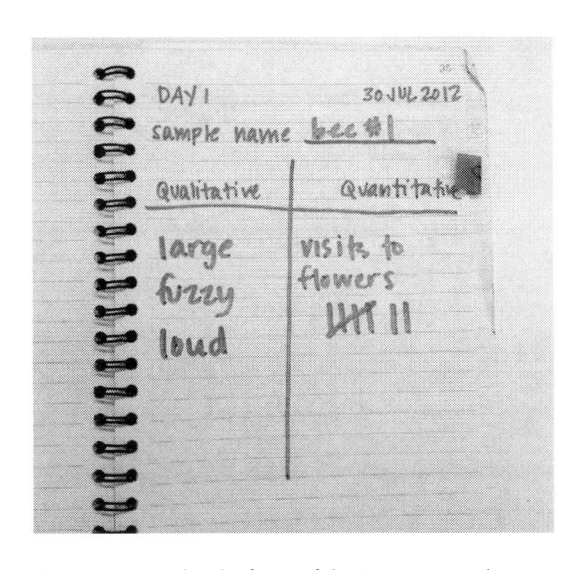

Figure 1. A notebook of one of the Environmental Adventurers documenting bees in her journal.

Planning to integrate mobile technology was somewhat more nuanced; how would we both enable teens to meaningfully document their own learning and self-direct their research, but also ensure they were able to build technological skills and social capital through access to cutting-edge technology used by scientific researchers when researchers own use of mobile is still evolving? We purchased iPod Touches to be used by each student as a way to collect data, take pictures, find locations, and research information at each outdoor location. We also purchased two iPads and paid for field-guide apps to identify local insects and plants. Our goal was for students to use the devices to document their learning through photography, and to learn how to capture images that would enhance the collected data, such as pictures of plants, that couldn't be identified in the field. We also wanted students to utilize the location-finding features of the iPods, given that field scientists document location in their field journals. Finally, we wanted to integrate a citizen science App for documenting bees called *BeeSpotter*.

PRACTICES AND OUTCOMES

During the week-long program, youth focused on two goals:

- Working in lab teams, students developed a research-based question of their interest about the behavior of native bees in Chicago.
- The youth compared the abundance of native bees in restored prairies (vs. ornamental gardens), both located in different spaces in Chicago.

While working alongside ecologists, students developed personal interest-driven research projects that examined native urban bee preferences for flower shape, color, smell, and sunny vs. shady areas. Youth used individual devices to collect data, record native bees in different habitats, track their study sites, collect bees, and take photographs of the prairie restoration natural areas within Chicago parks. Back in the lab, student teams used iPads to identify wildflowers and other insects during outdoor observation sessions (see Figure 2).

Figure 2. Kristian and Tajj use the Audubon Wildflowers App to identify local plants they observed in the field.

Each lab team recorded their notes in their journals. At the end of the week, each lab team provided the total number of bees they collected in restored prairies vs. ornamental gardens. The data was pooled together to compare the abundance of native bees in the two habitats.

Throughout the week, youth engaged with a wide variety of STEM professionals and scientists, wrote daily reflections on their experience, and participated in team-building exercises. Towards the end of the week, Becky led the youth through analyses of their collected data. The youth worked together in groups to create visual presentations, data representations, and practice explaining their conclusions from their research projects. On the last day, youth presented their findings, bee collections, and recommendations from their research to family, friends, and Project Exploration staff in a lecture hall at the University of Chicago.

A general template for the daily five-day schedule is as follows. Although the time spent on each of the items below may have been longer or shorter depending on the day, the following schedule outlines the core work of this intensive science and youth development program.

1. Warm-up led by our Teaching Assistant (a former Project Exploration student).
2. Introduction of science content and technology, data collection practice, and discussion.
3. Get in a van and go to a local site to place bee bowls to collect bees.
4. Lunch.
5. Return to the site to collect our bee bowls.
6. Drying and pinning bee specimens.
7. Document bees collected, in journals.
8. Journal, using a prompted reflection question.
9. Share journal reflections.
10. Wrap-up and share goals for the next day.

Bridging In- and Out-of-School Learning Environments

This program was designed not only to have an impact during the one week but also to extend into the classroom over the coming year. To do this, we included Stephanie Madziar, a Teaching Fellow[2] and Chicago Public School science teacher, as a co-facilitator of the activities. Stephanie

---

[2] Stephanie's participation was through the National Summer Learning Association *Summer Pathways for Innovation* teaching fellowship program, supported by the John D. and Catherine T. MacArthur Foundation. A full report about the fellowship—including highlights of Stephanie's fellowship with the Environmental Adventurers—can be found here: http://c.ymcdn.com/sites/www.summerlearning.org/resource/resmgr/publications/macarthur_policy_brief_final.pdf.

worked alongside Becky to facilitate activities, hone the ways in which mobile technology was incorporated into the program design, and support students. Stephanie's classroom experience helped us guide and evaluate the technology integration.

Stephanie also reflected on her experience in the summer program through a series of blogs for teachers describing her process and pedagogy. In addition, she developed content to use during the academic year in her own classroom. She applied her out-of-school experience to enhance her in-school ecology unit. As a result of the summer experience, Stephanie added activities such as observing the metamorphosis of a monarch butterfly, dissecting and learning the parts of a flower, understanding the importance of pollinators, using a microscope to diagram the parts of a honey bee, identifying and researching native pollinators, planting flowers in the courtyard of their school, and carrying out student interest-driven research projects about pollinators.

Technology in Practice

So how did mobile technology fit into this flow? We had some concerns about how our students would actually end up using these devices. Basic logistical questions came to mind first: How would we track the devices? What if something broke? How would we promote appropriate use? This turned out to be another area where Stephanie's classroom experiences informed the summer program. Stephanie recommended the following:

- Numbering each device and assigning one to each student for the duration of the program;
- Storing devices in a single location and providing them to youth when needed for an activity;
- Developing a signed-user agreement for appropriate usage;
- Modeling appropriate usage of the devices; and
- Engaging youth the first day with exploratory activities to learn how to use the devices.

Students were guided to use the devices as scientists would—as instruments to document the natural world. Stephanie facilitated an activity on how to take quality pictures in different settings (see Figure 3). They took pictures of pinned insects in the lab, flowers outside, live insects (and themselves!). They learned to take a series of photos from multiple angles and depths when trying to document a flower that may be hard to identify in the field. Students also learned to make sure that each picture had a reference for scale so it would be helpful back in the lab, and attempted to identify the plant or insect of interest.

Figure 3. Stephanie Madziar shows Kristian and LaShay how to capture focused images of active bees.

In addition to the convenience of portability, the iPods provided youth an opportunity to digitally document their personalized experiences and interest with nature. They took pictures of themselves with plants, their peers, holding monarch butterfly pupas collected from milkweed plants, and some good selfies! Students immediately appreciated the value of images in scientific documentation, and gained a sense of pride in work well done. One student said of the process: "the most memorable experience for me was taking my first picture with the iPod and having it turn out perfect and professional."

Students continued to use journals and pens to document data when they returned to lab. Every insect collected in bee bowls was carefully counted and recorded in their journals so that they could answer their research questions by the end of the week. The journals were also used for taking notes during scientist presentations and for writing reflections to journal prompts (Figure 4). The experience was as much grounded in literacy as it was in mobile technology.

Figure 4. Tavon and Ariel document bees observed at the Shedd Aquarium on data sheets.

USING MOBILE TECHNOLOGY: LESSONS LEARNED

The customizable nature of mobile technology can lead to unexpected usage and learning and an amplification of interests (Squire & Dikkers, 2011). We learned some things about the potential of digital technology in the Environmental Adventurers program that were surprising and unexpected. We observed what seemed to be natural progressions from unfamiliar to familiar use of the technology: moving from personal to professional use, expanded application from snapshots to stories, and student interest shifting from disengaged to engaged.

From Personal to Professional

Nearly all program participants had their own smart phones, and we anticipated there might be some digital competition between personal handheld devices and the iPod Touches being provided. The usage contracts were intended to help preempt digital friction by asking youth to put away their personal devices and focus on using the technology provided in the program. Surprisingly, youth informed us they preferred using the iPod Touch to their personal smart phones. One student told us her phone, with all of the text messages and social networking status updates, would have been a "distraction to her work." Consistently, the students said they liked using digital technology for learning and that having a separate device provided in the program facilitated this opportunity. As one student put it, "I think the biggest way that it [mobile technology] enhanced the experience in other areas is that it gave all of us participants ways to capture moments to look back on and to share it with others, in general, or the broader audience. "

From Snapshots to Stories

By focusing mainly on still image photography in our preparation of the students—we had dedicated time in the program to learn about taking good pictures for research purposes—we were placing inadvertent limitations to the creative techniques we imagined youth could utilize in the program. Our incapacity to imagine other uses did not however stop the students from thinking creatively with their tools outside the bounds we had set. One such progression of use we saw was their near immediate incorporation of video to document bee behavior and a readiness to incorporate these videos into their final presentations. Most of the bee videos made by students involved them following a bee as it moved from flower to flower. Some students got remarkably close to bees, and proudly showed their videos to their peers back at the lab. Youth immediately leveraged the media-making features to produce videos about bees despite not having any help from us (Figure 5).

Figure 5. Ariel, Tavon, and Becky Tonietto capture videos of bee behavior and movement.

The use of video as a vehicle to document bees was a progression of student learning and engagement, amplified and facilitated only by the integration of iPod Touches in the program (vs. a stand alone camera). We realized that we could have approached media making practices more broadly from the beginning, showing students not only good images taken by scientists, but videos as well.

When youth showcased their videos in their final presentations, they not only self-identified as students engaged in research, but also as scientists and documentarians of animal behavior. The context sensitivity of the devices afforded youth the ability to gather data unique to their location, themselves, their time, and their interests (Klopfer & Squire, 2008). For example, one of the students told us proudly,

> Using the video on the iPod made it seem more official. Going around collecting bees was important and I know it hadn't been done before in Chicago. But just having it be recorded and documented, made it seem official since a big part of science is getting stuff documented.

The multiplicity of capacities of the technologies enabled youth to develop multiple identities: they were not just Environmental Adventurers (ecologists and animal behaviorists in the making), but also documentarians of that adventure (historians, videographers, storytellers).

From Misperception to Awareness

During the Environmental Adventurers program we witnessed ways in which highly *engaged* youth were sometimes perceived as disengaged. Engagement actually came easily to our students when reading and writing were in context of authentic and purposeful activity—in this case documenting bees in Chicago. Reading and writing are critical skills in science, and serve as gatekeepers to pursuing STEM. All Project Exploration programs intentionally incorporate reading and writing on a daily basis, particularly because our youth are from populations traditionally underrepresented in science and often come from public schools with low literacy rates. As part of the general logic, we anticipated that youth would use the digital devices as note taking and self-support tools while in the field but—once again—did not imagine their use beyond these simple activities.

Students quickly progressed beyond these expectations and took initiative to use the note-taking features of their devices much more broadly, set reminders for themselves, and document their field site locations. During lectures, chaperones noticed the youth frequently interacting with their devices and assumed the worst. For example, some visiting scientists perceived students as "not paying attention" during presentations; other adults made assumptions that students were playing rather than learning. However further observation and communication with students allowed mentors to see that the youth were adding to the activity with new applications of their mobile devices rather than being off-task. We learned that the assumption that a young person looking down and using his/her smart phone is off-task—rather than amplifying or learning material—is stereotyping behavior incorrectly and requires professional training for adults to be able to see more nuanced differences in the use of mobile technologies. Students can, of course, get off track, but in Environmental Adventurers they were more often adding material and information to the conversation. We just needed to learn how to see this.

CONCLUSION

The practice of doing science is embedded in the social capital of its language, behavior, and tools. Young people who are the least likely to get involved in science—students of color and girls especially—often do not have access to the social capital needed to pursue STEM. Doing real science, alongside professional scientists, and using the actual tools of science helps build relationships, social capital, and ultimately, an identity in science.

In designing the Environmental Adventurers program, we anticipated mobile technology would be a useful addition because of its authenticity—field researchers use cutting edge technology in the field to document biodiversity and collect data—and its familiarity—students already have experience with mobile technology for listening to music, checking social media, and playing games. However, the unexpected ways in which the mobile devices were maximized by the students have forced us to further consider the potential of technology to highlight our participants' sense of agency, interest, and capacities. For those integrating mobile technology for the first time into youth programs, we hope that our experience and reflections demonstrate how both learning and student voice can be amplified by their use of mobile devices.

We suggest that personal technologies in learning contexts naturally cultivate professional practice, support storytelling with a variety of media, and encourage engaged student learners. From a sociological perspective, the use of mobile technology in a formal learning setting amplified the potential for youth to see themselves as scientists. Environmental Adventures participants used the iPod Touch as a science tool (Figure 6). They also reminded us that access requires not only a mission-driven approach to change, it requires that we stay open to possibilities—most especially the possibilities youth can create for themselves. As a larger digitally adept community of educators and facilitators, we are still learning how to navigate the potential of devices for amplifying youth agency, identity, and capacity. It is critical to engage youth in these conversations, and listen and watch carefully to what they say and do.

Figure 6. LaShay learns how to be use her iPod Touch on the first day of the program to photograph flowers and insects in an outside environment.

REFERENCES

Klopfer, E. & Squire, K. (2008) Environmental detectives – the development of an augmented reality platform for environmental simulations. *Educational Technology Research and Development 56*(2): 203–228.

Lyon, G & Jafri, J. (2010). Project Exploration's Sisters4Science: Involving urban girls of color in science out-of-school. *Afterschool Matters,* 11, 15-23.

Squire, K. & Dikkers, S. (2011) Amplifications of learning: Use of mobile media devices among youth. Convergence: *The International Journal of Research into New Media Technologies, 18*(4). 445-464.

ACKNOWLEDGEMENTS

The authors would like to acknowledge youth participants: Tavon B., Ariel D., Shelby G., Nailah H., Tajj H., LaShay H., Kaylyn M., Jordan P., Michelle V., Morgan W., and Kristian W. The authors would also like to acknowledge the guest scientists and partners, including Kelly Ksiazek, Hannah King, Jason Steger, Liza Fischel, Dr. Emily Minor, David Lowenstein, Peggy Espada, Hive Chicago, National Summer Learning Association, Shedd Aquarium, Chicago Park District, and Free Spirit Media. Special thanks to our teaching assistant, Jasmine Fleming. Environmental Adventurers program was made possible with support from the National Summer Learning Association and the Hive Chicago Learning Network. Project Exploration partnered with Northwestern University and the Chicago Botanic Garden.

CHAPTER THIRTEEN

Civic Engagement and Geo-Locative Media: Youth Create a Game to Discuss Political Issues

Juan Rubio

Recently, I found myself in charge of a project to foster civic engagement among youth through geocaching. *Race to the White House* was an initiative of the New York City-based non-profit youth development organization Global Kids' Online Leadership Program designed to teach youth about leadership, citizenship, global issues, and activism. The objective of the project was to combine geocaching—a global outdoor treasure hunting game—with presidential politics. A group of high school students would use technology, digital media, and game concepts, increase their understanding of the political process, do research, write content for the web, and practice public speaking and event planning. I was also interested in using location-based game design to help them gain awareness of how technology might be used to begin conversations with their peers and the public in general about social issues that mattered to them.

Did *Race to the White House* achieve those goals? Did we manage to create an experience during which youth gained game design knowledge and become civically engaged? Did the youth who participated in the program leave with new skills? In this chapter I will discuss some of my observations in designing and implementing the program so that other program managers and educators may benefit from the experience as they think of using mobile technology and a platform such as geocaching in their programs.

BACKGROUND: GLOBAL KIDS, GAMES, AND PLACE

Games are not a new topic for Global Kids. Over the years, the *Online Leadership Program* has used a game-based learning approach to teach youth about leadership, citizenship, global issues, and activism. Lately, that effort has focused on the use of location-based platforms for youth to create their own personal narratives, learn game design concepts, and explore their communities while at the same time developing computational thinking skills. When I joined Global Kids, one of my first projects involved the development of a location-based project with youth in the

Bronx using a geo-locative game platform. We used SCVNGR in a series of workshops for middle schoolers to create a geo-locative game that contained a narrative about the local history of their neighborhood. After some experience with that platform, I came to realize that the tool was not the best to achieve our goals due to its difficulty of use as a design tool and its focus primarily on supporting commerce. I also spent some time using ARIS with kids, and felt that ARIS had a more user-friendly interface and was geared towards use in educational programs. Given Global Kids' and my personal experience and interest in combining geo-location and rich educational content with our mission to engage youth in civics, using geocaching—a well known platform—was a natural progression. Unlike other more niche platforms, there is a large global community of geocachers creating content on a worldwide scale. This provided some of the appeal to pilot a program that would involve game based learning, be youth driven, and be able to be integrated with civic engagement.

Geocaching is an outdoor activity in which players participate in a digital scavenger hunt using mobile devices to find artifacts (caches) that have been hidden by other game players. The caches are created by players using receptacles that vary in size from large tupperware containers to small capsules the size of a coin. In addition to hiding and finding individually made caches, geocachers can purchase and use small metal plaques called travel bugs. Each travel bug can be registered by its owner on the website geocaching.com and has a unique number used to track its location. As the travel bugs are moved by other players around the world from cache to cache, they can be tracked by their owner: on the website their exact locations and trajectories can be seen on a map.

With the premise of geocaching and travel bugs in mind, Global Kids outlined *Race to the White House* as a two week activity involving the creation and play of a game that involved using geocaching to move travel bugs to discuss issues that were important to the students. The primary role of the students would be to fill in some details to complete the design of the game and integrate political issues they most cared about. Although I did not establish the original concept and basic parameters of the project, it was my main purpose to create from this outline a program that would develop in youth a deep understanding of the political process, introduce them to design concepts, prepare them to plan events, and take a leadership role in presenting about their project to their peers and the general public.

I began those two weeks in the summer of 2012 by meeting a group of high school students at the Grand Army Plaza Central Branch of the Brooklyn Public Library to discuss past presidential campaigns. I was interested from the outset in making sure the kids would decide on issues that were personally important to them and for that purpose a review of campaigns from the last few elections was necessary. Flash forward two weeks: this group of students had finished a prototype game, had it played by members of the community, and held two public meetings, one to discuss the results of their game, and another to teach the public about geocaching and other technologies.

MAKING DECISIONS BASED ON TIME CONSTRAINTS

The major challenge in implementing this program was the small amount of time we had to develop and complete it. *Race to the White House,* scheduled for only two weeks in the summer, was designed to bring together kids from high schools across New York City to work collaboratively and learn the technology around geocaching. In addition, they were to learn research skills and become better informed about the political process. All of these skills were embedded within the context of designing and developing a location-based game. And again, this was to happen in just two weeks.

Since the program was conceived from the start with a major time restriction, many aspects of the game design had to be decided in advance. In particular, the students would not be involved in the entire game design process—the actual mechanics of the game were already decided by program facilitators. We determined that kids would place travel bugs in caches around New York City and create the webpages corresponding to those travel bugs. On those webpages, players would be asked to move the travel bugs they found in student-placed caches closer or further away from the White House (towards or away from Washington DC) based on whether or not the player thought that a particular topic should be discussed in the upcoming presidential election. Students themselves would be asked to provide input on the issues attached to each travel bug and to write white papers about these issues to inform the players of their points of view and justifications.

Ideally, we would have the youth not only suggest content for a game like this but to be very involved in the game's design or maybe make multiple games together in small groups. However, designing a game, from ideation to prototyping, testing and changing the game based on feedback requires a significant amount of time and we had only two weeks to complete the project. These limitations led us to focus less on the design of the game and more on the actual implementation of that design. This left less opportunity for the students to engage in the design process. But it did allow us to spend time giving the youth an understanding of political participation and discussions about social issues within the context of media creation and game design plus teach them the technological skills to become effective playtesters and game developers for their game (Figure 1).

Figure 1. Participants from *Race to the White House* try to decipher the location of a geocache in Central Park prior to find it and place a travel bug attached to a political issue of their choice.

PRELIMINARIES:
FROM PAST PRESIDENTIAL CAMPAIGNS TO GEOCACHING

The program started in a Brooklyn library with a presentation of campaign ads such as the iconic Lyndon B. Johnson "Flower Girl" TV ad which captured the imminent threat of nuclear disaster during the height of the cold war. Other political ads were also featured from the presidential campaigns of Bill Clinton, George W. Bush, and Barack Obama. This review gave the students an introduction to political issues from a historical perspective and gave them a framework to start their discussions. The campaign materials also offered insights about several issues discussed and debated during presidential elections such as welfare, campaign reform, and the economy.

Starting the program with a review of past political campaigns proved to be effective. Since the political campaigns that I decided to show were recent—the oldest campaign reviewed was the Lyndon B. Johnson "Flower Girl" TV spot—the students were able to relate to them. They were familiar with the issues presented in the ads. In addition, they were familiar with the presidents in the campaign ads, most of them still alive. After reviewing their political campaigns, the students engaged in a lively discussion about the use of media, the issues themselves, and the effectiveness of the arguments presented.

Once they examined political issues, they were ready to learn about geocaching. Here, some of our connections came into play. Race to the White House was part of an initiative that included several partnering organizations: the Brooklyn Public Library, the Mozilla Hive NYC Learning Network, and the National Summer Learning Association. A teaching fellow from the National Summer Learning Association was responsible for facilitating some of the workshops and introduced the students to the inner workings of Global Positioning System (GPS), something we would have been hard pressed to do alone.

Going in depth with the students about GPS beyond what they technically needed to finish the game was about more than fitting in a lesson about technology. Because the part of the program included a peer education component, it was important for the students to fully understand the technology that was at the core of the geocaching platform. Preparing them to have a good understanding of the technology gave them the confidence to later explain concepts related to the game.

GENERATING AND DISCUSSING THE TOPICS, MAKING THE GAME

Once the students understood the mechanics of the game, the platform to use, and the overall theme of the program, they worked in groups to select topics significant to them for inclusion in the game. It is important to note that much liberty was given to them in selecting these issues. It was the goal of the program to have their voices come through and to include issues that were culturally relevant to them. To help them select the topics, they were introduced to research techniques and resources by staff from the Brooklyn Public Library—once again we made use of our partners in the community and program. After group discussions about their research, they decided to include the following issues: Medical Marijuana, College Tuition, Net Neutrality and Gun Control (Figure 2). Here are some of the things that our students said about why they selected their issues to be part of the game:

Net Neutrality. "We chose it as a group, because of SOPA and all the stuff that was going on, and it related to us and because of censorship. We decided it as a group and thought that was something that affected us. Because we are in the internet every time and all the time, if the internet was going to become controlled, we wouldn't be able to get the information all the time."

Legalization of Medical Marijuana. "It was not really a topic I liked but since this was a group activity even if you didn't like the topic I had to go with what other people thought it was important. I believe the main reason they wanted to do this issue was because of the benefits to people who are sick. Medical Marijuana could mask the symptoms they are experiencing, and it's a way to help cope with the illness. It was not a choice with some link to personal stories but more general, like what they heard and how it could help."

Gun Control. " Because we felt that the gun laws in different areas are very different, and that they are not equal creating different rates of crime, some areas have high crime rates and others low crime rates. It was a group decision to choose that issue. We wanted to bring attention to changing certain laws to prevent crime rates. Personally, I cared about the issue because I saw kids in my neighborhood of East New York being caught in that lifestyle, a violent lifestyle revolving around guns."

Figure 2. Students from *Race to the White House* brainstorm issues to include in their game, and do research to write entries on geocaching.com.

During the program, students became aware of the importance of being involved in the political process and how government officials can influence policy with a direct impact on the issues they were discussing. We invited a speaker from Common Cause—an advocacy organization founded as a vehicle for citizens to make their voices heard in the political process and to hold their elected leaders accountable to the public interest[1]—who clearly explained to students how citizens can get involved in the political process and shape policies by advocating for their causes at their local, state, and national level. Another factor that motivated their involvement in the political process was the fact that they cared deeply about the issues selected. This gave them more ownership over the program, and their investment in publishing the content for their game was higher than if the adults in the program would have influenced the decision on what issues to include.

With their researched topics in hand, students filled out the basic game template with an explanation about their topic and instructions on how to play the game. Once the travel bugs were attached to

---

[1] for more information about Common Cause visit http://commoncause.org.

a webpage, and the instructions for how and why players should move the travel bugs were created on geocaching.com, students moved outside to find geocaches in the parks around New York City to place the travel bugs. They found caches around parks in the city: Central Park in Manhattan, Prospect Park in Brooklyn, and Marine Park in Queens. During this part of the process, I noticed that the students became more invested in the program, working in groups and helping each other as they looked for caches to plant the travel bugs. They also spoke about leaving something behind, something tactile, something they had created. One of the students spoke about how he liked the idea of leaving something to be remembered for. "My legacy," he kept repeating as he deposited the travel bugs in the caches. Even though their game was simple, it was complete, and the students had already come a long way.

ENGAGING THE PUBLIC

A final step in our two week program went beyond giving our kids a chance to try these ideas out among themselves. We also gave them an opportunity to create media in the game to directly involve the public in a conversation about the issues considered. First, as part of the game development process, students created webpages attached to each travel bug on the geocaching.com website. Each webpage had a short introduction about themselves and the program. They included general information about the issue, and explained why they thought it was important to them. The sidebar provides one example, the webpage linked to the travel bug written by a group of students from *Race to the White House* on the issue of College Tuition.

SIDEBAR: TRAVEL BUG WEBPAGE FOR THE ISSUE OF COLLEGE TUITION

Current GOAL

This travel bug was placed by us, young people in Global Kids, Inc. and the Brooklyn Public Library in the summer of 2012. We placed a total of 48 bugs all over Queens, Manhattan and Brooklyn associated with topics we feel are important to society and should be discussed in the 2012 Presidential Election campaigns. This travel bug is racing against the other travel bugs. If you want to get your and our point across, will you help it run the race?

About this Item
The issue for this travel bug is:
College Tuition

The issue for this travel bus is the high cost of college tuition. The term "college tuition" refers to fees which students have to pay to attend collage in the United States.

The high price of college tuition is a major problem people are facing today. In order to pay for these high tuition costs students are forced to take out student loans which put these students in debt. Student loans for college tuitions have become one of the top debts faced by Americans today, rivaling credit card and car loan debt.

(con't on next page)

Another aspect of the program that asked students to collect their thoughts for outside audiences was time spent planning and producing public events. Students collaborated to produce two public meetings as a part of *Race to the White House:* one to release the game at the end of the program and another one to present the results of the game on November 4th, 2012, the day of the presidential election. During these gatherings and as part of the planning, students learned about producing an event, creating presentations, assigning roles, and speaking effectively to a public audience.

At the first event, students talked about their experiences and what they learned during the program (Figure 3). They also trained those attending, including other youth, on the use of geocaching and took a group of 25 participants to find geocaches in Prospect Park.

In the second event, participants from the *Race to the White House*, came together again to present to the public the results of their games, and how and where the travel bugs had moved. Since the event took place the day of the presidential election, students spoke about their program but also discussed how their experience during the two weeks in the summer had influenced their outlook on the political process. They answered questions from their peers about the game they developed, they showed how the travel bugs had moved (Figure 4) and how the public had participated in the discussion by leaving comments on geocaching. com as they played the game.

SIDEBAR

(con't from previous page)

When collage tuition is so high it discourages newcomers to not apply to college in the first place because in their mind they will think going to college will create debt for them in the future. If they are discouraged to go to college, they wouldn't be able to better their education as well as get a better job. If you graduate in debt, you'll have to pay your loans back. If the debts are large, then you are forced to take jobs just to pay off the debt.

We chose this topic because it's a realistic problem that we'll face soon. Most of us are starting college in the fall so raising the college tuition is not going to help us one bit. Along with tuition, we'll have to pay for books, room and board and also food to eat.

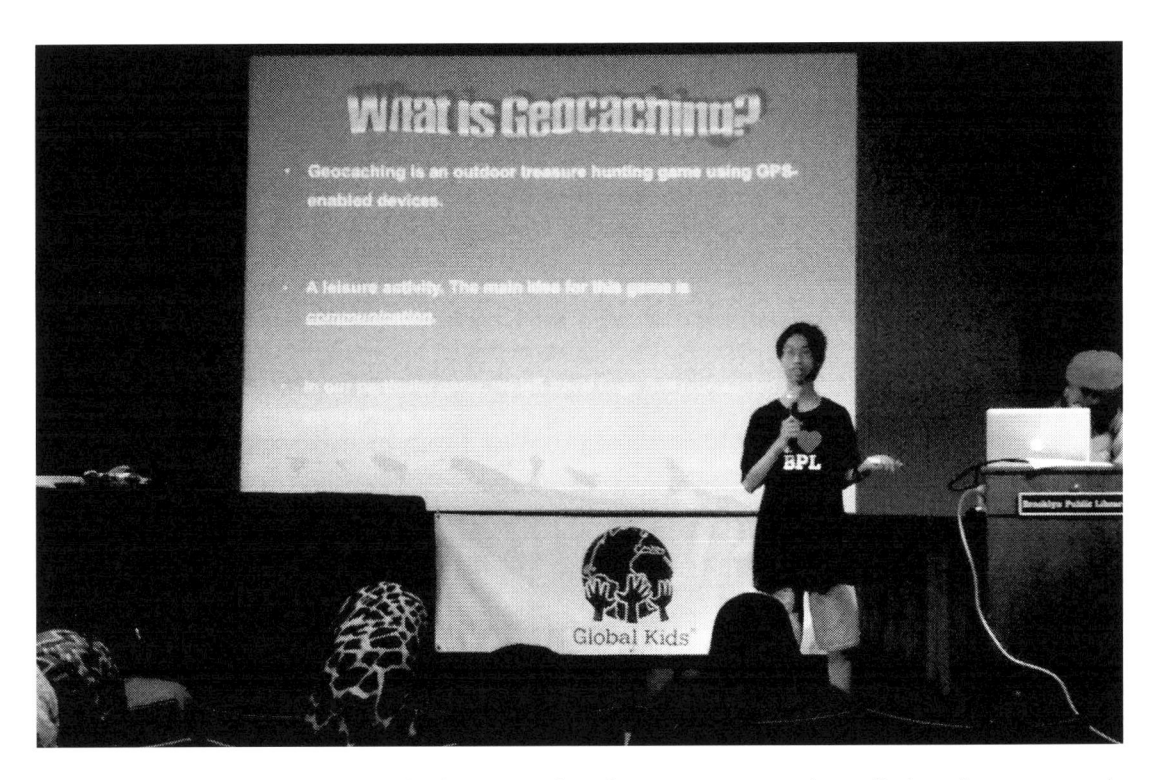

Figure 3. Before taking other youth to play the *Race to the White House* game, students talk about the program and explain the geocaching platform.

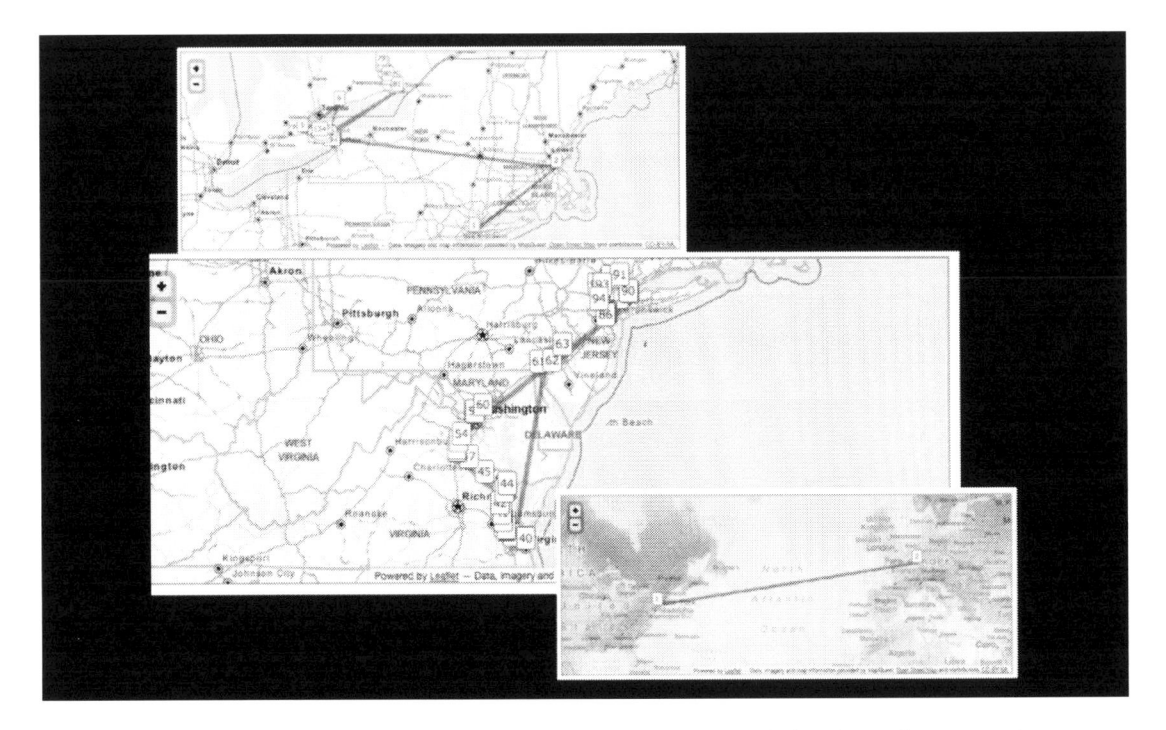

Figure 4. Map showing the distance and route that the travel bugs had moved after players from geocaching.com moved them following the instructions from the youth participants.

LEARNING, TECHNOLOGY, AND PLACE

The work conducted during *Race to the White House* successfully engaged youth in civic activities using mobile media, allowing them to think critically about political issues. It provided them with an opportunity to create content based on research about issues they found relevant and worth discussing with their peers. Creating a public virtual treasure hunt and selecting political issues that were important to them, the youth participated in a discussion and conversation with the community who visited the geocaches. They opened up this space for political conversations while applying design concepts to decide how the game could be more effective. Additionally, as they moved from looking for caches to planting the travel bugs (Figure 5), young people were learning how to negotiate group dynamics and collaboration: Who was in charge of reading the map? Who was leading the way to the cache? Who was logging the trackable to the site?

Figure 5. Youth find a cache and deposit a travel bug as part of the game *Race to the White House*.

The program also provided young people with an opportunity to use technology as a means to explore spaces that otherwise would be of no interest to them. Consider for example one of the participants in the program, a young woman who has lived all her life in New York City, but had never visited Central Park. Geocaching provided an opportunity for her to visit and explore a new space. She writes:

> In this program, I have visited Central Park and Marine Park for the first time. My experience in Central Park was awesome. It was cool to see all the different things that were going on in the park such as people renting bikes and riding around, horses pulling carriages, etc. It was beautiful and I would go back if I can. Marine Park was nice. It wasn't as entertaining as Central Park but it was nice and spacious.

This young woman's experiences point towards our ultimate intent: combining politics, technology, and place. With *Race to the White House,* we are re-examining the traditional model of teaching technology to young people. Rather than having youth gaze at computer screens, typing frantically at a keyboard and clicking mice, *Race to the White House* has asked students to mediate public spaces with the use of mobile technology and game play. It presented them with a new way to see their surroundings, using augmented reality to help them discover new facts about space and landmarks. One of the caches they found, for example, was placed in a large house near the library that was built by someone associated with the chewing gum industry in the 1800's. It was through the exploration of the space and the geocaching game, that students were able to learn the importance of that industry at that time in the United States.

New approaches to designing learning experiences include as a principle that students "become actively engaged in exploring, experimenting, and expressing themselves" (Resnick, N.D.). These new forms of engagement should consider the potential of programs that work with students in nontraditional settings and create environments for learning beyond the classroom and into public areas. *Race to the White House* exemplifies this form of learning by asking students to explore their surroundings and discover new places while mediating the space with the use of mobile technology.

CHALLENGES AND FUTURE ITERATIONS

While the program was successful overall, there are some challenges to address in future iterations of the program or in other similar endeavors. First, since the program took place over a two-week period with several field trips around New York City, attention should be given to the number of locations students visit during the duration of the program. Another challenge that comes from the short duration of the program is how to balance the development of research, writing, reading, and technology skills for strong educational outcomes with the implementation of the game. Because we needed to work towards a final event and to have a working game to release to the public on schedule, students were pressured to finish their research and writing in a short period of time. Future implementations of the program might consider creating groups of students with specialized roles. Some would work on the research and writing, while others work on finding the geocaches and planting the travel bugs. The groups then could rotate to allow all participants to benefit from all the learning opportunities offered in the program.

Moving to future iterations of *Race to the White House*, I would think of ways to connect civic engagement more directly with the game's design. Although the game was successful in engaging the students and making them think about civic life, politics and the government, I would have liked to have more participation from the public in general and the geocaching community in a richer conversation about the issues presented by the kids on the pages they created on the geocaching website. Because moving travel bugs is a practice that is only physical in nature—you find the travel bug and then you move it to another geocache—the game's design did not require players to take part in as much conversation as I had hoped. New iterations of the program could consider using a mechanic to create richer interactions between youth and those playing the game.

A strong part of the game's design I would like to see someone build upon is the visualization of the trajectories of the travel bugs. Even today our travel bugs for *Race to the White House* keep moving around the world. One of them traveled to Germany from New York and continues moving to this day. Creating a game that fuses the mechanic of moving or planting artifacts with exchanging ideas online could make the program stronger.

OUTCOMES

I had for some time been interested in designing a program that would use technology and game play to increase civic awareness. *Race to the White House* presented the ideal platform to integrate all of these aspects while developing in the participants media creation and other skills such as group collaboration, writing, designing and playtesting a game. There were several core takeaways for the youth participants of the program. They became more knowledgeable about how mobile technology can be used for meaningful learning experiences, they found new ways to collaborate and create consensus about issues that were important to their lives, they learned how to use digital tools for research, and wrote coherent instructions to explain the game and the issues they selected. Technology was used to facilitate exploration of physical space while at the same time help youth contribute to the political discussions around the upcoming presidential election. They also became familiar with event planning, working together to put a final presentation to release the game, and then—on the day of the presidential election—an event to show the results of the game. In the process, they also practiced public speaking skills and presented their ideas and game concepts to an audience of their peers and the general public.

Countering the trope that technology promotes isolation and antisocial behavior in teens, programs such as *Race to the White House* tap into the potential of technology to promote meaningful interactions that bring people together. Youth can create content to encourage communities to connect. We have the potential to develop agency in youth to create content that reaches larger audiences and ask the public to take an active role in what the youth create.

REFERENCE

Resnick, M. (N.D.). *Learning by Designing.* Accessed from http://pubs.media.mit.edu/pubs/papers/design-v6.pdf

CHAPTER FOURTEEN

Technovation Challenge: Introducing Innovation and Mobile App Development to Girls Around the World

Angélica Torres

New York-based photographer Zana Briski supplied children living in the red light district of Calcutta, India with cameras to teach them about photography. Observing their community through new eyes, they aspired to a future that transcended the invisible boundaries of their environment. The resulting Academy Award-winning documentary *Born into Brothels* features photographs and stories that share a world few people outside of their community had seen. Our program, Technovation Challenge, has a similar aim: we equip girls with mobile phones to open their eyes to the possibilities of technology and entrepreneurship, and bring their vision to the world. In this chapter we describe the evolution of Technovation Challenge and what we have learned about engaging middle and high school girls in science, technology, engineering, and mathematics (STEM) through running the world's largest and longest-running technology competition for girls.

WHAT IS TECHNOVATION CHALLENGE?

In Technovation Challenge[1], teams of girls identify a problem, create an app to solve it, code the app, create a business plan to launch the app in the market, and pitch their plan to experts—all in 12 weeks. Technovation Challenge's applied, project-based computer science and entrepreneurship curriculum reinforces the digital representation of information, algorithmic thinking and programming, and the societal impact of information and information technology. It connects girls with a network of professional women in business and technology while reinforcing life skills such as problem identification, designing and testing solutions, team collaboration, and communication to different audiences. Teams compete for $10k in seed funding to take their app to market. Between 2010-2013, approximately 1400 Technovation Challenge girls built 278 apps.

---

[1] Technovation Challenge is a program of Iridescent. Tara Chklovski founded Iridescent in 2006 with a mission to use STEM to inspire curiosity, creativity, and persistence in the pursuit of knowledge. Since its launch, Iridescent has helped more than 18,000 underserved families through mentorship and hands-on programs, with a team of more than 700 engineers and scientists.

WHY RUN TECHNOVATION CHALLENGE?

> "Because women account for one-half of a country's potential talent base, a nation's competitiveness in the long term depends significantly on whether and how it educates and utilizes its women." (Hausmann, Tyson, & Zahidi, 2012, p.31)

Technovation Challenge helps close the gender gap in computer science by teaching girls how to code and how to become successful entrepreneurs. Despite growing demand for employment in computing fields and pervasive social media, youth and particularly girls are not pursuing training in computer science in the United States. The Bureau of Labor Statistics expects more than 750,000 new computer specialist jobs by 2018 (Lacey & Wright, 2009); meanwhile, of the 3,000 students who took the Advanced Placement (AP) Computer Science exam in 2011, only 21% were girls (UCLA IDEA, 2012). By inspiring women to pursue computer science careers, we can bolster the workforce necessary to fill these jobs while also ensuring gender equity and the representation of various perspectives among the creators of new technologies and businesses.

Girls are avid internet users, but as Jane Margolis, author of *Stuck in the Shallow End: Education, Race and Computing* explains, "They're using it for communication, and that does not translate over to who is learning the computational thinking so they can create with technology" (Hing, 2012, p.1). But sparking interest is not enough; girls associate negative attributes to technology and face a computing experience and skills gap compared to boys (Teague & Clark, 1996). Many women enter programs enthusiastic about being a computer science major, but their interest erodes shortly thereafter (Sevo, 2009).

Girls need a long and strong base of support to imagine, invent, and engineer in the context of technology. Such a support base of positive experiences can propel them through a computer science undergraduate program. Our program provides powerful experiences to girls, allowing them to: 1) see themselves as leaders and inventors of technology; and 2) pursue STEM career trajectories in greater numbers.

PROGRAM HISTORY AND SCALE UP

Technovation Challenge started small and has grown large over the last few years. Rather than limit our influence to local audiences or those in proximity to large players in associated fields, we have found ways to expand our program to new audiences worldwide. By taking a brief look at our history, readers may get a sense of what it means to enact and support a new idea growing from a local experiment to a broad practice.

Small Beginnings: 2010

Anu Tewary, Ph.D., inspired by Startup Weekend[2], founded Technovation Challenge. Iridescent piloted the program in March, 2010 with 45 high school girls. Girls from different schools came together at the Google campus in Mountain View, California to form teams and attend two-hour classes twice a week for nine weeks. In addition to space, Google provided free mobile phones for the teams to use.

Technovation Challenge students use App Inventor[3], a software development platform created by Professor Hal Abelson from the MIT Center for Mobile Learning, to create mobile apps. App Inventor aims to empower people with no previous programming experience to design mobile phone apps. It is easy to start, inspires increasingly complex projects that build on each other, and embraces different interests and learning styles[4].

Twenty-five professional women from technology companies including Google and LinkedIn mentored teams throughout the program. Teams developed 10 mobile phone apps and pitched their business plans to judges at a final event at Microsoft. Good outcomes and a mention in the media (Rusli, 2010) convinced us that the program was worth repeating; the summer after the program, 12 Technovation Challenge participants interned at technology startups. Based on the success of the initial pilot, the Office of Naval Research awarded Iridescent a $2.4 million grant to implement Technovation Challenge in Silicon Valley, Los Angeles, and New York City.

Six Locations: 2011

In 2011, Technovation Challenge served 232 girls while expanding to six locations: Google in Mountain View, New York, and San Francisco; LinkedIn in Mountain View; the Berkeley Wireless Research Center; and the Iridescent Science Studio in Los Angeles. The program included 64 mentors who worked with the instructors at each site to walk the girls through the nine-week curriculum for two hours, twice a week. The program added 56 teaching assistants (TAs), college undergraduate and graduate majors in computer science, who were paid a stipend to provide additional support with coding. Teams created and pitched 55 apps.

---

[2] Startup Weekend (http://startupweekend.org/) offers weekend workshops all over the world; individuals get together to share ideas, form teams, and launch startup companies.

[3] See Chapter 5 in this book for more about MIT's App Inventor. - Eds

[4] App Inventor is used by universities such as MIT, the University of San Francisco, and Wellesley College, as well as other youth-oriented app development programs such as Apps for Good (http://www.appsforgood.org/).

500+ Participants: 2012

In 2012, Technovation Challenge allowed for leaders to emerge and organize participation themselves. As a result, 509 girls created and pitched 98 apps in Boston, New York City, Los Angeles, and the San Francisco Bay Area. We added an additional week to the curriculum (10 weeks total) to give teams longer to prepare deliverables. While TAs no longer received a stipend, they were encouraged to participate as volunteers. We added teachers, who were paid a small stipend to recruit teams at their schools and chaperone them to a technology company site. In addition to meeting at technology companies once a week for two hours, teams met at their school site with TAs to work on their deliverables approximately two additional hours a week.

Going Global: 2013

Moving the curriculum online allowed Technovation Challenge to go global in 2013, engaging 575 girls from 25 U.S. states and countries. The 12-week curriculum was hosted as a course on Mozilla's Peer to Peer University (P2PU). Finalists in 2013 included teams from Brazil, Nigeria, and the United Kingdom. We added two more weeks to the curriculum to allow extra time for teams to code their apps and polish their business plans (12 weeks total).

Through the first four seasons, we reached 1361 girls who created 278 apps (Figure 1). Winning apps included MASH in 2010, I.O.U. in 2011, StudiCafe in 2012, and Arrive in 2013.

Teams can now materialize anywhere in the world where girls can get together with a computer, internet, and a mobile phone, reflecting our changing ideas about how to engage girls who need the program the most. In our model for 2010–2012, girls traveled to technology companies such as Google, LinkedIn, Twitter, and Microsoft, where they worked in teams with mentors for a couple of hours each week over a period of 9 or 10 weeks. The technology company format was convenient for mentors who could participate at their home company and attractive to teachers who wanted to take their students to technology companies, but proved a challenging model to scale. Potential participants exceeded available spots and some girls had long commutes that

Figure 1. Technovation Challenge Scale Up 2010-2013, 1400 Girls Around the World.

affected program attendance and retention. Migrating our curriculum online in 2013 allowed teachers and youth directors at individual school and after-school sites to recruit girls and directly lead the program without a Technovation Challenge-provided instructor. Furthermore, relocating teams from technology campus settings to everyday settings brings the added benefit of fostering an everyday programming culture among girls. As part of the new scale-up and sustainable online model, teachers do not receive stipends to run teams. Some of the teachers who participated in 2012 continued the program in 2013; however, other teachers felt that the program should compensate them and opted out of the 2013 season.

Kicking Off Technovation Challenge: Hack Day

To meet our goal of empowering girls, Technovation Challenge begins with Hack Day, a boot camp where participants learn basic programming skills. Hack Days are one of the most successful components of the program. For most girls, the Hack Day is the first time that they see other girls coding and the first time they program their own app. While girls may be intimidated by boys their age who have more experience hacking at other events, the girls-only atmosphere of Hack Days levels the playing field. Girls seem to feel more comfortable taking risks when they do not have the option of letting a boy take over the activity.

Hack Days are full-day events hosted at schools, universities, technology companies, or community organizations in which girls acquire the basics of working with App Inventor. App Inventor is free and uses a visual programming language where code is organized into blocks. It is an ideal coding language for beginners because it is a visual, rather than textual, interface that teaches programming concepts in an intuitive and straightforward way. All instructions, PowerPoint presentations, and handouts for the Hack Day are available as part of the Technovation Challenge curriculum[5]. Girls can attend Hack Day as a team or on their own.

In addition to learning about programming tools, girls learn about programming practices at Hack Days. They take turns on computers with internet access and pre-installed with App Inventor. Working in pairs (pair programming), one programmer writes code while the other reviews each line of code as it is typed. The girls switch roles every 5-10 minutes. A Hack Day instructor leads participants through five step-by-step App Inventor tutorials: CrystalBall, PaintPot, MoleMash, NoTextWhileDriving, and CreateYourOwnApp. Concepts in the tutorials build upon each other and encourage girls to break out and hack the apps by incorporating their own twists to the code. Building these apps helps students gain confidence in making something that works. They also learn common app mechanics that they use as a base to build their own apps. To keep willpower high, Hack Days often include free lunch and snacks. The sidebar explains a bit about the five Hack Day tutorials and computer science concepts covered in the 2013 curriculum[6].

---

[5] Hack Day Tutorial Guide 2014: http://iridescentlearning.org/technovation2014/unit02.html.

[6] Since the release of App Inventor 2 in 2014, these are the apps included in the curriculum: http://www.technovationchallenge.org/curriculum/lesson-1/. (Wolber, David; Abelson, Hal; Spertus, Ellen; Looney, Liz, 2011).

One of our leaders in Orlando, Florida asks girls to reflect on the moment they first get the CrystalBall app to work. She encourages them to relish the excitement and pride of making an app work for the first time. "That," she says, "is the feeling you are always looking for as a programmer." The apps the girls create often go directly onto their personal Android mobile devices. They continue to reflect on their accomplishments as they share the apps they built with their friends. Teams have the opportunity to bolster their App Inventor skills through additional tutorials during the 12-week curriculum.

TECHNOVATION CHALLENGE THEMES

After Hack Days, Technovation Challenge moves on to the task of creating the best possible app in the time remaining. Each season, we announce a theme for the app competition before the 12-week curriculum begins. Our goal goes beyond incentivizing the creation of excellent, winning entries, toward motivating all teams to create an app from start to finish, and helping them grow as designers and programmers. The Technovation Challenge theme influences what the girls end up creating. Through research as well as trial and error we have arrived at themes that help participants produce their best work.

SIDEBAR: HACK DAY TUTORIALS AND PROGRAMMING SKILLS

CrystalBall (teaches event-driven programming and variables) Students create an app that predicts their fortune. Users ask a question such as "Will I win my soccer game?" and shake their phone to view the crystal ball's response.

PaintPot (teaches events, variables, camera, and pair programming) Students create an app that allows users to draw lines and dots of various colors on the screen.

MoleMash (teaches procedures and debugging) Students create a game in which a mole jumps randomly around the screen every half second. When users successfully touch the mole, their score increases by one point.

NoTextWhileDriving (teaches text-to-speech) Students create an app that auto-responds to text messages while users are driving. Users also have the option to have the app speak the message received.

CreateYourOwn App (teaches events, variables, lists, procedures, camera, buttons, accelerometer, labels, image sprites, timers, and sound) Students work alone or in pairs to design and develop their own original app. Note: Teams need not commit to their Hack Day app idea for the competition; this exercise is mostly for fun and to apply what students have just learned.

For the first two seasons of the program, challenges were open-ended and resulted in many fashion or "paper doll" apps (Figure 2). The instructors were somewhat disappointed that girls spent time customizing their app visually to their own preferences rather than making their apps useful or interesting for other users. We wanted girls to identify interesting problems and create apps as solutions, encouraging a departure from consumers of technology to makers of technology.

Figure 2. "Paper Doll" Apps, Technovation Challenge 2011.

Notable exceptions were apps that had well-defined problems. For example, one team made an app that hails a taxi from a phone as an alternative to stepping into traffic (Figure 3).

In an effort to inspire girls to explore STEM in the apps themselves and come up with interesting problems to solve, the 2012 theme was to create a science education app. However, the theme did not generally motivate deep, interesting app ideas. Most apps focused on quizzing and preparing for standardized exams (Figure 4). We realized that in classrooms where standardized testing in science is a top priority, the theme "science education" did not inspire innovation for students.

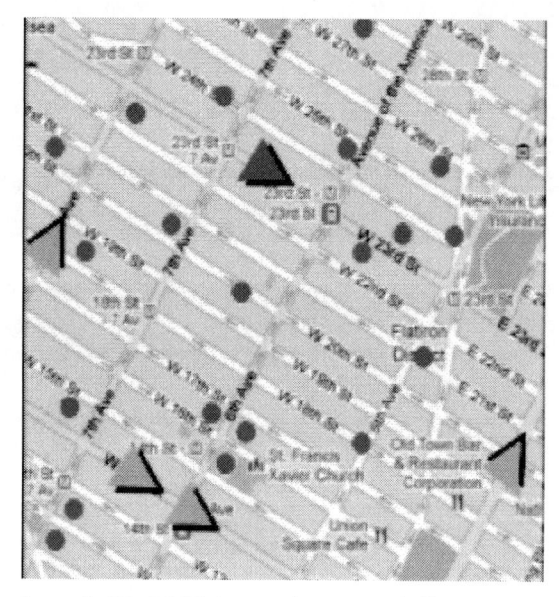

Figure 3. "HailNYC" App, Technovation Challenge 2011.

Figure 4. "Quiz" Apps, Technovation Challenge 2012.

As before, however, we saw notable exceptions to the general pattern. Some teams came up with apps that creatively interpreted the theme or selected an interesting problem to solve. For example, teams created an app that taught teens about safe sex to address the problem of teenage pregnancy, an app that helped teens navigate underage drinking situations, and apps that provided alternatives to costly and controversial organismal dissections (Figure 5).

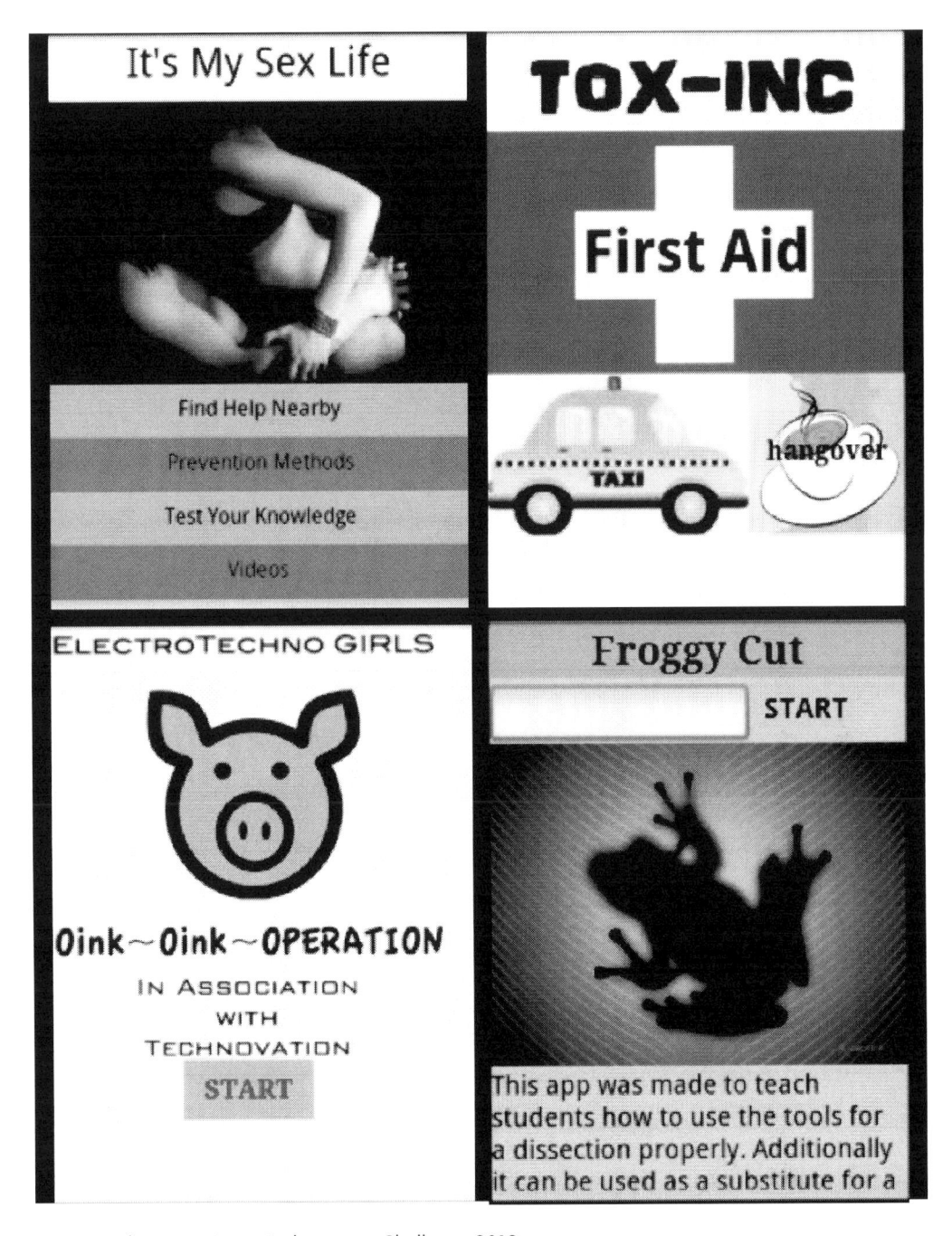

Figure 5. "Social Impact" Apps, Technovation Challenge 2012.

Notable apps in 2012 helped us revise the challenge for 2013. The 2013 challenge, "Solve a problem in your local community." was well received. Once again, however, many teams had a common and narrow interpretation of this theme. Out of 115 app submissions, 16 focused on the rather mundane topic of helping users identify volunteer opportunities (Figure 6). Without a clear problem to solve for a specific user, most teams that chose this theme did not generate innovative apps. Below are sample volunteer app descriptions.

Sample "Volunteer" App Descriptions, Technovation Challenge 2013

CommUnity: *CommUnity addresses these issues with an easy way to find and track volunteering opportunities that match your interests and help your community.*

Re-Genz: *Re-Genz is a free social mobile application, connecting volunteers to specific problems to regenerate local communities and help build up young people's confidence and experience.*

Do-gooder: *Do-gooder is an Android app that will allow anyone to find opportunities for volunteer work.*

Pass On The Kindness: *Do you love Facebook? Do you like helping people? Well, there's a combination of both in an unique application known as Pass On The Kindness!*

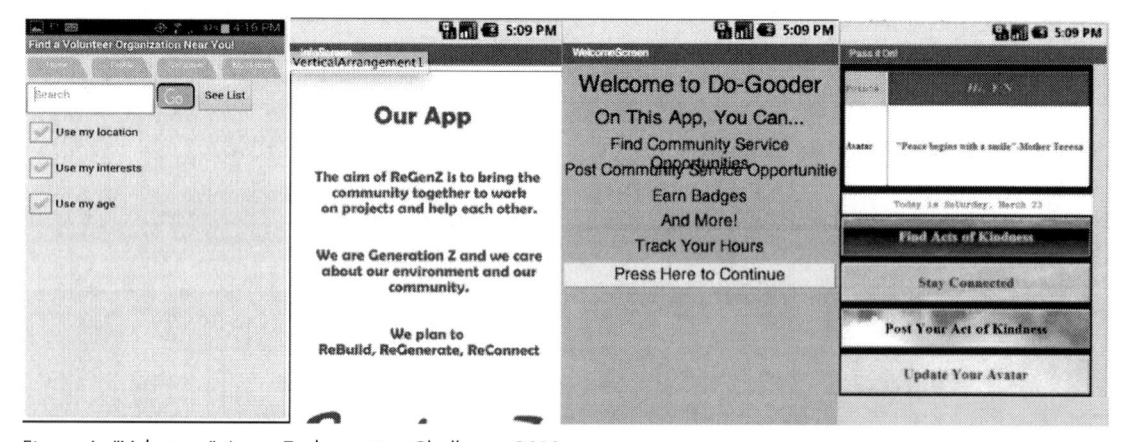

Figure 6. "Volunteer" Apps, Technovation Challenge 2013.

However, Team Solidárias from Brazil took third place at the Technovation Challenge World Pitch by refining the volunteering problem to their community and branding the app with the Brazilian cultural value of solidarity (Solidárie Sidebar)[7]. In addition to Solidárie, other notable apps in 2013 included a pet-finding app (Pet Stop, San Francisco), an app that instructs the user on when to call the police rather than emergency services (Who2Call, United Kingdom), a teen diabetes app (Diary of a Diabetic Kid, Orlando), an app for tourists (TranslateIndonesia, Indonesia), a directory of wheelchair-accessible places (EZ Wheels, India), and an early marriage education app (Early Marriage, Yemen) (Figure 8).

Figure 8. "Social Impact" Apps, Technovation Challenge 2013.

---

[7] Solidárias also promoted their app through social media: http://www.solidarias.com.br/, https://www.facebook.com/pages/Solidarie/498632113535123, http://www.youtube.com/channel/UCRC4ocWAnyRaMphE-rkPpOg

These apps responded to the challenge by deliberately picking problems that teams could research and test, thereby increasing the relevance of the app to their daily lives and taking full advantage of the Lean design cycle (we discuss Lean later in this chapter). For example, Tek5 developed Who2Call alongside the Nottinghamshire Police to implement in their community, regardless of the outcome of the competition.

12-WEEK CURRICULUM: ENTREPRENEURSHIP AND LEAN THINKING

Technovation Challenge extends over a 12-week period, giving teams enough time to dig into their development and incorporate ideas that go beyond simple hacking. The program timeline for 2014 appears in Table 1. Ideally, Hack Days and technology company field trips occur before the 12-week program to help with recruiting and team-building activities. The 12-week program begins in February to accommodate as many international academic calendars as possible.

The program prepares girls to succeed—teaching skills beyond learning to code—by introducing the entrepreneurial side of app development. The 12 weeks kick off with an introduction to entrepreneurship through a product design philosophy known as Lean (Ries, 2011). Nine of the top ten U.S. business schools teach the Lean methodology, and it comes recommended by Facebook COO Sheryl Sandberg.

The Lean methodology inspires persistence to keep improving and developing one idea in students. Each week, Technovation Challenge teams fine-tune their deliverables by considering

SOLIDÁRIE SIDEBAR

Solidárie App, Technovation Challenge 2013.

(con't on next page)

one aspect of the product design cycle. Teams learn about market research, user-interface design, and business plans. As they refine their ideas and pivot—making adjustments to their app or business strategy—they may revisit topics to fine tune their approaches. For example, a team may identify a sizeable market for their app idea, but when testing their prototype discover that the user needs will not be easily met on a mobile device. Based on this finding, they may create a new focus for their app or abandon their first idea altogether and restart the design process. Successful teams typically go through the design loop multiple times, improving their app, business plan, and pitch with each iteration. These teams proactively engage users and incorporate feedback at every stage.

SIDEBAR *(con't from previous page)*

Solidárie is a mobile application designed for people who want to find, connect and share volunteer experiences. Our mission is to give everyone who wants to help the ability to do so, and thus no opportunities for action or collaboration are missed. The app connects people to nonprofit organizations and charity institutions in need of donations or volunteer's support. For these institutions Solidárie will be vital to expose their needs, and get an almost immediate help. Through its social features anyone can post pictures and share volunteer experiences, creating a bond between volunteers and institutions and stimulating to volunteer more.

Table 1. The 12-Week Schedule for Technovation Challenge.

Date	Milestone
Early fall	Theme announced/course goes live, registration opens
October-February	Technology company field trips occur (in-person or virtual through our video series)
October-February	Hack Days occur (one day of App Inventor training, can happen anywhere, flexible format)
February-April	12-week curriculum runs with live support
Early April	Regions announced, teams assigned to regions
Late April	Submission deadline, teams submit and get confirmation email
Late April	Judging begins
Late April	Regional Pitch Night coordinators invite teams to Regional Pitch Nights
April-May	Regional Pitching
May	World Pitch Finalists invited and announced
June	Technovation Challenge World Pitching (San Francisco Bay Area), including technology company field trips and celebration luncheon for all finalists

Teams also receive help with effective presenting and pitching. A *What Is It Like to Work At...* video series features female engineers at companies such as Twitter, Google, and Facebook speaking candidly about their paths to technology as well as daily job responsibilities. These glimpses into the lives of women in technology as near-peers inspire girls to explore computer science and business careers. Guest blog posts by Technovation Challenge mentors and other experts provide additional content tailored to the 12-week curriculum (e.g. career exploration, how to make an effective visual presentation, video game design story, etc.).

After a regional round of judging, 10 finalist teams travel to the Technovation Challenge World Pitch event to demonstrate and pitch their apps to a live audience and highly esteemed panel of experts. The winning team receives $10k in seed funding from Iridescent to further develop their mobile app and take it to market. The idea that their team's app can become a reality proves to be a strong motivator for girls and distinguishes our program as a real business experience rather than a classroom exercise.

KEY ROLES IN TECHNOVATION CHALLENGE

Behind the program's curricular components, the adults who lead and teach teams throughout Technovation Challenge make the program a success. Below we describe the main roles involved with running teams[8].

Regional Coordinators. As our program has expanded, we have relied on regional coordinators, adult volunteers or partner organizations, to bring 10 or more teams together in a geographical area for events such as Hack Day, regional pitch nights, and mentor mixers. Regional coordinators also help match teachers with mentors. Potential coordinators often find us through social media and help generate buzz for Technovation Challenge in their areas; their similar personal or organizational missions as well as local networks allow them to hit the ground running. Successful regional coordinators connect with local technology companies, schools, after-school clubs, universities, and youth groups, are active on social media, and reach out to other regional coordinators as well as the core Technovation Challenge team at Iridescent to exchange ideas, contacts, and best practices.

Hack Day Instructors. Hack Day instructors are typically undergraduate or graduate students in computer science (preferably women) who lead teams and adult leaders through the five Hack Day App Inventor tutorials. While no previous experience with App Inventor is necessary, instructors ideally spend a week or so familiarizing themselves with the tutorials and have App Inventor pre-installed on all Hack Day computers. The ideal instructor thinks on her feet, modeling how programmers identify solutions to their problems. Teaching younger students also helps instructors improve their ability to communicate with different audiences.

---

[8] These roles are fluid and flexible, allowing teams to coalesce in ways that make sense for their situations. The descriptions below are intended as guidelines that may help others think about how to prioritize and provide for the important interpersonal work necessary to making a project such as Technovation Challenge a success.

Technovation Challenge Teachers and Coaches. Teachers and coaches are adult leaders in youth settings who run one or more teams. While some teachers work as regional coordinators, more often teachers focus on getting one or two teams through the 12 weeks, dedicating at least four hours a week to working with teams. They recruit students, find spaces to meet, and get required paperwork together, then partner with mentors to teach the programming and business sides of the curriculum. A few teachers with a strong passion for either programming or business have functioned as both the teacher/coach and mentor and successfully run the program on their own.

In addition to helping students code their app, teachers can help teams innovate faster by encouraging them to define a specific user profile and identify a realistic market. Many students have a one-size-fits-all idea about apps that relates to their understanding of Google and Facebook as businesses that serve everyone while making money from ads. For game apps, Angry Birds presents an unlikely economic success that takes reframing for budding entrepreneurs to understand in terms that help their own app development. Open-ended questions such as "How will users find your app?", "What will attract potential users to your app?", "What other apps like this already exist?", or "How many people have told you they have this problem and what do they do now to solve it?" help students think as builders and creators rather than consumers. Sometimes helping a student take the next step—for example, spending an hour on Google Play typing in keywords, downloading and testing free apps, and perusing reviews—will help students avoid the paralysis that often occurs during idea generation.

Technovation Challenge Mentors. Mentors function as role models for girls, providing a link to the technology and business industries. A mentor can be any woman in technology or business. The mentor partners with the coach or teacher to present the 12-week curriculum two hours per week during the program, enhancing the material with examples from their own work projects and experience.

Ideal female mentors are role models in the technology or business world, and as such they often have busy schedules or locations that prevent meeting face-to-face with teams. Working virtually with teams via Skype and other platforms addresses problems of access outside technology-rich areas like Silicon Valley while modeling how to reach girls in under-resourced regions. This kind of virtual mentorship can easily be applied to remote locales such as rural Ghana, as well as areas difficult for mentors to reach on public transit, such as New York City's outer boroughs. The virtual format works best when teams have a couple of in-person meetings with the mentor to build rapport. In one case, a team in the United Kingdom traveled to meet their mentor in San Francisco after the competition ended, taking the opportunity to tour her company and other technology companies in the area.

Finding good mentors has proven to be difficult. Mentors are hard to identify, and not every successful woman is a natural mentor. To help close this gap and find more successful mentors, we added a list of mentoring best practices in 2013 (Mentor Sidebar). Strategies for our mentor training stem from other Iridescent programs such as Engineers as Teachers (EasT) and Curiosity Machine—one of the many ways our programs improve through cross-fertilization[9]. A successful strategy for Technovation Challenge mentors and teachers has been to offer support by sharing "how I think" rather than "what I know." Sharing "what I know" intimidates students; it feeds the assumption that adults know best because they have more education and experience. Modeling "how I think" creates space for students to contribute as thought partners, which allows room for student innovation and leadership.

Women who do not have time to support teams through all 12 weeks can step in and help as needed, for example, as "pitch coaches" who help teams polish their deliverables or "regional/world pitch judges" who select winning apps.

With all this talk about curriculum and adults, let's not forget that the most important role is that played by the girls. Technovation Challenge students do not need any previous experience with programming. We encourage adults to think beyond high-achieving students and include girls with different educational profiles that may bring other skills to the team and take away more from the experience.

PROGRAM IMPACT

Unlike other programs that focus on learning specific coding languages and skills, the goal of Technovation Challenge is not to learn App Inventor; it is to create and pitch an original mobile app to solve a problem. App Inventor is a tool in meeting the challenge and not an end in itself. This use of App Inventor as a tool inspires girls to explore other platforms and programming languages on their own.

HANDOUT FOR MENTORS — BEST PRACTICES

*Lead by example. Be an **active** mentor* — You are the project manager and leader for your team. Some mentors feel nervous at first about taking charge and keeping girls on task, but strong leadership ensures that teams remain focused and meet deadlines.

Manage team dynamics — Working with different personalities can be challenging; some students may be shy, others may be talkative. Establish the "three-then-me" rule where each time a person talks she listens to three other people speak before speaking again. Encourage shy students to speak up by directing questions, they will eventually feel comfortable participating.

Stay neutral during discussion — At times you may experience tension or arguing in the group. Manage conflicts when they occur by helping each student share her concerns and feel heard without taking sides. While girls are brainstorming ideas, encourage them to make their own decisions and decide things by consensus when appropriate.

Show off your skills — Bring your own skills and talents into the mix, even if a given topic is not in the existing curriculum. Please customize the PowerPoint slides to reflect your own expertise and share what you do in your job with students. Exposing students to actual work projects helps them understand what engineers and designers do. If you are an entrepreneur, share copies of business plans and tips on how to pitch. Whatever your skills are, please share them with your team as often as possible.

(con't on next page)

---

[9] Iridescent Mentoring Philosophy, http://iridescentlearning.org/wp-content/uploads/2013/09/Iridescent-Mentoring-Philosophy-newer1.pdf

Technovation Challenge is not a destination in itself but a springboard for girls to pursue computer science courses, internships, and technology or business careers.

Many girls enroll in computer science courses after our program. Fifty-two percent of respondents to a Technovation Challenge survey, which captured the first four seasons of the program (2010-2013), reported enrolling in either high school or college computer science courses after Technovation Challenge. At Piedmont High School in Oakland, California, 10 girls from Technovation Challenge signed up for AP Computer Science in 2013, five times more than the number enrolled the previous year and a new record for the school. At the Nightingale-Bamford School, an all-girls school, enrollment in a computer science elective rose from 2 to 10 girls after the program.

In the same survey, 38% of respondents completed an internship after Technovation Challenge (18% at a technology company). Many alumnae have gone on to complete summer internships in technology through connections they make in the program, such as Jasmine Gao, who was mentioned in the New York Times as a data scientist at bit.ly (Seligson, 2013). Technovation Challenge mentors later become sponsors (Hewlett, 2013); Jasmine met her future boss Hilary Mason, former Chief Scientist at bitly, through our program.

SIDEBAR
(con't from previous page)

Be a role model — As your team's mentor, you give each student a window into your industry and what it is like to be a woman in that field. Get to know the girls, share your story with them, tell them about your career journey. What were your challenges? How did you overcome them? Help the girls relate to you by showing them photos of your pets, children, favorite vacation spots, and telling them about your favorite hobbies. Help them understand that being a working woman does not mean working all the time, you still have a fun and exciting life outside of work.

Provide one-on-one interaction — Get to know each girl on your team individually. Start a conversation with the shy student who is not very talkative, ask her what kind of food she likes, what she wants to be when she grows up, what her favorite classes are and why. Get to know each girl so they feel connected and supported.

Encourage and inspire — Hearing you say, "I think you are really good at solving complex problems. Have you ever considered becoming an engineer?" is one of the most transformative experiences a girl can have in school. Unfortunately, she may not hear it from anyone else if not from you. Your opinion may also carry more weight as an expert. Hearing your encouragement and feedback about her strengths might just change her life, particularly after you have built a relationship over time.

The largest takeaway for participants has been an appreciation for how to create a product, 17% of girls who responded to a 2012 survey continued to work on their app after the program. In addition to having created original apps, girls in 2012 reported a greater understanding of what engineers and computer scientists do (Figure 9).

% OF GIRLS THAT AGREE OR STRONGLY AGREE WITH THE FOLLOWING STATEMENTS

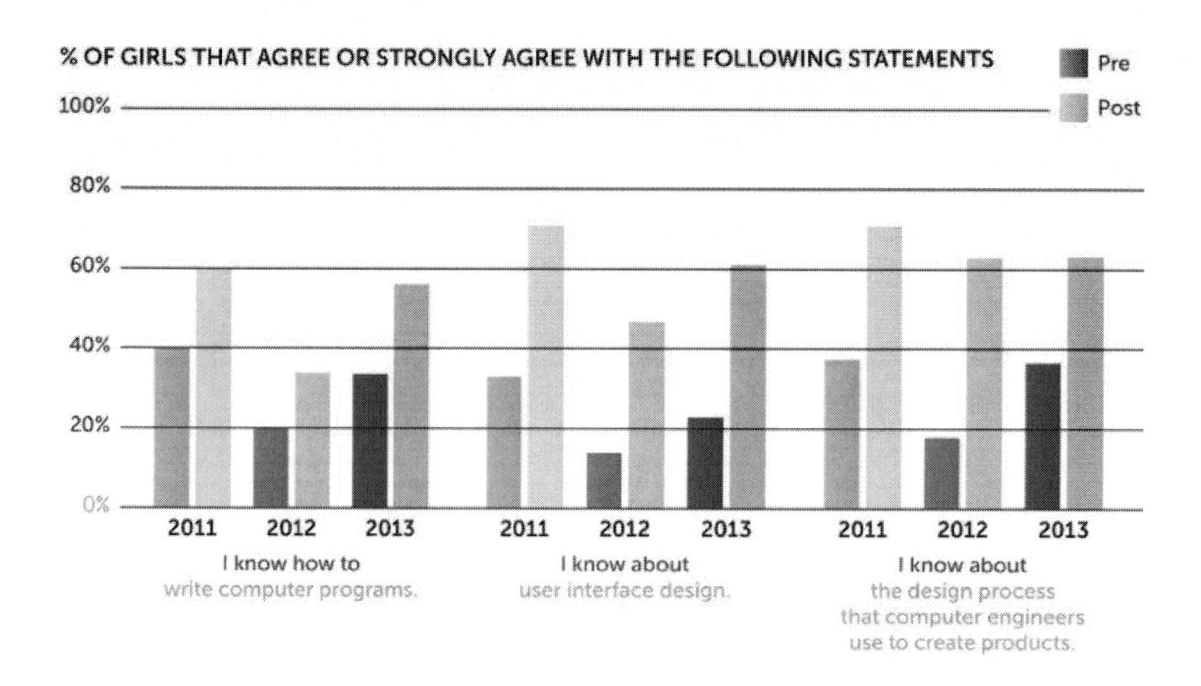

Figure 9. Pre- vs. Post-Survey Results, Technovation Challenge 2012.

A common assumption is that girls lack enough confidence to enter into a boys' world of technology. Many programs similar to Technovation Challenge seek to increase girls' confidence or self-perception of being capable in these fields. Interestingly, statements such as "I am confident using technology" and "I am comfortable making presentations" do not show significant gains here because girls rate themselves highly on these statements before completing the program. Most girls strongly agree with these statements in the pre-survey despite evincing considerable growth in how they interact with technology and pitch in front of an audience and experts.

After four years of results with Technovation Challenge, the notion that girls lack the confidence or wherewithal to successfully perform in a technology environment insults gender and observable data. For girls, a lack of belonging in a male-dominated field and a tendency to be overlooked by adults in favor of other (commonly male) students may play a part in keeping them from pursuing technology degrees and careers. We have witnessed how working alongside other girls and having a personal connection to a woman in technology inspires a desire in participants beyond meeting the current generation of female innovators to becoming their successors. Twenty-four of our alumnae have received the National Center for Women & Information Technology Award for Aspirations in Computing.

Technovation Challenge mentors benefit from their experience as well; they report that they enjoy networking with other women in technology (95%), increasing their knowledge of entrepreneurship (83%), learning to be effective mentors (88%), and improving their technical skills (63%). Mentors are inspired to keep growing professionally for example by starting their own companies, something Margaret Butler did when she founded Innovaspire. Many of our mentors return year after year. In the future, we intend to deepen the impact on the technology community by providing mentors with training that they can more directly apply to their careers.

WHY TECHNOVATION WORKS

> Technovation made programming real. What you're making is not just a project for a grade but it's something to impact somebody.
> — Technovation 2013 Participant

Figure 10 illustrates how Technovation Challenge serves girls through 12 weeks of applied computer science and business activities. The program activities emphasize technology as a collaborative effort; girls interact with other girls, mentors, teachers, and judges throughout the program. Girls personalize their learning by choosing what they want to work on for an app. They also choose what role and projects to focus on within their team.

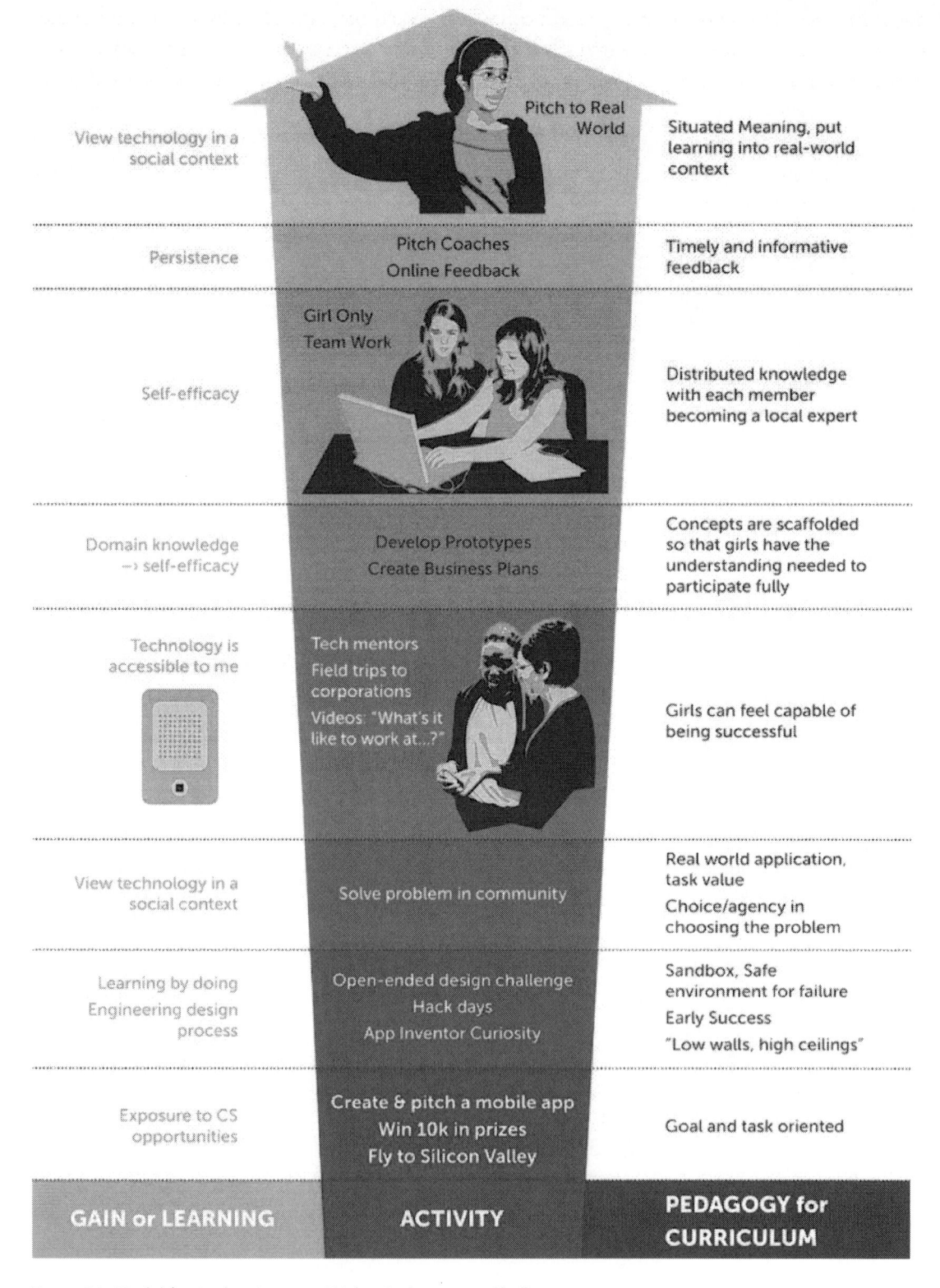

GAIN or LEARNING	ACTIVITY	PEDAGOGY for CURRICULUM
View technology in a social context	Pitch to Real World	Situated Meaning, put learning into real-world context
Persistence	Pitch Coaches / Online Feedback	Timely and informative feedback
Self-efficacy	Girl Only Team Work	Distributed knowledge with each member becoming a local expert
Domain knowledge → self-efficacy	Develop Prototypes / Create Business Plans	Concepts are scaffolded so that girls have the understanding needed to participate fully
Technology is accessible to me	Tech mentors / Field trips to corporations / Videos: "What's it like to work at...?"	Girls can feel capable of being successful
View technology in a social context	Solve problem in community	Real world application, task value / Choice/agency in choosing the problem
Learning by doing / Engineering design process	Open-ended design challenge / Hack days / App Inventor Curiosity	Sandbox, Safe environment for failure / Early Success / "Low walls, high ceilings"
Exposure to CS opportunities	Create & pitch a mobile app / Win 10k in prizes / Fly to Silicon Valley	Goal and task oriented

Figure 10. Model for Student Learning Within Technovation Challenge.

SciGirls, a weekly television series and educational outreach program for elementary and middle-school children, scoured the research literature on evidence-based practices and proposed seven proven strategies for engaging girls in STEM (SciGirls Seven), summarized below. Examining these strategies helps explain why our program succeeds in engaging girls in computer science and entrepreneurship. In addition to the programmatic aspects that support these criteria, the basic activities of app building, tinkering on mobile phones, and creating media are a good match for engaging girls in computer science and entrepreneurship. Reflecting on how abstract criteria play out in a concrete program such as Technovation Challenge may help others apply these criteria to create their own STEM opportunities for girls.

1. Girls enjoy working in teams. Girls often express excitement about sharing what they learn with other girls. They benefit from settings in which they are rewarded for collaboration and flourish from the ability to communicate freely on a team. They also become comfortable sharing responsibilities and taking turns being in charge. The positive feelings they derive from working with their friends can become associated in their minds with technology. These feelings may help them seek out internships or declare a computer science major.

Technovation Challenge students work and learn in teams of four or five middle or high school girls. Our program can run as an after-school club or even as a formal course. The DSST Cole Middle School in Denver, Colorado, for example, taught the Technovation Challenge curriculum in a STEM enrichment course of 35 sixth and seventh grade girls. Their teachers shared that girls who barely knew each other before the program became best friends by working toward a goal as a team. As girls code their apps, they do not go it alone. Girls learn pair programming at Hack Day and continue to use this technique throughout the program. Programming apps on their phones makes it possible to share what they are building with friends and family.

2. Girls find motivation in projects that are personally relevant and have societal impact. Girls enjoy projects that are meaningful and have personal significance. While a career in technology may not be an automatic aspiration for many girls, girls demonstrate a general inclination for professions in which they can serve their community. Reframing technology and business as a way to solve social problems can make these stereotypically cold careers more appealing to girls.

The importance of this factor can be appreciated in our struggle to develop a productive challenge over the years. We have designed themes with the hope of motivating girls; even though we have not been entirely successful at inspiring great work in every case, our app submissions improve each year. Stand-out entries often come from teams who are able to make the challenge personally relevant. For example, Team RoundofAPPlause at Thomas Jefferson High School created NaviCar, a carpooling app, as a solution to being shuttled around by parents to after-school events in the daunting Washington D.C. metropolitan area traffic. Team PrincetonGirlsinIT from Lagos, Nigeria redefined "daunting traffic" for the Technovation Challenge World Pitch 2013 audience at Twitter when they shared how daily traffic fatalities in their city inspired them to collaborate with traffic security agents to create TrafficApp. TrafficApp allows users to report traffic violations the moment they occur.

3. Girls enjoy projects that are hands-on and open-ended. Innovation typically results from exploration and a series of failures that pave the way for success. This format is more easily digested when learning occurs within a hands-on and open-ended project-based framework. A girl may be more inspired to persevere when designing an app that does not work the first time than when receiving a low grade on a computer science assignment or exam.

Although we started off Technovation Challenge with an open-ended theme for apps, we quickly realized that most teams had no idea on how to begin. In our iterations of the theme, teams identify interesting problems, then decide on the process they will use to create and pitch an app that solves their problem. Girls report that they enjoy working on Technovation Challenge because, unlike a prescriptive assignment, they have complete ownership over their apps. The ability to display their work on personal mobile phones for some girls also makes the experience rewarding.

4. Girls enjoy bringing their own unique set of interests and talents to a project. Concepts in computer science may appear boring on their own, but when applied to students' own interests, take on new life. The applied nature of project-based learning allows girls to draw on other skills that enhance their chances for success.

While building their apps, girls learn to take advantage of other interests and talents such as artistic ability. In 2011, "paper doll" apps suggested that girls sought an outlet for self-expression. In 2012, we began to see this self-expression channeled into ways that were more conscientious of the app's end user. ElementQuest, a 2012 app, teaches users about the periodic table of elements by having them identify elements in original, illustrated panoramas (Figure 11). Likewise, the creators of Arrive, a school attendance app, used their knowledge of robotics to create a robot that opens a door after users check in using their app.

Figure 11. "ElementQuest" App, Technovation Challenge 2012.

5. Girls gain confidence when they receive positive feedback on things they can control, such as effort and strategies. Problem solving promotes a growth mindset, where bad solutions can lead to a better solution. When hard work and perseverance pay off, girls may be less inclined to believe that their knowledge and skills are inherently not a good fit for certain subjects or careers. The best feedback that a girl can get in Technovation Challenge is watching her own app work for the first time. We have assembled a team of adults—regional coordinators, Hack Day instructors, teachers/coaches, and mentors—to make these moments happen as often as possible for girls. Our training for mentors and guidelines for teachers emphasize strategies for scaffolding and inspiring students to create their best work. We also share best practices with judges at pitch events on how to ask questions and give feedback so that girls leave motivated to do more with their apps.

6. Girls gain confidence from critical thinking. Learning can occur from simply questioning assumptions and lines of thinking. The ability to evaluate ideas and repeatedly incorporate feedback allows girls to realize that they will eventually build a great app. Girls gain critical thinking skills as they cycle through Lean methodology to keep improving their app and business plan. Improving critical thinking is a major reason we use the Lean methodology; students immediately incorporate feedback into the next version of their product, entering another iteration of the product cycle. Girls also grow in their ability to present and communicate their ideas to colleagues and experts.

7. Girls are inspired by role models and mentors. Meaningful interaction with role models helps dispel stereotypes about careers in technology, and affords girls an opportunity to consider various identities. "Side by side" interactions with mentors encourage positive and expanded interpretations of technology and business careers. In Technovation Challenge, a mentor and teacher guide the girls through the curriculum. Girls interact with other women in technology through events, video interviews, blog posts, and activities with other teams. The online platform gives girls the ability to access and connect with teachers and mentors from all over the world, and provides them with a community that supports and rallies behind them throughout the program.

INNOVATION IN TECHNOVATION CHALLENGE

Before digital cameras, photography happened in a dark room; only the few people who entered a dark room had the privilege to consider themselves photographers. Similar to the revolution of digital photography, mobile phones have brought programming into new light. In Technovation Challenge we capitalize on the ubiquity of mobile phones to give every girl in the world the chance to become a programmer and entrepreneur. Our program has proven innovative in its scale and the uniqueness of its product, original mobile apps created and pitched by teams of girls to solve community problems. In closing, we would like to highlight three key lessons our experiences have taught us for how to get more girls into technology.

Reach one girl at a time. Despite working with an online platform that is limitless in the number of students it can support, Technovation Challenge's influence increases through intensive recruiting, one girl at a time. Even though teenage girls are active users of mobile phones, they rarely see themselves as inventors of technology and do not always realize our program applies to them. "People follow the lead of other people they know and trust when they decide whether to take it up. Every change requires effort, and the decision to make that effort is a social process" (Rogers, 2003, p. 576). During Hack Days, girls experience firsthand the rewards of programming small, working apps. After this powerful, positive experience, girls sign up for the 12-week program. Hack Days are a successful and critical part of our recruiting strategy; however, they can be effort-intensive. We have divided this effort among partner organizations and volunteers (regional coordinators, teachers and coaches, mentors), and disseminated online training kits that detail sample resources and best practices. These strategies promote one-on-one recruitment and support.

Maintain quality at scale through research and evaluation. Evaluation data support the finding that Technovation Challenge changes girls' attitudes toward and engagement with computing, while still growing the program to large scale. We achieved these results by a combination of vision, persistence, and data collection. Our process echoes the Lean methodology our girls learn; we analyze the program for its most effective and scalable features, and have the courage to pivot, making changes to the program as guided by evaluation findings. For example, we moved our program to school sites and refined themes to encourage better apps.

Encourage apps with a social mission. One of the most unique and innovative contributions of Technovation Challenge is the apps girls create, 278 original apps through 2013. The mobile nature of the phone implies that the apps solve problems that traditional desktop computers and websites do not. Furthermore, the inventors of the apps are girls, providing a new perspective to problem solving in this space as compared to traditionally male software engineers. As a result of this diversity of perspectives, apps are innovative, often addressing unique interests and problems. Girls who experience the potential social impact and meaning of their ideas are better positioned to pursue computer science and entrepreneurship careers.

REFERENCES

Hausmann, R., Tyson, L., & Zahidi, S. (2012). *The Global Gender Gap Report.* Geneva, Switzerland: World Economic Forum. Retrieved from http://www.weforum.org/reports/global-gender-gap-report-2012

Hewlett, S. A. (2013). *Forget a Mentor, Find a Sponsor: The New Way to Fast-Track Your Career.* Cambridge, MA: Harvard Business Review Press.

Hing, J. (2012). Can a Black Girl be the Next Steve Jobs? *Colorlines, Jul 31.* Retrieved from http://colorlines.com/archives/2012/07/black_girls_code.html

Lacey, T. A., & Wright, B. (2009). Occupational employment projections to 2018. *Monthly Labor Review, November,* 82-123. Retrieved from http://www.bls.gov/opub/mlr/2009/11/art5full.pdf

Ries, E. (2011). *The Lean Startup: How Today's Entrepreneurs Use Continuous Innovation to Create Radically Successful Businesses.* New York, NY: Crown Business.

Rogers, E. M. (2003). *Diffusion of Innovations* (5th ed.). New York, NY: Free Press.

Rusli, E. (2010). Fixing Silicon Valley's Gender Gap One Pitch at a Time. *TechCrunch, April 22.* Retrieved from http://techcrunch.com/2010/04/22/fixing-silicon-valleys-gender-gap-one-pitch-at-a-time/

The SciGirls Seven: Proven Strategies for Engaging Girls in STEM. Retrieved from http://www.pbs.org/teachers/includes/content/scigirls/print/SciGirls_Seven.pdf

Seligson, H. (2013). The Apprentices of a Digital Age. *The New York Times, May 5.* Retrieved from http://www.nytimes.com/2013/05/05/business/enstitute-an-alternative-to-college-for-a-digital-elite.html?_r=0

Sevo, R. (2009). Literature Overview: The Talent Crisis in Science and Engineering. In B. Bogue & E. Cady, Eds. *Apply Research to Practice (ARP) Resources.* Retrieved from https://www.engr.psu.edu/AWE/secured/director/assessment/Literature_Overview/PDF_overviews/ARP_Talent_Crisis_in_SandE_Overview.pdf

Teague, J., & Clarke, V. (1996). Improving Gender Equity in Computing Programmes: Some Suggestions for Increasing Female Participation and Retention Rates. In *1st Australasian Conference on Computer Science Education* (pp. 164-170). Sydney, Australia: ACM.

UCLA IDEA (2012). State's AP Computer Science Exam: 29 African Americans, 21% Girls. Retrieved from http://idea.gseis.ucla.edu/newsroom/our-ideas/themes-in-the-news/archive/august-2012/states-ap-computer-science-exam-29-african-americans-21-girls

Wolber, David; Abelson, Hal; Spertus, Ellen; Looney, Liz (2011). App Inventor: Create Your Own Android Apps. O'Reilly Media, Inc..

SECTION FIVE

Connecting to Curated Spaces

15. Quest for the Cities of Gold
16. *ParkQuest:* Mobile Media Learning as a Large Group Activity
17. *Lift Off:* A DIY Addition to a Smithsonian Space
18. *Horror at the Ridges:* Engagement with an AR Horror Story

---

This section is comprised of chapters which have the design and trial of an Augmented Reality game at their center. Also at the center of these projects are the places these authors have sought to interpret and transform for their audiences. The spaces and the audiences who fill them to play the authors' games are by design informal. Each game was created for a setting where those present could choose to play the game or not. In addition to offering perspectives on MML as a ubiquitous feature of our future world by creating learning experiences for ad hoc, non captive audiences, these chapters remind us of the value of voluntary action in the learning process by meeting it head-on. If you build it, will they come?

CHAPTER FIFTEEN

Quest for the Cities of Gold

Gianna May

In August 2013, I had the opportunity to watch a seven-year-old read a description of an 18th century New Mexican textile on display at the Albuquerque Museum of Art and History in order to answer a question in a mobile game that I created with help from a few other University of New Mexico students: Ann Christmas, Brian Martinez, Sara McGinnis, Paul Strasser, and Sam Strasser. We had built this game, *Quest for the Cities of Gold,* over the summer using free software to provide a new kind of interactive experience with history in a museum space. We wanted to help museum patrons, especially children, engage more with the history they are exposed to in the exhibits.

Often, museum patrons look at the artifacts on display, bbut do not necessarily connect the items in the museum to the larger historical moments they represent, nor do they take the time to read every information plaque located throughout the space. Their experiences are fairly passive. We created *Quest for the Cities of Gold* to remedy this situation; we wanted the game to engage players in an exhibit at the Albuquerque Museum and connect the artifacts on display, the information contained in the description boxes, and the history and people that the exhibit represents. We wanted to encourage our players to interact with the museum space and become participants in the historical narrative in-game by answering questions and making decisions based on artifacts in the exhibit. The seven-year-old mentioned above was searching for the answer to a question asked of him by a New Mexican weaver in the game, and in doing so, was connecting the textiles on display to this historical figure while acting as a player in the in-game narrative.

BACKGROUND

My interest in mobile games and history began in 2013 with my work as a history intern at the Albuquerque Museum and with a course I took at the University of New Mexico, *Games for Change,* which introduced me to the use of videogames beyond entertainment.. My work in the course centered around using videogames to make history more interactive and participation-based by inserting the player into the history they were learning about as a character and active participant. After the course ended, I used connections established through my internship and established an independent study with the professor of *Games for Change,* Dr. Christopher Holden to continue this work in videogames as a way to facilitate learning about history and enhance the experience of museum exhibits. I wanted to build a game for history education at the Albuquerque Museum that patrons would get a chance to play and experience. Further, the Albuquerque Museum lacked any digital interactive elements in their displays, so I also wanted to make a game that had the potential to be used after the project was complete; this videogame could further act as a prototype for future mobile gaming experiments to enrich the exhibit space.

In May 2013, I recruited a few volunteer students who also wanted to help out with the creation of this game. The museum provided guidance for what they wanted to see in a mobile game and who they wanted it to be for. As a prototype for future gaming projects, the museum wanted a game that targeted children, from nine to twelve years of age, and combined teaching history with experiencing an exhibit and interacting with the artifacts—an important goal they set for their own exhibit designs as well. Their main idea was to have a game that allowed children to slow down and connect items on display to the periods they were from. They also requested that the game focus on the *Along the Rio Grande* exhibit, which features an overview of Albuquerque history from pre-Spanish contact to World War II. The narrative we developed follows the conquistadores in Coronado's 1540 expedition. The game also has a bonus level set in 19th century Albuquerque, where the player becomes a trader along the Santa Fe Trail.

The independent study itself was meant to be fairly simple. We did not have a lot of outside resources and chose to build the game with free game design software, ARIS, which could be downloaded and played for free on iPods, which we had available for playtesting. Throughout the process of putting the game together, we were constantly trying to balance what the museum wanted, what we wanted, and what ARIS was capable of.

Quest for the Cities of Gold took roughly three months to construct and was released in August during a Family Day event at the Albuquerque Museum. The creation of this game was a team effort. As a group, we brainstormed and debated over how to create a successful game in a museum space that would be the most entertaining, educational, and approachable for players. Together, we created the outlines, narratives, and promotional material that we would use. During Family Day, around twenty museum patrons played our game. Overall, these players received this game positively. The final version of the game and the response we received suggests that we had achieved a significant step toward learning how to engage players in history and museum spaces through videogames.

DESIGNING *QUEST FOR THE CITIES OF GOLD*

Creating *Quest for the Cities of Gold* involved balancing considerations of design, technology, and the overall end goal for the project. At the beginning, we made initial decisions about the technology and design as well as the historical narrative we wanted players to experience. To do this, we had to take into account the space we would use in the museum and how it would influence our game. These considerations ultimately resulted in a prototype version that would be developed over the course of the project.

Technology

We chose to create the game using ARIS due to its user-friendliness, accessibility, and familiarity. The tools to build the game were fairly easy to understand and did not require an in-depth knowledge of scripting or computer programming. Further, ARIS is free to download on the iOS App Store; players could easily get the app on their own devices. For Family Day, we loaned iPods to museum patrons to play our game and also encouraged them to download ARIS on their own iOS devices if they had them. With our iPods, we also launched the game on pre-established accounts to put players immediately into the game without needing to create accounts in ARIS themselves. This last step turned out to be key for patrons to overcome the complexities and friction featured in playing *Quest for the Cities of Gold* quickly on deivces often new to them. The use of ARIS and our own iPods (loaned to us by Dr. Holden, purchased through a UNM Teaching Allocation Grant) allowed us to create and provide the game without any expenditure on the software or devices for us or the players.

At the same time, our decision to use ARIS only partially settled the question of our game's design. ARIS is a generic tool, malleable to different situations in multiple ways. At a basic level we knew we wanted to use virtual conversations with characters as the main mechanic,[1] but the rest came the hard way, down to the decision to navigate the game space within the museum using QR codes instead of GPS coordinates or Quick Travel. We went through many iterations trying to figure out how best use the features available to meet our goals for creating player interaction through a story told in the exhibit space.

One instance of how our thinking evolved through this process comes from our use of quests to help direct players. Before we included the quests as an aspect of the game, players would become confused as to what tasks they were supposed to complete.. They would scan QR codes out of order, which would throw off the game sequencing created via dialogue in ARIS. As a result, players could find themselves unable to progress through the game. Quests provided a way to direct the player and serve as a reminder to what they are supposed to do next. The characters in the game would first prompt an action, such as "Go talk to the Blacksmith," and then a quest would appear to remind the player who to talk to, where they might be, and what they look like. Figure 1 is an example of a quest presented to the player in *Quest for the Cities of Gold*.

---

[1] For information on the basic features and mechanics of ARIS see Chapter 6 in this book.

Figure 1. The first quest in *Quest for the Cities of Gold.*

The structure of the narrative in the game allows players to interact with the exhibit and uses augmented reality to make the connection stronger. Characters had to be accessed through QR codes in the exhibit, so we placed these codes around the space which further encouraged players to physically move around the area to play the game. Quests that require players to find a particular artifact and interact with it—such as asking them to find the chain mail on display and lift it up to see how heavy it is—promote interactive engagement with the exhibit and items on display. Characters even ask questions that are answered by reading certain exhibit panels and inserting one-word answers in the decoder section of ARIS to trigger specific in-game plaques. Players themselves are characters in the narrative, and therefore feel more invested in the exhibit and history. Instead of simply reading about what others in the past did, the game allows them to embody a character from this time period who interacts with historical figures and their stories. Through our game, we create a relationship between the player, the history, and the exhibit.

In-game Historical Narrative

Along with the general description above and the basic technology we used to connect museum patrons to history, much of our design efforts went into the creation of a story for players to inhabit. Many of the specifics of figuring out how to tell a story through a game have been instrumental to accomplishing our goal of connecting the player to history through the exhibit. Revisiting a couple of these details may be helpful for others who pursue a similar goal.

In *Quest for the Cities of Gold,* the player is a conquistador in 1540 who is about to embark on a journey north from Mexico with Coronado. This expedition was the first Spanish exploration of what would become New Mexico, and is perhaps most famous for the search for the seven cities of gold at Cíbola. The game begins with Coronado telling the player to find proper armor for the journey. The player then goes to talk to the blacksmith, who tells the player about the different forms of armor and their benefits. The blacksmith encourages the player to look in his "shop," a section of the museum that features different types of armor. The player is also specifically directed toward a chain mail tunic, which can be touched by museum patrons (Figure 2).

Figure 2. The chain mail is one of the interactive, touchable displays in the exhibit. In the game, the player is asked to lift it up and see how heavy it is, revealing a QR code for the game beneath.

Figure 3. The player's dialogue options after Coronado asks why they went on the journey. Their response will affect their ending.

After the player has chosen their armor, they talk to Fray Marcos de Niza, who led the initial expedition in 1539 to what he thought was Cíbola; his journey would serve as a guide to Coronado's initial expedition. The player is asked to find the right map of this expedition, which can be found on an information panel on the wall. The player must enter the year Fray Marcos de Niza went on his own expedition. After that, the player sets off on the journey with Coronado and is asked a few questions regarding what path to take, which ultimately results in success or failure. For example, if the player chooses to go along a desert path with no source of water, they will die of thirst and the game will end. However, if the player chooses the right path, they will end up in New Mexico where they will be asked why they, personally, went on the journey with Coronado (Figure 3). Their response will bring up one of three different plaques that concludes their story with a short narrative.

These small choices give players a chance to reflect on the nature of the journey and the motivations of the conquistadores. In playing through this narrative, players are immersed in the information present, but often overlooked in the exhibit, and are asked to connect artifacts and the museum space to history. They become active participants in these historical narratives, as opposed to a passive observer of history and museum artifacts.

The Museum Space

A third element we sought to unify through our design was the museum space itself. One of our goals in creating *Quest for the Cities of Gold* as a game to engage children in museums and history was to make the museum itself more child-friendly. The Albuquerque Museum does contain some interactive, child-friendly elements in the exhibits. However, their placement and design does not always allow for children to fully interact with them. One example is a toy Model-T in the Route 66 section of the museum. While you are allowed to pick the toy up and drive it, it is placed on a ledge only big enough to hold the car itself and the wire that is tied around its wheel is too short to allow children to move it to the ground to play with it. Most of the plaques in the museum are eye-level for a typical adult—inaccessible to children and others whose eyes are closer to the ground. Further, interactive and touchable elements of the exhibit are are not always labeled well and are consequently easy to bypass. *Quest for the Cities of Gold* tries to draw attention to these more interactive displays—like the chain mail—while also making other displays—like the map of the conquistador expeditions—accessible to children by making it a part of the game.

We chose the conquistador narrative in *Quest for the Cities of Gold* because of the content the exhibit provided and because one of the most popular objects in the entire exhibit are two conquistador mannequins and a horse in armor (Figure 4). These objects have the most potential to engage players due to their size and the ideas they represent about journeys to New Mexico.

Figure 4. Two conquistadores clad in 16th century armor. This display is one the focal point of the *Along the Rio Grande* exhibit.

However, working with this space in the museum had its shortcomings. The area of the exhibit is relatively small, which prevented a lot of movement. This limited how far apart we could place characters and created congestion in areas where players were standing to "talk" to characters after scanning their QR codes. The room was separated by a center oval divider where the conquistador display was located which allowed visitors to walk around in a circle to see the exhibit, but also made it confusing for players to discern a suitable starting point and know which direction to go in order to progress.

In spite of this, we created the game to use the small area as an advantage. The game was well contained in the space and could be structured into short narratives. While there still were issues with congestion and the flow of the game in relation to the space, the area was ideal for playtesting. We were able to watch multiple players move through the game and see how they interacted with the mobile device and physical artifacts as they progressed.

Figure 5. Museum patrons playing *Quest for the Cities of Gold* during our launch of the game on Family Day. Behind the conquistador display is the armor section where the blacksmith is located.

Figure 6. Coronado's plaque in *Quest for the Cities of Gold*. In order to talk to Coronado, players would scan his QR code.

COMBINING THE PHYSICAL, IMAGINED, AND TECHNOLOGICAL SPACES

As a whole, our design for *Quest for the Cities of Gold* was a combination of three different dimensions of player interaction: the physical museum space, the in-game imagined space, and the technological space produced in ARIS. All three factors had to work together in order to achieve our objective; the imagined space was pulled out as much as possible in order to be experienced in the physical space and was facilitated by the technological space, allowing players to interact with these different layers using an iPod and ultimately drawing them into the history and museum space.

An example of how we utilized these three dimensions is illustrated in how we placed characters in-game to fit with the small physical space of the exhibit and further had these characters emphasize the player's physical surroundings. At first, we used the map feature in ARIS to locate in-game characters, who could be interacted with by touching their icons on the map (i.e. Quick Travel). This character interaction was later changed due to the difficulty in placing several characters in a small space indoors and the disconnect it established between the in-game world and the museum space. We replaced the map-based interaction with QR Codes that represented characters and other objects and required players to find and scan the codes to talk to them and continue the narrative (Figure 6). This allowed players to interact with the space and the exhibit without having to completely separate from the game world whenever they looked up from their screen or moved to a different location.

Figure 7. The yellow plaque contains several maps of the Spanish expeditions into New Mexico. Unfortunately, they are placed high on the wall, preventing children from getting a good look.

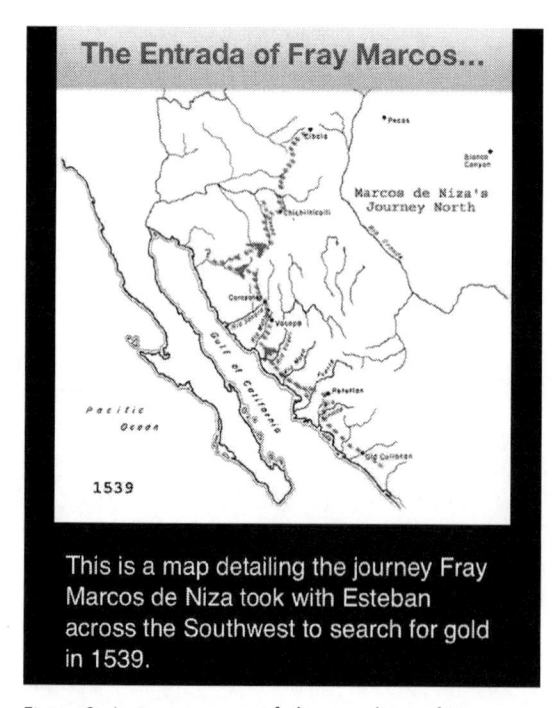

Figure 8. An in-game map of the expedition of Marcos de Niza. It contains the same information as the museum's mounted map. By putting this map in the game, we allow players to view the map regardless of height.

The physical, imagined, and technological spaces of this game were further blended in our attempts to make the exhibit and museum experience more child-friendly. To provide more objects for players to interact with, we moved information that children normally would not be able to read—such as the conquistador expedition maps (Figures 7, 8)—to the game itself. This created a connection between the technological space players were using and the museum space the map was present in. This brought the objects down to eye level so young players could view them on their own.

CHALLENGES IN DESIGN

Throughout development, there were certain roadblocks that affected and altered our design choices and the general format of the game. These problems ranged from ensuring the historical integrity of the narrative to choosing a title that both described the game and its connection to the museum and appealed to younger children as an interesting and fun game to play. Unfortunately, not all our problems had outright solutions.

In constructing the narrative, our first concern was maintaining historical accuracy within the game. Part of our goal was to teach children history, and so our facts and details had to be as accurate as possible. At the same time, we took some liberties with the narrative to make the experience of playing the game more interesting and engaging and suitable for a short narrative. For example, Governor Coronado would not have asked the player about what route to take on the expedition, but this narrative element was a good opportunity to give players a reason to look at the historical maps. This allowed players to become participants in their inclusion of the expedition and gave them some agency within the game. In the end, our compromise between historical accuracy and fictitious elements feels natural and productive.

When retelling history, in addition to historical accuracy, we confront the question of perspective. It is difficult to craft an effective conquistador narrative without considering how Native Americans fit into the picture. The representation of Native Americans in our game was a huge topic of debate, as was how to present conquistadores in light of the brutality of their historical expeditions. We were constantly aware of how we presented the narrative and how we portrayed the different characters within in it. At the same time, our narrative still focuses on a colonizing-centric perspective with the conquistadores, as opposed to Native American experiences of the same event. We did not want to directly glorify the Spanish conquest. However we felt compelled to work with the information that was available at the museum. The exhibit, along with our game, addressed the history from a neutral, but conquistador-focused perspective—it does not over-glorify their expeditions, but neither does it condemn them or address their more violent actions. Like the exhibit in the museum, we did not deviate from the standardized historical narrative usually taught in school and found in textbooks. As a result, our in-game narrative was rather devoid of a Native American presence and focused mainly on the expedition itself.

We made a choice to teach children about what the museum had to offer in their exhibit and artifacts and provide a brief overview of the conquest of New Mexico rather than present a complete and balanced historical narrative. A number of factors played into this decision. We felt we did not have the time or resources to add interaction far beyond what was already available within the exhibit. The time spent in the exhibit and playing the game are brief. Our narrative reflects this lack of depth for the sake of presenting a playable and comprehensive game. Finally, we did not necessarily feel free to challenge the perspective the museum's curators had decided upon when confronting this same dilemma as they set up their exhibit. While this decision worked for us at a level of convenience and logistics, we realize the potential loss of information and dangerous implication of enabling the conquistador character to identify as the "hero" in the narrative. I do not think that we were able to solve this problem, but recognizing it at least feels like a small victory.

PLAYTESTING

The public playtest for *Quest for the Cities of Gold* took place during Family Day at the museum. We stationed ourselves in the exhibit to observe players' progress and offer guidance if they got stuck. We did run into a few technical issues and had to walk a few players through the game (especially those who were not acquainted with touchscreens), but overall the game was well-received.

Issues that affected the playtest included software bugs and a poor WiFi connection. While playing the game, ARIS would occasionally stop working and the program would crash or otherwise prevent the player from moving on in the narrative. Often the only solution was to restart the app which would also erase the player's progress because they would be logged out of the custom accounts we had prepared. And, while the museum had WiFi available in the building, the connection was weak at points. If a player was on the network for too long, it would disconnect them and they would have to log in again. This disrupted the flow of the game and risked losing the player's progress too. These issues were the most commented on in our surveys, but we were unable to find a good solution to them during the playtest. The best we could do was log players back in and get them playing again as soon as possible, hopefully without losing their progress in the process.

Not all of our players were acquainted with ARIS or touchscreens before playing *Quest for the Cities of Gold*. The ability for players to navigate the technology varied, and so we had to establish specific guides outside and within the game to help those who became lost. After players understood how to operate the devices and progress in the game—such as using QR codes to initiate conversations with the game's characters—they were able to play the game and progress smoothly. We created a brochure for the event (Figure 9), which included a guide for scanning QR codes. Even with knowledge of how to scan QR codes, the process was not perfect for players. Uneven lighting sometimes made it difficult for the iPod's camera to recognize the codes. Explaining how to scan codes as well as suggesting potential errors and troubleshooting tips became a necessary part of running our game.

As part of the playtest, we requested that players fill out a post-game survey. Children and parents expressed excitement for having this game as a new way to learn about history. Over half the players made it to the end of the game, and in doing so were able to navigate the game successfully and also interact with the museum space as intended. Some frustration was expressed over the technical difficulties, but many of the players were very receptive toward the idea of having such a game in a museum to facilitate learning and engage players, and were happy to struggle with our game, in spite of the glitches.

How to Scan a QR Code:

A QR Code is a barcode-like symbol that can be "scanned" to unlock different parts of this game and to "speak" to the characters in the different narratives.

To scan a QR code, simply hold up your Apple device to the code when the decoder screen is active (it will almost look like you are taking a picture). The QR Code will register with the Apple device and a new screen will generally pop up once the code is scanned.

Please stand about a footstep away (about 1 foot) from the code; you do not need to be close up to view it and it registers better if you are not too close to the QR Code.

Figure 9. Our brochure includes a description of what a QR code is and how to use it in the game. Because QR codes were such an important aspect of progressing in the game, understanding how to use them was vital.

Parents, in particular, commented on the game as a useful tool to engage children in the exhibit. The seven-year-old I mentioned earlier was there with his parents. They commented that he was not looking forward to coming to the museum, but once he started playing the game, he began to enjoy himself and still learn about history. Siblings who played the game at the same time would compete or would help each other through difficult points. One girl played through the game and when her younger sister joined her, she excitedly shared what she learned and the experience she had in playing the game.

CONCLUSION

As a project, our game accomplished its goal, but further development is required for it to be used in a museum space without outside help. To more fully engage players in history and a museum space, the technical difficulties will have to be dealt with and a smoother method to start people playing, regardless of familiarity with touchscreens or ARIS, needs to be established. Further consideration and development is also required to build a more complete and in-depth narrative that does not just follow the conquistador point of view and avoids glorifying or condemning their actions while still maintaining its identity as a game where the player is a participant in the history.

But in spite of the issues still to be resolved, the interest expressed by players and their interaction with history and the museum space suggests the potential such a game has. A typical museum experience does not always encourage engagement or immersion. We wanted to directly ask the player to be more than a spectator of artifacts. *Quest for the Cities of Gold* allowed players to interact with a museum exhibit in a new way, highlighting aspects that often go unnoticed. Throughout, players could draw connections between artifacts, history, and people. *Quest for the Cities of Gold* gave players a chance to feel like participants in history, experiencing the narrative on display while interacting with the museum space in a unique and engaging way. The excitement we saw during Family Day affirmed the hard work we put into *Quest for the Cities of Gold* and convinced us that it, or more games like it which are built by non-professionals using free tools, could potentially change the ways in which museums engage people in history.

CHAPTER SIXTEEN

ParkQuest: Mobile Media Learning as a Large Group Activity

Seann Dikkers, Ryan Rieder, & Tamala Solomon
Ohio University

Last year, our design team was approached by the *InsideOut!* organization. They wanted help encouraging urban youth to explore the many trails found at a nearby state park, and thought a 'game' might motivate kids to try hiking. The game would be a small part of a larger event called *Let's Go Outside*. Over the last year we made our first attempt to introduce kids to hiking for fun and created *ParkQuest*. It wraps story, digital maps, and real-life hiking trails together in a mobile game that lead kids into the forest—some for the first time. This chapter reviews the design, implementation, results, and lessons from a playtest of *ParkQuest* at *Let's Go Outside*. Moreover, *ParkQuest* should be an idea others can rather easily use or modify for similar outdoor spaces and gatherings. This game could be a model for many other home-grown outdoor learning experiences that include elements of both story and game.

Figure 1. An aerial view of Alum Creek State Park where *Let's Go Outside* is held.

211

DESIGNING FOR THE PARK

Let's Go Outside is an eight-hour expo at the Alum Creek State Park, north of Columbus, Ohio, sponsored by the *InsideOut!* organization. Over 400 youth from the urban Columbus area, and representatives from supporting community organizations were expected, and organizers hoped to encourage urban youth to take more of an interest in nature and outdoor entertainments of all sorts. They asked our design team at Ohio University to create an activity to address these goals. They noted that youth growing up in urban centers have limited access to wild or green-spaces, so events like *Let's Go Outside* are important in creating awareness to the opportunities they do have.

Alum Creek State Park features a large central green where most of the event takes place, as well as a lake, and extensive paths and trails that venture into the surrounding woods, prairie, and low hill country around the green. *Let's Go Outside* includes a variety of activities on the green like archery, kite-flying, rock climbing, and a geology dig. On the lake, youth can fish, canoe, or learn to kayak. In previous years, the trails had remained unused by the event. Previous *InsideOut!* activities for the wooded areas at the event had not successfully encouraged youth to go hiking. Organizers guessed that urban youth were hesitant to explore wilderness areas. They tried handing out park maps, setting up tables in remote locations, and offering adult chaperones to no avail. In approaching our team, they wondered if it was possible to engage and motivate urban youth to want to trek down forest and prairie lined paths.

By adding *ParkQuest* to the event, our team and the program's sponsors and coordinators hoped to:

1. Introduce urban youth to map reading and navigation,
2. Encourage kids to explore the outdoors, and
3. Introduce both plant and animal life found in the Ohio wilds along the way.

We were inspired to this line of thinking by John Martin's *Mystery Trip* (2012) where a GPS-based mobile game was used to encourage off-trail exploration. Recognizing that a similar game might also encourage hesitant kids to travel new paths during *Let's Go Outside*, we created a map-based mobile game for the event to introduce hiking and following maps—and perhaps indirectly—jogging, geocaching, and life science topics like botany or zoology. We built this game in the ARIS platform. The result is a cooperative effort between *InsideOut!* and our team at Ohio University to investigate the use of digitally mediated experiences for learning. Collectively, we explored how a game might inspire a sense of adventure and reward exploration. In the following pages, we briefly review the design and implementation of the game, but focus on the real-world issues that emerged when coordinating a larger event on location.

DESIGN THROUGH CONVERSATION WITH PARK ORGANIZERS

An essential process for the game's development was to discuss with organizers their goals and to use a prototype of the game as a central aspect of moving that conversation forward. Iterations based on feedback from the organizers of *InsideOut!* highlighted deficiencies in our initial designs and helped us create a game that blended with the existing event goals.

Our original design highlighted 'Freddie', the mascot frog, looking for tools he suspects 'Mr. Snake' had stolen. When players visit Mr. Snake, the sneaky critter readily admits that he took them, and left them with a variety of animals that were too big to eat. Players are left with the task of exploring a nearby wooded area to gather tools from virtual animals. Event coordinators embraced the use of hand-held technology and 'quests' that challenged players to explore, but shared concern about taking participants off-trail (guessing that the youth may not be ready to hike in tall grass). Consequently, we decided to use designated hiking trails instead of encouraging off-trail exploration.

Second, the tools taken by Mr. Snake in our story were initially random, but we changed them to match those used in a soil conservation dig-station—another activity planned for the *Let's Go Outside* event. Connecting tools in our story with another activity (even promoting it a bit) seemed like a natural fit.

A third shift was to redesign the game so students finish it at the dig-station, providing an opportunity for the geologist running the station to strike up a conversation with them. Though the dig-station could be experienced independently, it could also be a connected experience from the mobile game.

Based on our conversations with park organizers, we also integrated a new design idea *outside* the mobile game that would connect to it: stations with animal handlers for each animal in the game. To further engage players, organizers sought out experts to manage tables with real animals (partnering with the local zoo), animal models, furs, teeth, and energetic curators to talk about the animals with students who find them in their lairs. We matched the cartoon abstractions of animals used in the game with real animals at the newly suggested expert stations. The game was then designed to direct traffic to stations along the paths where experts could point out animal trails, markings, and talk about plants that the untrained eye may overlook.

Adding information tables not only sought to strengthen our game but, similar to the dig-station, would hopefully benefit the informative tables themselves. We hoped that by connecting the mobile game to these tables, players of the game would be both prompted and encouraged to initiate conversation with volunteer experts; organizers were aware of difficulties with previous attempts by these experts to attract attention to their tables. Handlers could reference the storyline of the game as conversation starters and youth would quickly discover very natural and authentic discovery rewards for hiking into the woods.

Editing the game with organizers also helped our team edit and update the text used in-game, selecting words more appropriate to the participants, and shortening and clarifying the activities to provide less 'screen time' and more 'tree time'. Conversations needed to be easily read and goals clearly expressed both in conversation *and* in quest directions. Finally, coordinators asked for courtesy expressions such as 'please' and 'thank you' to be added to each dialogue to reinforce and model polite discourse. Though small, these updates improved the game's overall quality and fit for the event's audience.

MURPHY'S LAW: WHAT CAN GO WRONG, TYPICALLY DOES

Previous experience with making mobile games told us we needed to not only prepare our game in terms of design but to thoroughly test it to make sure it worked on location and for a fresh audience. Along these lines, we tested and iterated our design several times to get it right. We conducted both remote and on-location walkthroughs of the game to test for bugs, glitches, and playability. These uncovered a few minor bugs that we fixed on the fly. Prior to the larger event, we made sure the technology worked—including our internet connection, mobile devices, charging stations, and player instructions. We thought we were ready to go, but our preparation was not sufficient.

Game day. September 21, 2013, just north of Columbus, Ohio. The rain has been going on all night, making the park soggy and muddy. The morning weather report announces ongoing rain and all-day clouds. Coordinators have food ready for over 400, providing the 152 actual attendees a handsome feast. Upon arrival, the coordinators moved most of the remote stations—the ones we designed to line the path of our game—into the larger meeting tents. Paper guides, promotional handouts, and mobile devices were packed away in boxes. Weather, of course, is a real risk for any outdoor activity. Still, some students wanted to get wet and go mobile (Figure 2).

Figure 2. Less youth than expected turned out for the event due to the rain.

The inclement weather also meant the animal experts were unable to attend. The rain had caused leaks in the roof of their facility the night before and they had moved all of their animals to a new location. The animals were tired and we imagined the keepers were ready for bed too. We planned for actual animals and their keepers to be at each location where the players met a character in the game, but now the game would need to work without them.

The map function of our game also did not work as planned. ARIS requires internet connectivity to function, in particular to provide a player with their location and a map of their surroundings. We had planned for this by providing portable routers to give our WiFi mobile devices the connectivity they need (Figure 3). However, on game day the heavy clouds interfered with the portable routers' ability to receive cellular data and the map wouldn't load properly inside the game. Later, when the rain stopped, the game itself loaded but players had to find their next station without the blue navigational dot, partially nullifying the navigational benefits of the game. Students who did play had to do so during infrequent moments of optimal reception.

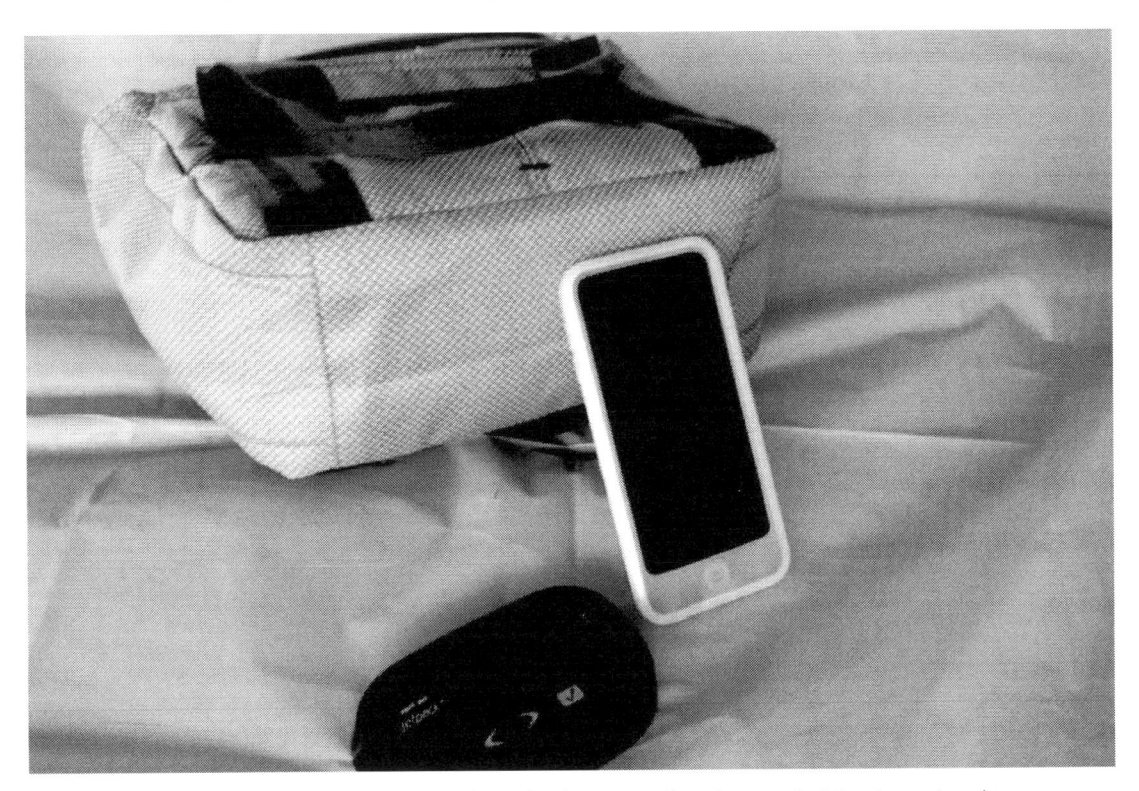

Figure 3. A Jetpack Portable Router and an iPod Touch. The game, played on an iPod Touch requires data over WiFi. The portable router wsa to provide that data, but on game day failed to perform.

Despite the ongoing rain, pre-play interviews revealed that all players were interested in the technology and using maps. They naturally grouped themselves into teams of 3-4 as anticipated, each team traveling with one device. No players tried the game on their own and some stopped the game after talking to the Snake and realizing that the next stop required them to walk a distance from the tents. Still, others happily splashed through puddles. Some wanted to stay close to the tents, others ventured out. Tenters shared passing interest in playing "if the weather was better" because "this looks cool." Those who tried when the WiFi was weak or batteries ran low did not return later to try again. At first glance, the weather, technology problems, removal of live animals, and lower attendance at the event seemed to make our first effort less successful than we hoped. For those that did play, they returned to the tent excited about: 1) the kind of game it was, 2) the ability to use the devices, and 3) their ideas for future "awesome" stories. Their feedback was consistently positive. While we didn't get hundreds of youth to play as we had planned, we did get about 40 of them to enjoy the soggy outdoors.

DEBRIEFING OUR DAY AT THE PARK

We approached the event coordinators discouraged about the level of interest in the game, and the technical issues. After attempting to apologize, the organizers interrupted us and said they saw significantly more interest in this activity than with their previous attempts to encourage exploration, and were looking forward to next year. They explained that previous efforts produced nearly no adventuring map readers. The fact that we had any participants tromping off into the woods at all, despite all the issues, was a significant win for all the veteran planners involved—kids were actually hiking the trails! Despite Murphy's Law, this was the day at the park they were hoping for.

Having participated in the walkthroughs, coordinators knew firsthand that the game was functional and that the weather was an unpreventable variable that shut down the canoes and the animal handlers too. They minimized the importance of our difficulties with the map function and noted that the mobile adventure still provided enough hints to be completed without the aid of a map. For instance when the character said to "look in the woods to the north," players discussed which way north was and debated how to figure that out. Then they looked around to see woods in that direction. Unintentionally, we provided directive hints in the quest descriptions as a way to maintain awareness of context for our players; in the absence of the maps these instructions sustained the adventure effectively.

As designers we missed having live animals, handlers, and stations. The players, on the other hand, didn't miss what they didn't expect. Players expressed concern for the cartoon versions of the animals; we had small facts and information embedded in the game dialogue and item descriptions, so players were still able to connect to the wildlife in the game. Coordinators and players felt their objective to have players learn about the animals was met by what they saw.

We learned that the narrative combined with location still held attraction for play. As the narrative is constant, the environment is an interesting variable that will have its story elements that it brings to gameplay. For instance, for those that played, the soggy weather made the game more adventurous than otherwise expected, and they embraced it. Splashing in puddles easily replaced seeing live animals as physical rewards for players.

Additionally, parents were making a point to thank coordinators for the experience, as this letter from a parent to coordinators illustrates:

> It was also nice to hear all of the good feedback from my son and daughter about their experience exploring nature and even interacting with mobile learning games that were included as an activity. Rarely do they have the opportunity to assemble outside for a full day of play and fun without the distraction of new-aged media and television at home. - A.R. Murray

It was encouraging to hear from this parent, as well as through our conversations with the organizers, that our game felt like something that coordinated with the outdoor activities it was meant to inspire and be a part of rather than the mindless entertainment they associate with other media and television.

Though the smaller attendance to the event was disappointing, feedback indicated that participants and organizers both appreciated that the game successfully: 1) motivated youth to enjoy the outdoors, 2) respected the physicality of locative play (even as a contrast to television), and 3) warranted integrating mobile learning for future events. In short, even with challenges, coordinators saw increased exploration and navigation of park space, and parents and supporters were excited to see kids engaged in map-based navigation activities with what they perceived as cutting edge learning designs.

PLANNING FOR PUDDLES

We were interested in how we could have planned better and learn from the unplannable elements. We were happy to note that the part of our game that was plannable was surprisingly functional. Sun, animal and dig stations, and internet access in a second iteration will of course improve the experience for players. In addition, we have considered four more elements to help our game respond more robustly to changing conditions—just in case.

- An effective Plan B could be to create paper versions of the game and a map that could be handed out in waterproof ziplock bags. This low-tech solution might substitute passably if we need it (similarly Macklin and Guster (2012) used grocery bag kits to deliver quests and challenges to players in New York).

- Similar to what is done with other outdoor activities for participants who might not be prepared for bad weather, we could have various sizes of flip-flop sandals available to loan out to youth as part of the event. If we could have easily pulled out sandals and held their nice shoes for them so they could freely pounce puddles, this would have allowed more players to adventure—not only in the game but in all the activities.

- We could find more robust options to provide internet. In fact, the coordinators of *Let's Go Outside* have arranged for the Best Buy Geek Squad to bring out a van to provide a more robust WiFi signal for the expo next year. Best Buy agreed to volunteer this service, so this alternative option is still free for our players. Generous local businesses may be able to help solve logistical details that are otherwise burdensome with just a couple calls.

- We could do more to make it easy for those who volunteer to help run the game. Volunteers are often recruited on the day of the event and although happy to help, may not know the lay of the land. For our game, this means having ready for them short and clear written instructions and details for any live stations. With a mobile game, the technology itself can be intimidating. Making volunteering as easy and as low-tech as possible can potentially smooth the road for new helpers.

CONCLUSION

Despite the issues mentioned above, we were happy with how the game addressed our primary goals of encouraging navigation, trail hiking, player engagement, and delivery. We also maintain that despite requiring adjustments for more robust play, the game garnered positive feedback from players. Coordinators and parents saw enough of the gameplay that they were excited *ParkQuest* was added to the *Let's Go Outside* event. Players were able to navigate and engage in a hands-on learning experience in an outdoor environment while hiking through trails in the park. *ParkQuest* was, in the end, quite robust and adaptable in the face of unforeseen problems, especially as facilitated by adults who were monitoring the situation and ready to adjust. The portions that worked were exceptionally engaging and built enthusiasm for a new way to interact with the park space.

Our initial question of engaging urban youth in nature adventures may have not been answered fully with the first iteration. However we did: 1) create a park adventure game that echoes Martin's *Mystery Trip*, 2) found that the game was resilient even under 'Murphy's Law', and 3) recognize that we still have an opportunity to refine the design in coming iterations. It is more than possible, even under challenging conditions, to build a story and mobile gaming experience that encourages pathway exploration in a park setting.

Due to the simplicity of the actual game, *ParkQuest* should be easily replicable, resilient, and refinable. If you have a park near you, and kids that would benefit from time outdoors, this may be the kind of basic adventure game to start with. Mobile media learning, as with any learning, is as much about dealing with real-world conditions, people, and hiccups as it is about design and technology use. We suggest you expect and anticipate the need for back up plans and that this planning frees up concerns over technology function in favor of flexible learning models that bring story and game into outdoor learning experiences.

REFERENCES

Martin, J. (2012). "Mystery Trip". In Dikkers, S., Martin, J., Coulter, B. *Mobile Media Learning*. ETC Press.

Macklin, C. & Guster, T. (2012). "Re-Activism". In Dikkers, S., Martin, J., Coulter, B. *Mobile Media Learning*. ETC Press.

CHAPTER SEVENTEEN

Lift Off: A DIY Addition to a Smithsonian Space

Christopher C. Blakesley and Jennifer McIntosh

How can a team sustain the integrity of a vision in less than ideal circumstances? What solutions work when pioneering a mobile game activity in a museum-like space? These questions are addressed in this story of our team who made a helicopter artifact area more interactive and engaging for a day at the Smithsonian Air and Space Udvar-Hazy Center.

Our teamwork began as Christopher Blakesley, a learning technologist living near the Udvar-Hazy Center, met and discussed mobile game possibilities with Jennifer McIntosh, the Center's Interactive Education Program Manager. We (Chris and Jennifer) discussed the many aircraft artifacts in the Center, their associated histories and stories, mobile technologies, and game-based learning approaches. Through several discussions, a shared vision began to take shape: To create a proof-of-concept mobile game activity that enhanced visitor engagement with aircraft artifacts.

Soon after our initial discussions, we decided it would be mutually beneficial to create and facilitate a mobile activity at an upcoming event called Super Science Saturday: "Helicopter Day." This was recognized as one of the the most popular events for the Center, with approximately 10,000 participants expected to attend. During this event exhibitors from the aerospace field facilitate hands-on "discovery stations," where visitors can learn hands-on about aspects of aviation. Visitors would even have the opportunity to see functioning helicopters outside of the museum.

We wanted to create a meaningful experience in which visitors could briefly take on a gameplayer identity—to playfully strive for a goal while interacting with responsive artifacts. We hoped for a memorable experience imbued with affect and curiosity. To inform our approach, we considered the following "five properties of handheld computers that produce unique educational affordances" (Klopfer, Squire, & Jenkins, 2008):

1. *Portability* - can take the computer to different sites and move around within a location.
2. *Social interactivity* - can exchange data and collaborate with other people face to face.
3. *Context sensitivity* - can gather data unique to the current location, environment, and time, including both real and simulated data.
4. *Connectivity* - can connect handhelds to data collection devices, other handhelds, and to a common network that creates a true shared environment.
5. *Individuality* - can provide unique scaffolding that is customized to the individual's path of investigation.

We particularly favored the features of portability and individuality, as we wanted players to walk through the center with mobile devices that could augment their perception of the space around them. The devices needed to make the experience personalized and replayable. Building upon the concept of individuality, we identified fitting features from the role-playing game (RPG) genre to incorporate into our game. With a RPG approach, players would take on the identity of a protagonist immersed in a fictional world. Players also would explore the world and move a narrative forward by completing quests—challenges that usually end with some kind of reward.

Based on the concepts of portability, individuality, and RPGs, we could envision an engaging player experience. Players would walk around the Center with a mobile device, start the game, and be assigned a virtual identity (a pilot). Next, the player would consider a quest, such as fueling an aircraft to enable lift off. This quest could require the player to find, collect, and return virtual fuel to a plane or helicopter. Finally, a rewarding moment would occur by watching an aircraft take off via video. We also planned to use our small budget to buy prizes to give players who completed the game. We eventually decided to buy Flarbles, a small propeller-like plastic toy that proved to be very popular among visitors.

In addition to formulating a game concept, we selected a tool to build the game upon, as well as recruited volunteers interested in helping to build the game. In terms of choosing a tool to run the game, we chose ARIS. ARIS offered an inexpensive, experimental, and flexible platform needed for our goal to create an initial, proof-of-concept mobile learning game[1]. In addition to having a usable mobile authoring tool, we needed help building and facilitating the game, so we decided to recruit interested, local youth. This seemed like a rich learning opportunity that young people may find personal interest in, or potentially an item for a resumé. The involvement of youth also aligned with the mission of the Smithsonian to increase and diffuse knowledge. After communicating through our networks, 4 local youth and 2 Smithsonian volunteers joined our team.

---

[1] Below, the authors reference a few specific features of ARIS. For more information about them and ARIS generally, see Chapter 6 in this book. -Eds

THE ORIGINAL GAME DESIGN

Our team quickly developed a mobile game concept in which participants would take on the role of an aviator faced with three possible quests involving the collection of fuel for one of three selected helicopters in the Center. The helicopters we ultimately chose were the Engineering Forum PV-2, Bell U-H 1H Iroquois "Huey" Smokey, and the Sikorsky UH-34D Seahorse. We envisioned the participants collecting virtual fuel tanks scattered around the center, walking to and "fueling" a helicopter, and viewing that helicopter in flight—in a video we could play in ARIS—as a reward.

We quickly figured out how this idea would work in ARIS: A participant would find and scan a QR code to collect fuel. Each scan of a fuel QR code would increase the fuel in the virtual inventory within the participant's mobile device. To fuel up a helicopter, the participant would scan a representative QR code in front of a helicopter (see Figure 1). In terms of game design, we aimed to make this activity engaging through the action of collecting and a light narrative in the form of a role, and a video cut scene as a culminating reward. We chose to use short YouTube videos to show each helicopter in flight.

We also designed the quests so that one was more challenging than the others. For the hardest quest, we chose to involve the PV-2 helicopter, since its location was harder to find than the other helicopters. We also added a second task in this quest, requiring participants to take pictures of the helicopters located outside of the Center—In the game story, the pilot was researching other helicopters for future purchase. The ARIS platform contains a data collection tool that enabled users to take pictures and save them in a virtual inventory; we wanted to use it to instill a feeling of interactivity and closeness to functioning helicopters both inside and outside of the Center. In sum, players would need to successfully collect fuel and take pictures of the helicopters outside before viewing the final video. The YouTube video we selected for the PV-2 flight was also unique, a commercial that argued for cars being inevitably replaced by helicopters as the main commuter mode of transportation. This video's entertaining futurist angle made it our choice to provide a satisfying ending to the hardest quest of our game.

Figure 1. A Helicopter QR Code easel near the Sikorsky UH-34D Seahorse helicopter. The easel displays a QR code for "fueling" and an advertisement flier created for the activity.

However, during our game development process we discovered several jarring constraints that threatened our vision for the game. While we were welcome to facilitate a mobile activity during Helicopter Day, we would unfortunately be on our own for funding. We would need to secure our own mobile devices, and we agreed that we would not want people taking the devices we used away from our station table. This decision was reinforced by the low cellular and WiFi reception in the massive Center, meaning that even if players could use our devices or personal devices, they wouldn't necessarily have a good Internet connection needed to run the ARIS app.

We found ourselves at a crossroads. On one hand, this initiative seemed destined to be nothing more than a grounded information table with iPads. On the other hand, we recognized that this might be the only opportunity we would have to test our ideas in front of such a large audience and in such an impressive space. A successful, proof-of-concept activity could lead to future possibilities at the Center, and we didn't want to pass up the opportunity. While the solutions to our challenges were not clear, we decided to press forward and trust that creativity, collaboration, and a shared vision of our project would result in it's success. Also, if we did not succeed we had little to lose!

After three weeks our team completed preparations for our activity, which we dubbed Lift Off!. We decided to create the original concept of the game for players with personal mobile phones as a starting point. While we anticipated low participation in this option due to limited cellular reception, and the required steps of downloading the ARIS app on their phones, we nonetheless decided to make this option available. Players had all the information they needed through the instructions located on the easels in the center. They could collect fuel indefinitely, fill all three helicopters, and view all three videos of the helicopters in flight. Creating this game, with it's high fidelity to our original vision, provided us with a conceptual starting point from which to create an alternative game that would be accessible to the majority of our participants.

THE ALTERNATIVE GAME DESIGN

To design the alternative game, we started by intentionally retaining the (1) game action of collecting fuel and the (2) light narrative feature of a video cut scene reward at the end of the play experience. Our primary constraint was that the mobile devices were not mobile—the iPads volunteered for the event by members of our team had to remain at our station table. We decided that players would begin at our table (see Figure 2), where they would hear a description of the game and then be invited to collect a required amount of fuel by walking and collecting QR code printouts found in envelopes on easels located throughout the Center. For simplicity, we created one fuel QR code that would work for any helicopter rather than separate codes for each helicopter as originally envisioned. While participants would be encouraged to collect codes from different locations, they would be able to game the system and collect all required codes from one location. We were actually curious to see if any participants would be engaged enough to investigate this issue. Fueling the PV-2 helicopter required 6 codes, the Huey 4 codes, and the Seahorse 4 codes.

After collecting fuel QR codes, participants would then return to the table and select one of three images of helicopters to fuel (see Figure 3). The images were photographs of three helicopters located in the Center. Participants would use an iPad running ARIS to scan the QR codes attached to the images to view a video of their "fueled" helicopter in flight. We also decided to offer participants a

Figure 2. Members of the *Lift Off!* team (from left to right): Jack Sorensen, Chris Blakesley, Jayson Call, Yamelet Alvarez, and Joselid Alvarez.

Figure 3. The three helicopters players can refuel for lift off after collecting fuel tanks by scanning the QR codes at the bottom of their sheets within the *Lift Off!* game in ARIS.

Flarble as a prize. The brightly colored Flarbles, along with the iPads at our table proved to be an appealing draw to players, and provided motivation for participation.

FACILITATING THE ALTERNATIVE GAME

During the Helicopter Day event our team revised the game as needed in response to feedback from participants. The gameplay actions of collecting and viewing videos were areas we prioritized to retain in the game design. We quickly noticed that the abstraction of collecting fuel by finding and returning QR code printouts proved to be a challenging concept for participants. During the first hour of the event, our team developed a useful approach for introducing the activity to participants. We would say some version of this statement to passers by:

Do you want to play a game? You get to be a pilot who collects fuel to send a helicopter into the air. You need to find at least two "tanks of fuel" (hold up QR code papers) and bring them back here. Then you can watch a video of a helicopter and win a prize.

It usually took a few more minutes to explain that the card-sized QR code printouts represented fuel, and that the act of bringing the QR codes back was intended to be the act of getting fuel. Many participants at this point were still not sure what to do next. We found another improvised solution. We moved an easel containing QR codes next to our table and directed players to get their first fuel-code there (see Figure 4). For the remainder of the event, this scaffold helped participants quickly understand the concept of the game and get started with the collection activity.

Figure 4. We placed an easel near our table as a scaffold to guide players with the main gameplay action of collecting fuel tanks by scanning QR codes.

We also adapted to the needs of family and children participants. We noticed that our original requirement of 6 or 4 QR codes for fueling was too aggressive for parents of very young children, who were primarily motivated to get a flarble, and didn't understand the game concept. We adjusted the game requirements in ARIS (on the fly!) and on the image printouts so that the fueling the PV-2 helicopter would require 4 codes, while the Huey and Seahorse would require 2 codes, allowing families to complete the game more quickly.

At the same time, many adolescent participants engaged in the collection activity with zeal. They frequently returned with many more QR codes than were required (see Figure 5). One discovered a QR code flaw—the fact that all the QR codes were in fact the same, mentioned above. His mother approached the table asking in a doubtful tone, if her son was correct about all of the QR codes being the same. I informed her that he was correct and that he was the only one who discovered this feature out of all the people to play our game. I explained that this was a deliberate decision—to use the same QR code for all fuel tanks—for design simplicity.

When we wondered if any participants would try to game the system and discover this minimal flaw, our team wondered what reaction this discovery would bring. Scorn? A feeling of being cheated? The mother told her approaching son that he was right, which led to a euphoric celebration. I asked them how they felt about this discovery and they indicated that they didn't feel cheated, but rather happy that they were the only ones who had discovered this secret. The collecting activity itself, rather than the video it led to, could have been the greater reward for many participants.

Figure 5. A large stack of collected QR codes despite the minimum requirement of two codes to play the game.

Figure 6. Participant families watch a video of "their" helicopter in flight.

The sequence of scanning QR codes and unlocking a video was an engaging moment for many participants, evidenced by commitment to watch the videos to their conclusion, and conversation occurring during video play. Several parents commented and posed questions to their children while watching the videos together (see Figure 6). Comments like "This is a helicopter they thought would replace cars..." and "What do you think that helicopter is used for?" Our team increasingly described context to the videos or insights afterwards to participants, such as pointing out where the actual helicopters were in the Center. While we believe the experience would have been even more engaging if the videos were viewed in front of the representative helicopters, participants still seemed to appreciate the activity. Our hope was that participants would notice or seek out "their" helicopters during the remainder of their time in the Center.

REFLECTIONS

Overall participation at the alternative table version of *Lift Off!* was high, with a total of 436 players, the second-highest player total among all the other Discovery Stations at this event (See Figure 7). In addition, the original mobile-only version of *Lift Off!* was actually played by two people, a modest success. Given that we simply made the original game available in the space, without providing any hands-on support, we did not know if players with iPhones would be drawn to playing this game, let alone be engaged enough to complete all of the quests. To our delight, two participants went to the trouble of downloading ARIS and playing the original version, and one of these participants completed all 3 quests. These participation results demonstrate that a minimally funded mobile game project can successfully engage players in a museum-like space.

Figure 7. Players learning about and completing the *Lift Off!* game at a Discovery Station.

We also learned several lessons from our experience. We found it was important to move forward with commitment to the vision of a project while also adopting an adaptive attitude. When tough problems appeared—and they did appear—a tactical flexibility led to effective solutions. Our team originally set out to make a mobile activity that engaged visitors with aircraft artifacts through a game-based approach. Due to constraints of limited funding and tabled mobile devices, our team got creative with the game mechanics while staying as true as possible to the original project vision. Although players couldn't take devices with them around the Center, we still incorporated movement in our game. Although players wouldn't necessarily be able to see the aircraft during gameplay, the experience still promoted a measure of individuality through player choice of helicopter to fuel.

We learned that while design tactics may need to change because of constraints, a team commitment to a shared vision can still bring a concept to successful, unique fruition. Despite daunting challenges, our team made aerospace artifacts more interactive and engaging for a day at the Smithsonian Air and Space Udvar-Hazy Center. We hope our lessons can provide insight for other teams working to innovate with mobile tools in museum-like spaces.

REFERENCE

Klopfer, E., & Squire, K. (2008). Environmental detectives - the development of an augmented reality platform for environmental simulations. *Education Technology Research and Development, 56,* 203–228.

SPECIAL THANKS

Thank you to the volunteers whose preparation, enthusiasm and commitment brought this project and chapter to fruition. No one could create and facilitate this project alone; everyone's help and adaptability as a whole was the key to a great experience. We extend sincere gratitude to Joselid Alvarez, Yamelet Alvarez, Jacob Bixler, Emily Blakesley, Mary Blakesley, Jayson Call, Tom Caswell, Josh Freeman, Sruthi Poduval, and Jack Sorensen.

CHAPTER EIGHTEEN

Horror at the Ridges: Engagement with an AR Horror Story

Rebecca Fischer and Seann Dikkers
Ohio University – Athens, Ohio

The year is 1900 and you are here to report on the advances being made in medicine for the clinically insane. The newly opened Athens Lunatic Asylum is touted as a gem of innovation in both architectural design and care for the ill. You think, 'This is a place that the sick can get a little air and let nature heal as it should'.

It's beautiful indeed, but there is something else that unsettles you here. Perhaps it was just the long ride in the train.

We designed the game *Horror at the Ridges* to build horror through an augmented reality (AR) experience. As part of a series of games we are building around established genres of entertainment, *Horror at the Ridges* explores how a mobile game can draw an emotional reaction from its players. We drew from the conventions of horror movies, novels, and past AR games to successfully build anxiety, create imagined narrative outcomes, and even scare players. Through a conscious attempt to develop an engaging story through AR, *Horror at the Ridges* also seeks to expand our thinking about informal learning design. In this chapter we provide a brief discussion of engagement and horror media, outline some of our design considerations for using AR games to produce an engaging horror story, and discuss qualitative findings from our playtests. Player reaction was a central part of our iterative design process and analysis, so through our observations and reports from our players we gain a glimpse of players' engagement with the narrative we created. We conclude that an AR game—through the unique constraints and advantages of mobile media technology—can effectively build the emotional states necessary for engaging narratives.

MOTIVATION

One reason for our experiment is to explore the possibilities of AR gaming as a medium. AR gaming is currently a niche activity. There are small AR fan communities drawn to location-based activities (e.g. geocaching) and more recently massive social territorial marking (e.g. Ingress), but nothing like those gathered around the artifacts of truly mass media. In addition, a small number of educators—like those found in this book and the previous Mobile Media Learning—have built educational AR experiences for students, often using story or narrative as operative design. Most of these previous efforts with a learning focus have been largely confined to the classroom and similar spaces. We wanted to follow this lead, but specifically explore how AR can be used to create an engaging story outside any compulsory context. We wonder, will AR have a proper place among other popular media formats to tell immersive stories and build fandom? Can we create narrative experiences that draw informal players into a story—enough to care what happens next? Can we ever expect to have truly popular AR games that might compete with console titles? We postulate that emotional reaction and caring about a story, or engagement, is the first step to being a fan, sharing an experience with a friend, and eventually to the popularization of the medium.

At the same time, *Horror at the Ridges* is an experiment in game-based learning. We see our investigation of an audience's uncompelled engagement with an AR game as a stepping stone to designing compelling learning experiences. Connecting learning to engagement is not a new idea. Research in the fields of education, media studies, anthropology, and psychology all suggest that engagement can be a powerful force for learning (Hirumi, Appelman, Rieber, & Van Eck, 2010). When engaged in a game, learning can be a natural outcome of participation (Squire, 2011), invite players into social networks or third spaces (Steinkuehler & Williams, 2006), and be as rigorous, gritty, and complex as the game affords (Gee, 2005). To accomplish these positive ends however, game designers focus on an essential experience first, and playtest for engagement as confirmation of design (Schell, 2008). Previous thinking about engagement and games and the possibilities for AR games to explore narrative genres by placing the audience in the story convinced us to try and make an AR game that was worth playing. Though we have a long term desire to use these experiments to think about learning—Horror at the Ridges is an effort to focus on creating an essential experience first to further design and contribute to a conversation about engaged media.

HORROR AS ENGAGEMENT

Our specific question for *Horror at the Ridges* was whether we could make an AR game engage a player well enough for the player to report a feeling of horror. H.P. Lovecraft called horror "the oldest and strongest emotion of mankind". Fear connects us viscerally to an experience as well as providing thrill-seekers with a rush of sensations. We do understand horror to play into our unease, but when we engage in the experience, it can fill us with a feeling of accomplishment, survival, and courage. The audience pay off for their engagement in horror can be a very positive experience.

Although our team sees the horror genre as but one example among many in theory representable through AR, in this case we hoped to leverage existing author expertise in horror writing/film for compelling AR narrative writing, to make a game that could scare people in a good way. In short, if we can scare players with an AR game, we can reasonably conclude that engagement with the story, place, and/or empathy with the fictional characters is possible more generally within the medium.

In addition, the emotion of fear is often an easily observable phenomena that allows researchers clear, observable indications of engagement. It should be easy enough to see when our game is working in the ways we have intended.

To produce engagement, a work of horror requires the audience to develop a strong emotional connection to the narrative; to be afraid, or horrified, one must fully realize characters and events mentally and become repelled by or anxious about the imaginary or real outcomes that await. Being scared while experiencing a fictional narrative is to be empathetic with fictional characters and their bad situations. For the purpose of making our game, we used the AR storytelling tool ARIS and operationalized fear as:

1. Having limited sensory inputs (sight, sound, knowledge), causing one to imagine awful things they might experience if they had the chance;
2. Heightened attention to potential negative outcomes to a situation; and/or
3. Unexpected or startling sensory input ("Boo!").

AR can literally place the player in the physical space of the narrative (See Chapter 2 of this book - Eds) so the story is all around them and thus remove a layer of unreality from the player's perceptions. If they are playing our game in a creepy place, players are not distracted by a comfortable couch or theater. Imagined negative outcomes are easier to compose when you hear real wind, feel real dirt crunching under their feet, or when you smell real mildew and decay.

THE ATHENS LUNATIC ASYLUM

To make an engaging AR horror narrative, we needed a place that would effectively set the proper tone and mood and we found the perfect location. Nestled in the Ohio Appalachian foothills is a bucolic multi-building campus called The Ridges—formerly known as the Athens Lunatic Asylum. *Horror at the Ridges* uses dreadful—and actual—historical medical archives from that closed state asylum, and takes place at The Ridges.

Founded in 1874, and used for over a century, the former asylum has been host to over one hundred years of unique and "innovative" medical philosophies. Locals claim the campus is one of the most haunted places in America and tell stories of lost patients, crocodiles, hidden tunnels, and ghost sightings. It has already found its way into television and books.

Closed in the 1970s, The Ridges has fallen into disrepair. The whole place has a brooding sense of loneliness and decay—a sense of a former gilded age, or greatness, for the campus and those that came here. While there have been cursory attempts at refurbishing the buildings, a closer inspection reveals many of the structures are still boarded up, with flaking paint, covered in danger signs, and seemingly abandoned. The entrance to the main building (Figure 1) looms over nearby Athens.

Walking around the grounds one quickly understands how the rich history of myths and local legends have flourished. Our current disconnect with early 20th century medicine creates compelling curiosity. Functionally named buildings today sound unfamiliar to visitors: the suicide ward, lobotomy labs, and the ballroom. The human-sized heat ducts (that housed a crocodile in the winters) are bewildering. Many tourists are uncomfortable with the history of electroshock therapy, lobotomies, isolation treatment, and management practices employed by a medical staff that largely lived in isolation on site with the patients. For instance, when they buried their inmates in the on-site graveyard, the leaders of the Athens Lunatic Asylum chose to mark the graves only with an ID number. The patients were left nameless. This already creepy place is a natural location to stage a horror game.

Figure 1. The Main Entrance and Early Game Location.

The location offers many nooks and crannies particularly suited to setting the mood for our players. Some of the first floor rooms look like sets from popular horror movies and games: there are boiler rooms (*Nightmare on Elm Street, BioShock*); workshops with old tools still laying around (*Saw, Texas Chainsaw Massacre, Doom*); broken porcelain restrooms and living quarters (*The Shining; 7th Guest*); and rooms like those in Figure 2 look like cells, including writings on the wall (*Portal; Batman: Arkham Asylum*). Many of the windows into these room/scenes have been overgrown by plants and cobwebs. This makes these locations feel cramped even while viewed from outside.

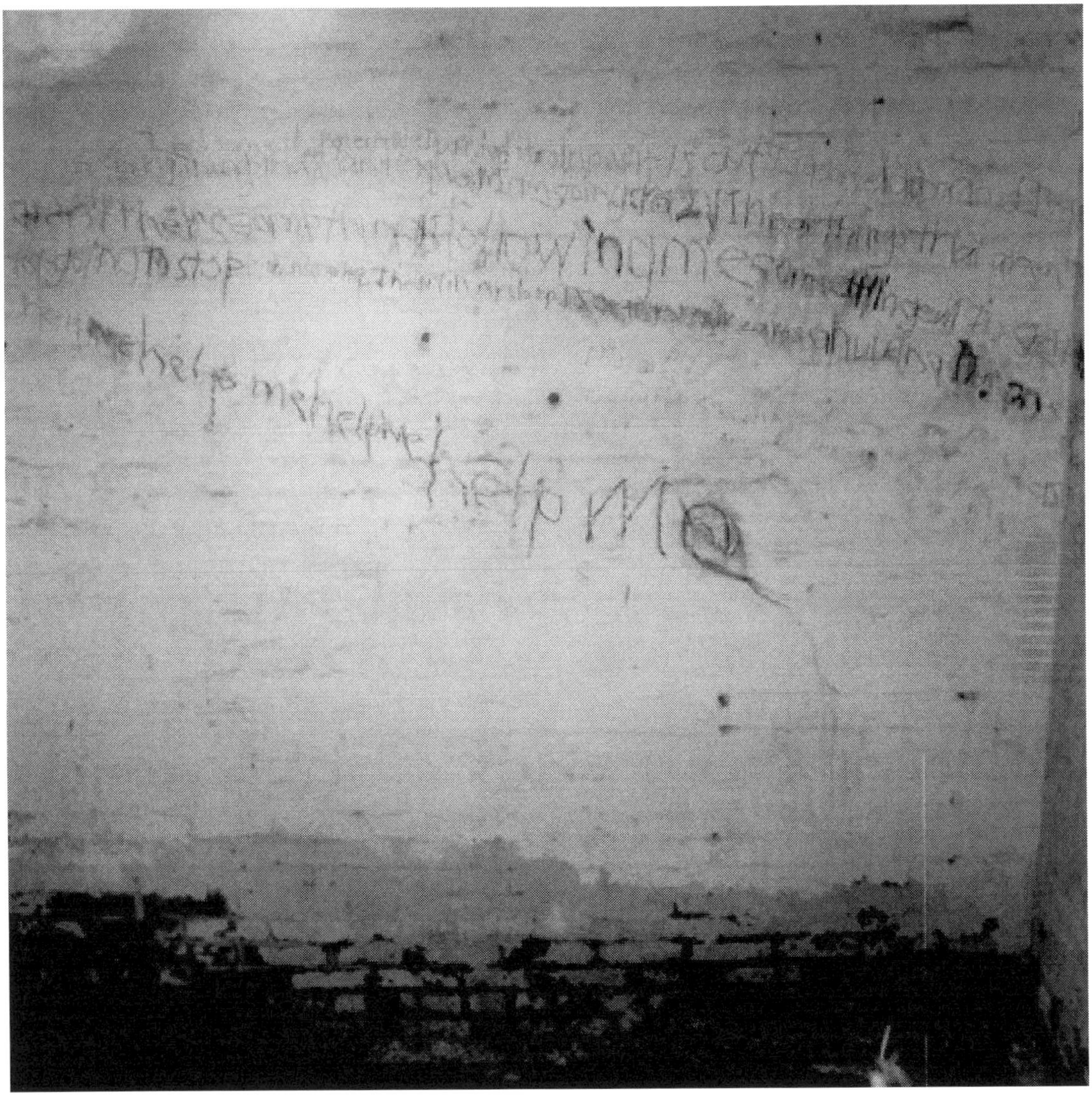

Figure 2. The View into Lucy's Room.

Prior to designing our game, we spent an afternoon as visitors and observed natural tourist behaviors. We informally observed that visitors did not necessarily walk up to windows to see these sites, most chose to drive by or stay on the marked sidewalks. One might expect many visitors would be looking into windows or through doorways to get a peek at the preserved history and horror of the location, but they do not. Some of the best views of the location were being lost to the casual tourist in favor of a single repurposed art gallery in the main building. As a partially abandoned and public space (it is currently owned by Ohio University), players were free to walk around, but it is not a curated space that gives active permission to look around. Visitors' current use of place fell short of what the location could actually evoke, which created an opening for us to use an AR game to create new, stronger experiences.

We began to imagine how narrative, and specifically the mechanics of horror stories could be applied to leverage the evocative qualities of this place to draw players in and really scare them. The story could prompt players to leave their usual paths and venture further into the buildings and grounds. Not only would this get them to the areas that make for varied creepy sets or backdrops for storytelling, but also give them permission to do something they would not otherwise feel they had permission to do. This could actively build anxiety, contributing to a player's feelings of isolation and being somewhere they are not supposed to be, inducing a fear that they could be caught. The obscurity of the darkened rooms and windows could be opportunities to limit a player's sensory input (our first common element to horror stories) and anticipate the horrors within.

CREATING A NARRATIVE FOR HORROR

An old, and some say haunted, asylum goes a long way towards achieving our goal of making players afraid; what brings us one step closer is crafting an effective narrative. We had a location that was in and of itself unsettling, but none of the visitors to the Asylum who we saw expressed the verbal or physical horror that we expect from the genre. Could our story actually deliver on this promise? Would players actually leave the beaten path? Would players engage with these unsettling windows if prompted by an AR narrative guide? Would the experience connect emotionally with them, or would it feel like just another tour? The story still had to pull back a layer of knowledge about the place, and allow the player time and clues that would inspire.

Writers often use history as backdrop, as do films like *National Treasure, Bill and Ted's Excellent Adventure,* or the recent *Mr. Peabody.* Current game franchises like *Assassin's Creed* also allow players moments of connection when they first see game versions of the Hagia Sofia or Rome's Coliseum; designers recognize the delight of historical cameos and the excitement in meeting legendary figures for players. Learning, in all of these media, is a positive outcome, but not a necessarily or centrally planned outcome. For instance, in *Assassin's Creed,* the central activities of the player are to move, climb, hide, fight, and solve problems to move the story forward. Though you can learn much about renaissance Italy from *Assassin's Creed*, this is a small part of what the game was designed to do. Likewise, entertainment and engagement remain our central design goals for *Horror at the Ridges,* and learning benefits were secondary. The experience of the player includes walking, looking, sharing, or even running in fear. We want them to experience horror first, and we use archived history not for learning design, but for engagement.

We wanted to make use of the reality of the asylum to come up with an engaging story, but we had to be careful to do so ethically. There are people still living who worked at or were patients in the Asylum. While we used many local legends and bits of history in the game, we also looked to movies like *A Beautiful Mind* and *Shutter Island* to help build a narrative where the people in the game (and by extension the institution) were not the real enemy as a way to distance our story from that reality.

Our story unfolds in five chapters, and follows an arc commonly found in horror-style narratives: Context (Horror at the Ridges!), Introduction of Characters, Harbingers of Doom, Rising Tension, Confirmation of Fear, Chase, and Climax and Resolution.

1. Players are introduced to the game in the role of a reporter, freshly arrived at the Athens, Ohio train station and ready to do some research for his or her next article on the new asylum (establishes Context, funnels visitors to the location and introduce basic game navigation interface).

2. Players freely explore The Ridges through the game, exploring the grounds as well as meeting and interacting with recreations of some of the people who created and shaped the institution (Introduction of Character).

3. Players become more familiar with some of the fictitious residents of the asylum and their needs. It is here that players discover the cheerful outer exterior might be hiding something more sinister (Harbingers of Doom!).

4. Players discover they cannot locate either of their new friends (Rising Tension) and the horrors happening at the asylum (Confirmation of Fear).

5. Players attempt to escape and return to the newspaper (Chase) to report on the clear corruption at the Athens Lunatic Asylum (Climax and Resolution).

Horror comes not from elements that startle players, but rather from the gradual unveiling of the horrors around them.[1] Early chapters of the game are almost cheerful, meant to lull players into a false sense of security while giving them the opportunity to learn a little history about the asylum and interact with some of its founding members. Players know this is written as horror, so the carefree nature serves to build imagined realities, behind the veil, prior to actually unveiling them later. Hints indicate something might be amiss despite characters describing compassionate patient care and beautifying the grounds. Later chapters reveal secrets about characters and places that invite the player to rethink their motives, previous script, and how closely they are tied to real history.

---

[1] For horror buffs, this follows a Hitchcockian style of suspense and anticipation, rather than a Wes Craven-style shocker.

In producing this storyline, we were able to leverage actual history of the place and mental health practices. For instance, the actual horror of early medical experiments comes into focus when, in the game, you find one of your co-conspirators is completely incapacitated due to a lobotomy treatment given by the facility. Doctors and nurses in the game treat the surgery as routine because it actually was. This allowed the narrative to take on a level of reality that players could react to. Also, when playing, you discover one character is a ghost—following a local legend that claims many ghosts still walk the Asylum today. We also studied patient files to create mentally ill characters loosely based on real people who had passed through the asylum's doors. The game takes echoes of the past—the people, the places, the events that happened—and weaves them into an experience for the player. Some of the scariest elements of the game were not the ghosts we created—rather horror was realized in the discomforting knowledge that many of the most disturbing narratives at *Horror at the Ridges* were based on the real history of what occurred there and the full understanding that these horrors are not confined to fiction.

PLAYING *HORROR AT THE RIDGES*

With the location and game ready, we invited players to come and try a new game at the former asylum. If anyone actually showed up, this would at least prove our AR game could draw an informal audience. When they did arrive, we asked if they would be willing to talk briefly after the gameplay to share more about the experience and give us suggestions. We did not offer any incentives other than a chance to play *Horror at the Ridges*. Even though this was a preliminary playtest of a small prototype, we wanted to get as close as we could to the question of recruiting natural interest in AR gaming.

We hosted nineteen players over three sessions. Those who tested the game varied in ages from 13 to 42. Gender was balanced. Playtesters consisted of mostly undergraduate and graduate students at Ohio University. All but two came with a friend or family member. This served as what we considered a small sample, however for a new medium, travel distance, and the size of the community, we considered this a positive first effort. The largest playtest attendance came on a foggy, misty day—iconic for horror stories—making us wonder if weather actually helped recruit for the event or if this was a coincidence. Observations of their play combined with interviews provided data concerning their engagement with the narrative and explanations of their experiences.

When participants were done playing we conducted a short interview with each group. We asked players their opinions on several of our design choices and considerations and how they thought we could make the experience better. Was the game scary? What was captivating and what elements of the story were engaging? In cases of specific and observable shock or horror, we asked what exactly made them react while noting where they were in the story and what they were thinking at the time. Playtesting over three iterations meant we could learn from our players and refine the elements of our game with each group.

Overall, we see promising evidence of engagement with the narrative and successful reconstruction of horror elements in the AR medium. From the data, we have organized and summarized key findings around indicators of engagement: 1) narrative-driven navigation, 2) space as anxiety builder (primarily looking in windows), and 3) building dread through narrative and how it links to interest in history.

Changing Paths

One of our hopes was that we could use the game to draw people further into the asylum. The game provided license to leave the sidewalks, and our players took the bait, even as they felt unsure about walking up to windows. Players shared that they did not think they would have gone off of the paved path if not for the game,

> "I had to move off the course to get where Ms. Jefferson was … I wouldn't … I wouldn't have! Why should I go like step on places that are not protected … fenced and grass growing when there is a clear path that I can follow. I would not have gone there had it not been the game."

The use of the phrase "not protected" hints that the player thought he was being slightly deviant. Yet the grounds are public without any fences, signs or other indication that it is not acceptable to walk on the grass. The player here was attempting to comply with the game—even with confliction or discomfort in leaving the path. That we could coerce players to change their behavior and go against their instincts is a positive sign of the possible effectiveness of the medium.

Other players liked being directed to unusual places and commented on them as a rewarding aspect of play:

> "… more secluded places. Places that no one can ever think of going to. Such elements can develop the sense that it's getting more … more even strange. I felt that was good … secluded building. Like uh, dark places."

The game changed how players would have otherwise visited the former asylum. This was positive confirmation for us that the game and place were in conversation with each other. Narrative driven navigation, in AR, requires engagement not with the place as visitors normally experience it, but through experiencing the place in new and different ways.

Moments of Horror

Players compared the overall experience of *Horror at the Ridges* to being in a horror film; a clear example of this was a player who exclaimed, "I love horror movies and it's neat to come and live one." Rather than playing a game, they saw *Horror at the Ridges* as allowing them to be inside the story. The connection to the genre was of course first encouraged by the location selection, "The way the buildings look reminds me of the Haunted Mansion or Tower of Terror at Disney World," but also fostered by the discourse and story design within the game that augmented the location and conditioned the players' experiences within a commonly known genre. It was clear that players recognized the genre and began to connect the AR narrative with familiar media experiences within it.

The most welcomed aspect of *Horror at the Ridges* turned out to be the opportunities for players to look into the windows of the old asylum. Players appreciated seeing things at the ridges that they would have "never seen otherwise". Having to shield your eyes to see inside the windows meant not quite being able to see what was around. We imagined these interactions around windows would contribute to our ability to deliver horror because this moment of waiting involved our players having limited sensory input and the opportunity to imagine awful things inside. They also would have to risk something in getting close enough to see the interior.

Throughout the game digital characters ask the players to look inside windows on the ground level to find clues, evidence, or other narrative elements (Figure 3). We found that groups would playfully challenge each other, saying things like "Who wants to look first?" Players took turns, creating an interaction where the first looker would display a reaction that the other lookers would react to. Excitedly one would ask, "What did you see?" This was either followed by a verbal description or physical reaction of anxiety from the first viewer like shrugging with a grin, shaking with a chill, or a poker face, "I won't say. You have to see this one. Take a look". In interviews, players explained that they were imagining what they were about to see and comparing expectations to actual views inside the windows.

Some players felt that looking in windows was the tipping point for building anxiety and a sense of horror. One remarked,

> "It was all well and good until we got to the room over there, then it was 'help me, help me' [written on the back wall of the room]. It was like, 'No, No we're moving on'. That was scary."

Another stated, "That's when it got real for me and that's when I felt the connection, I guess." Looking in windows also served to confirm that the place was real. Players knew on one level that the game experience was not real. Yet on another level, the history used for inspiration was; confounding, cruel, and/or bad, things happened here. These historical links were

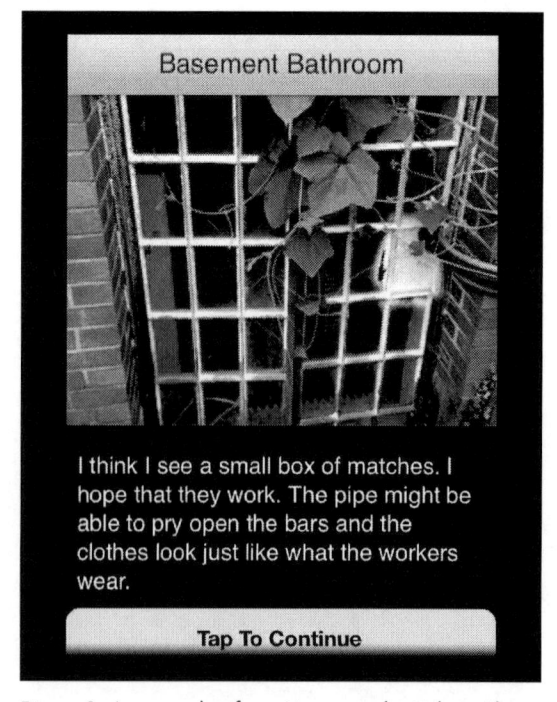

Figure 3. A screenshot from *Horror at the Ridges*. The player is asked to look inside the window.

powerful connection points for players to engage with the narrative. For instance:

> "You remember the girl? The girl in the basement? That is something that could have made me very very like sad, peeping in that building and you see a piece of cloth very deserted for one time there's no sense of life in the building. And you imagine somebody is there and that person is waiting for some help from nowhere … I felt sad."

Finally, one player expressed that he enjoyed a sense of accomplishment from not being scared—another common reaction to horror stories told through other media. But to claim you were not scared is to confirm that you have overcome a risk and/or that you are superior to normal reactions. As the player put it,

> "Maybe it was my personality or being a risk taker and I don't want to sound very, very stereotypical but boys are not scared. So I like to be like a hero."

Looking in windows was a chance for this player to be brave, to encourage others he was playing with, and to express a disconnect with worry. His desire to see himself as a hero is part of his comfort and attraction to horror stories.

Building Dread

Recall that an important part of the horror story we were trying to create is not just the delivery of the disturbing truth, but to set up this discovery with a sense of unease. Players did feel unease early in the narrative and did find some of the interactions with characters to be creepy even in the initial parts of the game, indicating a general sense of unease and worry that something might go wrong.

> "I like how the things that the characters are saying don't quite add up. It, it makes it seem like the characters are actually mentally ill. Everything isn't quite right … I like that. It contributes to the realism … all was not as it seemed in this nice, supposedly friendly place."

> "It's kind of creepy when Lucy talks about flipping a switch to make the patients feel better."

After the game was over, players reflected on the experience and the way the game stuck with them.

> "At first it was a little creepy but it wasn't really terrifying but as the night wore on and it got darker, the story sort of got scarier and scarier as it got darker outside … It had a sort of growing effect."

One player sought us out to explain a week after the event that:

> "Lucy's story—how she was murdered and kept in a room and then buried in an unmarked grave—is disturbing to think about ... That Lucy will follow me ... it's creepy ... It makes me want to look over my shoulder everywhere ... Stuff like that just really gets me, the idea of a ghost who was murdered going around with you ... it's scary to me."

The game was not actually over for some when it ended; residual consideration of the plot and story caused fear to linger after the AR game. These responses indicate success with cultivating dread, the slow, uneasy aspect of telling a horror story.

TOWARDS A BETTER DESIGN

Although we were happy that our basic design was received well by our players, that is not to say that everything went perfectly. Our players also were helpful in informing us about how our design or use of the possibilities of AR might better fit their purpose. By listening to the difficulties and missed connections of our players, we can learn to make AR games that do more. Here are a few examples.

Early on, players had difficulty with the level of physicality required by the game, about two hours of wandering the site. We responded by making later revisions shorter in length and distance, bringing the narrative playtime to about an hour. Yet exploration could take longer for those that wanted to discover remote, non-essential, elements of the plot. The level of time and physicality were not mentioned after these changes, indicating that this might be a sweet spot for an AR game session of this nature. Walking time should be a key design consideration for AR games; we will target 45-60 minutes for future games.

Our game is rather text heavy. Clearly we could do better by taking advantage of more modes of experience. One player described their desire for audio to compliment the story: "I wish there were actual, like audio dialogue rather than just reading it. It would be nice to be able to hear the characters saying the dialogue." Audio could amplify the effects of looking in windows, add ambiance, and even create startling moments that were unexplored in this study.

Players followed the historical connections from our game to the asylum's past, indicating a way for us to deepen the opportunities to learn history through the game. Players expressed an interest in learning more and claimed they felt they already had more of a connection to this history by playing the game. Some players were expecting to learn more facts about the asylum, and others felt that they learned enough to make the topics worth pursuing more.

DISCUSSION

Horror at the Ridges was our first attempt to combine AR and horror design elements to create new media to engage players. We combined narrative, place, and historical authenticity to create emotional reactions among our players. We saw strong signs that players were engaged with the narrative enough to alter their walking tours of the space, fearfully enjoy the supposedly simple act of looking in windows, and embrace a sense of dread throughout the experience and afterward. Slowly revealing horrors through an unfolding story connected to the players through history of the place can contribute to the player's growing sense of unease and horror.

There is much room to grow in the genre of AR horror. By refining the design techniques used here—use of space, re-direction of walking to new paths, familiar genre-based narrative structures, and continuing to build on more engaging digital and non-digital elements for players—we can continue to move forward. Further, our preliminary work left clear targets for improving the game and our future research; we anticipate adding audio, taking better advantage of looking in windows, monitoring walking time, and attempting engagement across media and with an increasingly diverse player base. Finally, we seek to monitor play counts over time to see if engagement is also leading to sharing the experience with friends.

Preliminary engagement is not our ultimate goal, but a waypoint on the path to fandom that emerges from sustained, shared interest. The possibility of recruiting attention is an important precursor to the production of worthwhile programming directed at specific learning goals. We value our work on *Horror at the Ridges* as a step toward building a range of engaging AR games that people will increasingly engage with as informal experiences. We are further haunted by the possibilities of how mobile media engagement can lead to increasingly powerful mobile media learning.

REFERENCES

Gee, J. P. (2005). *Why video games are good for your soul: Pleasure and learning.* Melbourne, Vic.: Common Ground Publishing.

Hirumi, A., Appelman, B., Rieber, L., & Van Eck, R. (2010). *Preparing instructional designers for game-based learning: Part 1. Techtrends, 54*(3), 27–37.

Schell, J. (2008). *The art of game design: A book of lenses.* Amsterdam: Elsevier/Morgan Kaufmann.

Squire, K. (2011). *Video games and learning : teaching and participatory culture in the digital age.* New York: Teachers College Press.

Steinkuehler, C. A., & Williams, D. (2006). *Where everybody knows your (screen) name: Online games as 'third places'.* Journal Of Computer-Mediated Communication, 11(4), 885-909.

SECTION SIX

Discussion

19.   What Have We Seen, What is Missing, and What is Next for MML?

In finishing this book, let's consider what we have seen, who or what is missing, and what is to come. A brief discussion of these themes may add texture to your reflection and further planning in your investigations of new learning contexts with MML. We return in the end to a more general discussion of MML in reference to the actual stories presented.

CHAPTER NINETEEN

What Have We Seen, What is Missing, and What is Next for MML?

Christopher Holden

WHAT HAVE WE SEEN?

There are a couple of final points to be made in the name of interpreting the myriad approaches you have now seen. One concerns the role that technical difficulties play in the design and use of technologically intensive educational projects. Another point is about the role of place. Finally, we recognize the projects here all employ concrete ways of looking outward from their own immediate settings as an expression of design; despite their differences, each references a context external to their own educational setting in their production and use of mobile media. Productive failure, interacting with place, and the extroverted side of design are uncommon features in many educational settings. They can help us understand MML a bit better and may provide direction in considering how designers, instructors, and students can play complementary roles in collaborative processes where everyone is involved in the learning.

Failure

Many of the stories contain segments about failures of technology and advice about how to avoid or handle such problems. Technical difficulties are expected when using developing technologies. Not only was the technology our authors used new to them, but it was new to the world, and on top of that they were often combining several technologies at once. Most performed their experiments without the benefit of a test group or other nets into which they could fall safely. If you search the book for the word "disaster" you will find many hits. Yet, the overall tone from these authors was not one of failure but excitement and resilience. When our authors' internet connections went down, when the software was glitchy, they did not chuck their devices in the trash and give up. They did not swear off advanced technologies until the day they become bulletproof. They are all excited to try again.

One reason for this: the technology is not all-or-nothing, and it is surely not everything. Projects went well while the technology failed because the technology was not at the center of what our authors were working towards. A clear example is provided by Garza and Rosenblum's work in chapter 9. Their neighborhood trip featured a rather large failure of the technology. But the success of the ARIS tour wasn't their main goal. Through a successful debrief, and because the tour was only important for getting the students to think in better ways about East Austin—a focus on place—their project that contained the tour was a success. As a design course, such understanding was a corequisite to finding the skills and voice to put something new back into the world. If we think too narrowly about Mobile Media and Learning—if we think about it as a new kind of content deliver—we may miss the comprehensiveness of their design.

But there is more to success than resiliency in the face of failure. The way we usually talk about technical difficulties in relation to educational technology—to be avoided by the competent educational technologist so teachers and students have something bulletproof to implement—misses something important about the role of failure itself in learning. Failure is an important part of learning and should be designed to be a natural and productive aspect of learning experiences. One example from this book is Frandy's students' first attempts at ethnography (chapter 8); the expected variability among students' work early in the semester, made communal through ARIS, was used to improve all students' ability to conduct ethnography later on. Technical difficulties turn out to be a concrete aspect of a generally productive attitude toward failure, something MML may help make more common.

Place

Places—locations with significant meanings and not just any old classroom—were primary features of most of the projects in this book. Place took on meanings in many ways for our authors, their students, and the learning they were trying together to make happen. One strategy was to use real places as theaters for academic content. A real setting can make ideas concrete and come alive. MML can take a museum or a classroom—places designed for learning—and reimagine them. Place has also been considered as a fundamental part of the mobile medium and hence incorporated as a natural part of authors' designs, as seen, for example, in Fischer and Dikkers' *Horror on the Ridges* game (chapter 18). Others look to directly explore places with MML through data collection activities, or more complexly such as in the case of Adam and Perales' experimental cinema (chapter 9), where place is both setting and subject, and as cinematographers, they are both audience and participants.

Even the seemingly place agnostic projects in the book depend in key ways on specific aspects of place. Bressler's game *School Scene Investigators* (chapter 5)—made with the intent of being portable to any other school—actually reimagined the school itself as a place for student activity; instead of working within a single classroom, students moved throughout the school. The game had the front office and principal conspire to become part of the mystery, involving their locations and actions in the design of the learning experience. With Technovation Challenge, the idea is to scale to reach girls everywhere. But to actually set up and facilitate the Challenge, much has been demanded of the places that have and will continue to host it. They have worked hard to locate aspects of local culture that can be successfully reproduced or created away from the techno-business centers where these elements already exist and where the Challenge began. Cultivation of local place is an inherent part of their plan to scale.

Place and mobile are closely intertwined. Certainly their relationship derives in part from the basic affordances of mobile devices to interact with location (e.g. knowing location via GPS), but there are subtle yet pervasive ways that mobile interacts with place as well. There are many perspectives to consider; mobile and place are not simple to disentangle. In *Mobile Media Learning: Multiplicities of Place*,[1] Kurt Squire posits that when it comes down to it, the main thing mobile does—generally, not just within designed learning—is enable people to remediate the spaces they inhabit. Mobile technology is how we transform ourselves in new places and what places mean to us. Interacting with place also can be seen as an application of the values we borrowed from Papert (chapter 2). Places have a specificity, and our actions in them and interpretations of them pull us into the concrete, connecting us to the lives of others.

Advocates of place-based learning such as David Sobel, David Gruenewald, or James Mathews would say we should go farther, suggesting a reversal of the previous implication: being involved with place is a central value; concreteness and connectedness are how that value is articulated. Their and other diverse views about why and how we can and should encounter the dimension of place when designing for learning will take time to sort through. But they do coincide in noticing, with our authors, the new access given to educators by mobile for availing themselves of a too-much ignored resource for learning.

Design

We mentioned in Practical Considerations (chapter 3) that imagining the real world as a destination for student designs can be a motivating factor in their production. When we talk about design we can refer to many different acts and means of creation, but at the center is this act of imagination, the hope that what you make might have purpose for someone else. And while it is noteworthy to involve students, it is just as important that this same attitude is shared by the educators in our book, that they are motivated by the prospect of design. Our authors imagine their projects have something to contribute to a world outside their immediate use; they took the trouble to write about them for you.

Technovation Challenge (chapter 14) has grown so big because of its organizers' commitment to enable girls everywhere to make something that might matter in the world. The creative software our authors and their students have used offers another perspective on this theme:

---

[1] Squire, K. (2009). Mobile media learning: multiplicities of place. On the Horizon, 17(1), 70-80.

This software is produced for other people to directly take up and use in any setting they choose and for whatever purpose they desire. The developers at some point made a conscious decision and considerable effort to make their tools appeal to and available for a general public. Their software is the result of a dream that somewhere, someone else might do something interesting with this tool. It is a contrast to the common but myopic concern in instructional design, curricular planning, and educational research with only one's classroom, one's students, and their performance on designed educational tasks.

With everyone—students, instructors, software developers, etc.—designing, it may be easy to become a bit pessimistic about the quality, utility, or reach of what has been designed. But you have seen how the success of an MML design can happen in many ways. Evaluation of MML design will typically involve some consideration of both process and product. Torres (Chapter 14), for example was very careful to note that large commercially successful apps make poor models of success for girls making apps in Technovation Challenge. This is not just because that kind of success is unlikely, but because focusing on it can blind them to what other forms of success look like. It is doubtful that any of the actual designs mentioned in this book will directly achieve true scale at the level of any mass market. But it is not the ability to deliver a mass market winner that makes the designers' dreams viable. It is the fact that these dreamers are neither idle nor alone and that the internet creates many small opportunities, not all of which run on money. Some are local and immediate, others dispersed through time and space.

A focus on design that contains modest but real external ambition is in agreement with Papert's values of "inherent virtue of informal learning" and "creating publicly" (see chapter 2). It is also an important instance of the kind of grassroots collective action we considered as means of educational change in the same chapter. It can be used to connect educators and learners together by providing shared goals, and is itself a direct expression of our desire to increase agency through MML. It is a statement of independence through interdependence. Like Place though, there are many theories and expressions of learning through design to be sorted through as we move forward.

WHO/WHAT IS MISSING?

This book has yielded a small, though important, sample of who is out there doing MML and in relation to what. It would difficult if not impossible to achieve a complete representation in this sense. But it is imperative to now ask, as we look forward to what has not yet been done instead of reflecting on what has been tried, "Who isn't at our party? What educational contexts, groups of people, and job descriptions are not represented here, not just because an author did not write in our book but because work there is generally lacking or talked about in non-overlapping circles? Why are they missing?"

Those without advanced devices. Access to capable devices and the internet is still a barrier to participation for many. We can note that the bar is getting lower all the time as smartphones reach worldwide saturation or the programs that make devices available in some unlikely situations, but we shouldn't be too smug about these problems going away entirely, or soon. Devices will become even more plentiful, but internet access, necessary for so much that these devices can help us do, remains in this country rather expensive and, even worse, difficult logistically for schools and institutions to help provide. This is especially true when we leave school grounds or other WiFi-enabled bases. Finally, the complexity of privacy issues raised by mobile technologies, along with a history of institutions making the legally safe but horrifyingly defeatist decision to try to ban outright anything they cannot totally control or guarantee as safe, may continue to prevent educators and learners from exercising creative and purposeful use of mobile and the internet as part of their official business of learning together.

The examples presented here do add one statement to the well-discussed issue of access: it too can be successfully dealt with on a contingent, local level. Large institutions balk at the cost to provide everyone with devices and service, but small initiatives can depend on BYOD—devices that students have—and fill in the gaps with relatively little funding. In situations like these, there is the added benefit that the use of these technologies is directly planned and motivated by the end users.

Difference and Disability. A large part of our message with MML is about diversity, inclusion, and multiple paths to success. But none of our stories specifically involve those differently-abled, take place in a therapeutic learning context, or focus on specific ways that MML can enable participation by those who might often be considered incapable. We do know that mobile may have a key role to play in how we can provide equal opportunity to all learners. In particular, we can see assistive devices in a less stigmatizing way now that we are all using them (and we are using the same devices). We know that mobile devices like the iPad are replacing and augmenting legacy assistive technologies due to their affordability and flexibility. It is obvious that formerly strong distinctions about how a person is able to communicate with the outside world might begin to fade once we get used to doing so with the help of multimodal communication through these devices. Idiosyncratic rather than mass-market software development, as we have already discussed, helps small groups with diverse agendas design for their needs. We know these ideas and stories are out there, but we need to make connections with those working in specifically in these areas and pay particular attention to issues of difference and disability in our own work to say anything substantive about them. More than for the sake of completeness, meaningfully broadening discussions of MML to include disability and difference may help uncover the commonality in what all educators are working towards.

The Very Young. Perhaps the most common revelation bestowed by the advent of mobile technologies for learning is the ease and facility which even the youngest of children find in using these devices. Planned or not, these days a smartphone or tablet is likely part of a child's learning experiences before they ever set foot in a school. And because one and two year-olds can and are using these devices, software development for them has suddenly become a big business. Depending on who you are, it is either fascinating or terrifying to watch a young child learn how to play a mobile game that was made for someone their age. Many of these titles are meant to appeal directly to parents by emphasizing a learning that maps easily onto typical expectations for School learning (letters, shapes, numbers, etc.) similar to a large portion of physical children's toys. But another class seems to tap more directly into this audience's inherent and developing abilities and desires (Toca Boca is probably the most well known publishing house for this kind of toddler software design). Here too, we have no concrete information or expertise to add to this massive area of MML. And once again, we suspect that this is an oversight or lack of communication on our part. What these devices and their ecologies can do for young people should share much with what we are collectively exploring for older learners.

Other Disciplines. There are many disciplines, academic and otherwise, represented in this book and elsewhere with MML. Our enthusiasm for MML is closely bound to the way it connects to so many ways of seeing, thinking about, and acting in the world. Some disciplines however are absent from this work. Certainly there are disciplines not directly represented in this book but which are known to have found their way under the umbrella of MML elsewhere. For example there are no chemistry-based projects mentioned in the above chapters, but Bressler (chapter 5) has made another School Scene Investigators game since writing her chapter, this time based on a chemistry activity. But we do not yet know what the natural limits are, if any, to the breadth of human experience capable of being enlivened through MML. Paleontologists may not be excited to share the exact locations of long-dead vertebrates through a mobile app, and mathematical thinking is somewhat typified by learning to do paper-based, abstract work, purposefully disconnected from embodied examples in the real world, but does reasoning like this actually correspond to some material disaffinity? We don't yet know.

Design Software. General purpose, easy to use, media production software is absolutely essential to the utility of MML for large audiences. The software that our authors have mentioned in this book (ARIS, App Inventor, NoTours, Traveler, Taleblazer) and popular favorites in use elsewhere (Garage Band for example) is not beholden to a specific educational agenda or use, and that is exactly what makes it so useful. Since we discuss such software frequently in this book, it may seem strange to list it among those aspects of MML that are not yet in place. But we need more tools like these. Outside mobile, there are more examples, from web design (Google Sites) and media production (iMovie) platforms to modding tools that ship with commercial games (The Sims) and indy game design software (RPG Maker). MIT's Media Lab has established a reputation as a perennial producer of these kinds of tools; we need more outfits like them. And we also need others who will follow different paths like those taken in the development of ARIS, Traveler, and NoTours—small development efforts willing to and capable of reaching large outside audiences with tools not only to use but to help define through our interpretive uses. There are also important decisions to be made about how the software is developed and distributed. Open source is a model that fits MML in two ways: 1) free software is software that is accessible to all, and 2) the ability to yourself become a developer of that software is yet another path to increasing agency.

WHAT IS NEXT?

As you can see, there's still a lot to work to do concerning MML. Compared to the first book, this book is a deeper dive into what MML is about, with more numerous and diverse examples to work from, but the ideas here have a ways to go before we begin to see closure. Some possible themes worth looking into further:

- Place and learning. We know place is important, but we have yet to sort through how in a way that squares with both what people are doing and what has been said before about what place should be about.

- Boundaries and overlaps. MML intersects significantly with many more areas of thought and action about learning, for example "games and learning" and "learning through design". Where are the boundaries between shared ideas important or superficial? How can considering practices that do not include mobile strengthen our understanding of it and when is it a distraction to do so?

- Growth and collaboration. When does this action begin to look collective instead of individual? How can it grow within and across settings? Does growth that is non-hierarchical and non-compulsory mean that schools will not often be sites for it?

- Comprehensive Plurality. As we bring in more concepts to think about MML and as work with it multiplies, how do we do so in a way that doesn't pave over the complexities for the sake of unifying the message? How is it possible to continue to respect simultaneously the diversity of perspectives among those employing MML and the need to put these ideas and projects together through summative descriptions and analyses?

- Developing the Medium. We have lauded the inherent value of mobile media creations beyond their utility for specific learning outcomes. What projects are moving the medium itself forward? Where is it headed?

In opening up discussion of MML to perspectives that resemble theory, let us not forget the value of concreteness. The lived learning experiences of educators and learners are the fodder for the evolution of practice. We need to keep sharing practical ideas and stories from our own backyards for MML to organically grow. Theory can help us find the words to make sense of those experiences for others, but it should serve a cause, not become a cause of its own. Like musicians, artists, or any community of creative expression, we need to not only make and share our work, but to be students of others' work too. We look forward to an emerging MML scene that can feed its own creative energy toward better design.

Closing

When we put together our first book about Mobile Media Learning (MML), our primary goal was to simply share the unique, daring, exceptional work that we were seeing emerge around the globe using mobile devices. For our readers, we hope they enjoyed reading about them and perhaps were inspired to make their own trials and experiments. That was then.

This new book has taken on a slightly different timbre. MML, while still not a common feature of educational environments, has been employed by an increasingly numerous set of educators in diverse settings. Tools for producing and enacting MML experiences—hardware, software, and inspirational—have multiplied and improved, expanding options for educators to take advantage of mobile affordances more easily, effectively, and interestingly. As you've now seen, MML is being employed not so much as a way to keep up with technology or to appeal to the younger generation, but to reinvigorate learning experiences for everyone involved. So, our goal in this book has been to share the edges and innovations still challenging our understanding of what MML is and what it can do for how we think about and design learning experiences. To this extent, we hope that this second effort has inspired you to move to those edges or to share your stories of the work you do with MML. You may not be ready to test for emotional response or have learners playing with bees, but you may be ready to start by using MML to enliven a field trip, or build a scavenger hunt on campus.

As pleased as we are with the work we have put into this book, on its own it necessarily falls short of opening up communication among educators about MML. That is because it is a book. Messages from us to you, frozen in time. Within these pages, there are no comments or follow-up, no further details to be had or way to respond to your ideas and questions. But we do hope this book can bring you into conversation about MML even if it cannot directly provide it.

If you haven't yet, we hope you start making something amazing to increase the agency of youth and adults in the name of education in your own way. As you work with MML, please get in touch. Ask any of us for help. Or maybe you already have stories to share. Maybe you're working in one of our missing areas. Share your stories informally and broadly. We want to hear from you to and to help you reach others. We want your story in our next book.

- The Editors

Mobile Media Learning: Innovation and Inspiration

Editors and Authors Biographies

In order of appearance

Christopher Holden is an Assistant Professor at the Honors College of the University of New Mexico. His research revolves around place based game design for learning. He makes games and helps others to make games for a wide variety of learning contexts, from language learning to community action, from classrooms to museums and community centers. He also helps produce ARIS, an easy-to-use, open source, augmented reality game platform. Chris teaches classes involving mobile game design, and directs the *Local Games Lab ABQ,* a fancy name for supporting unfunded faculty, students, and community members to make games and other interactive experiences to develop new forms of meaning within their local natural, cultural, and educational environments. Chris was once a number theorist but at some point went rogue thanks to the Games+Learning+Society folks at UW-Madison. As compensation, the group has generously set up Dance Dance Revolution for him each year at their annual conference.

Seann Dikkers is an assistant professor in the Educational Technology division of the The Patton College of Education at Ohio University. Formerly, Dikkers served fourteen years as a middle school history teacher, high school principal, and education consultant. Dikkers' work focuses on the integration of new media technologies for formal and informal educational settings. His books, *Real-Time Research, Mobile Media Learning,* and *TeacherCraft: How Teachers use Minecraft in the Classroom* are helping educational innovators to integrate technology into classroom learning. His projects include CivWorld, the Comprehensive Assessment for Leadership in Learning (CALL), Mobile Game Design, TeachOn!, and co-director of Playful Learning - Ohio. His current partnerships focus on the development of *Life Master: The Card Game that Just Happens* and *Just-inTime* teacher professional development systems.

John Martin has been integrating technology to increase learning in higher education in various roles since 1998. He is currently a Senior Teaching & Learning Consultant at the University of Wisconsin–Madison, where he teaches and develops socioculturally-rich teaching and learning practices. For his Ph.D. in Curriculum & Instruction, he broadly considered the motivational and sociocultural learning affordances of video games, and specifically focused on learner-designed place-based mobile games. Drawing on a background and interest in technology, art, writing, outdoor education, and with a commitment to environmental and social sustainability, John investigates tools of inquiry and expression that promote greater understanding and appreciation of the social and physical spaces we inhabit.

Breanne Litts is a postdoctoral fellow at the University of Pennsylvania where she investigates STEM learning and computing through electronic crafts as part of an NSF-funded project. Her scholarly interests coalesce at the intersection of identity, learning, design, and technology, particularly from a learning sciences perspective. Broadly, she studies how people learn through making, design, and production within makerspaces, mobile augmented-reality applications, and game-based learning environments. Breanne has conducted myriad research and evaluation studies in out-of-school contexts, especially focused on designing makerspaces and investigating the learning that happens within; much of this work has been in collaboration with the *Learning in the Making* team, an NSF-funded research partnership. Moreover, she helped found the Mobile Learning Incubator (now the Field Day Lab) as their lead researcher by examining mobile technologies as tools for field research, design, and games across a range of contexts. She remains an active member of the Games+Learning+Society research group at the University of Wisconsin-Madison.

Lohren Ray Deeg is an Assistant Professor of Urban Planning at Ball State University in Muncie, Indiana, where he has taught beginning design studio and visual communication courses for fourteen years, serving as the College of Architecture and Planning's common first year program coordinator from 2010-2014. Mr. Deeg collaborates with multidisciplinary design / planning practices in Muncie, Indiana, and maintains an illustration practice as a member of the American Society of Architectural Illustrators (A.S.A.I.). Lohren resides in Muncie, Indiana where he is an avid cyclist and advocate for healthy communities.

Kyle Parker is a Senior Software Engineer for Developing Technologies at Ball State University in Muncie, Indiana, where he has worked in Information Technology since graduating from the university in 2000. During his time at his alma mater, Mr. Parker has served as a web developer specializing in Microsoft products and tools; a group leader overseeing project management and other developers; and most recently, a software engineer working with a variety of mobile and wearable technologies. With a focus on the mobile app space, Mr. Parker is collaborating with instructors and students to imagine, create, and develop apps; deploy and integrate emerging technologies; and provide the students with new learning opportunities beyond the classroom. Kyle currently resides in Muncie, with his wife and daughter.

Shaileen Crawford Pokress is an advocate for gender and racial equity in computer science and engineering. Ms. Pokress earned a bachelor's degree in computer science from Cornell University and a master's degree in education from Harvard. Through her work at TERC, a national non-profit, she facilitated the development and curation of MSPnet.org, the groundbreaking online network supporting thousands of math and science educators working under grants from the National Science Foundation. Ms. Pokress later served as Director of Education for MIT App Inventor, a blocks-based programming platform that allows a wide variety of students to engage in the power of building mobile apps. Leveraging two decades of experience, Ms. Pokress joined Project Lead The Way to develop and deploy problem-based computer science curricula for K-12 students. Ms. Pokress is passionate about giving all students the opportunity to become technology creators who can fully participate in their 21st century world.

Denise Bressler is passionate about the potential for learning with mobile technologies. Formerly, Denise worked as an Exhibit Developer and Project Manager at Liberty Science Center in Jersey City, NJ. She developed the mobile learning initiative called *Science Now, Science Everywhere*. Recently, Denise received her Ph.D. in Learning Sciences and Technology from Lehigh University. Her research revolved around mobile game-based learning and mobile augmented reality (AR) experiences. Denise created a series of mobile AR games called *School Scene Investigators* which can be played with WiFi-enabled iOS devices and QR codes posted in a school environment. Denise is now an Education Researcher with the Center for Innovation in Engineering and Science Education at Stevens Institute of Technology.

Tim Frandy is a folklorist and outreach specialist for Native American communities at the University of Wisconsin—Madison's Collaborative Center for Health Equity and the Native American Center for Health Professions. In this work, he supports indigenous cultural revitalization efforts that improve the health and wellness of the community. These projects include birchbark canoe building, the revitalization of traditional Anishinaabe wintertime games, and the building of the first winter lodge in Lac du Flambeau in centuries. Frandy earned his Ph.D. in Scandinavian Studies and Folklore from UW-Madison in 2013, and he has conducted extensive fieldwork in both the Upper Midwest and in the Nordic countries. His research interests involve indigenous cultural revitalization, ecological folklore, cultural worldview and belief, identity, and traditional health and healing. He has taught folklore, literature, and language at both UW-Madison and Washington State University.

Kim Garza is an Assistant Professor of Graphic Design at St. Edward's University in Austin, Texas. As an educator, she employs innovative methods to create an engaging learning environment for her students. As a designer, her work moves across the print, interactive and motion mediums. Prior to teaching, she worked in a variety of professional design settings — an advertising agency, boutique design firms, in-house design departments and as a sole proprietor. Kim received a Bachelor of Arts degree at Anderson University and a Master of Graphic Design degree at North Carolina State University. In her spare time, she works on experimental short films in collaboration with her singer-songwriter husband. She is also the proud mother of two beautiful boys.

Jason Rosenblum is an Assistant Professor of Digital Media in the Bill Munday School of Business at St. Edward's University. He teaches courses that range from interactive technologies to digital music and audio, the business of gaming and social media and digital analytics. In addition to 20 years of experience as an educational technologist, Dr. Rosenblum holds a Master's degree in Computer Education and Cognitive Systems from the University of North Texas in addition to a Ph.D. in Curriculum and Instruction from the University of Texas at Austin, with an emphasis in Learning Technologies. In his dissertation research, Dr. Rosenblum studied people's experiences with sound in educational games. His doctoral studies include a focus on game-based learning, game sound, music psychology and innovative applications of learning technologies to support curriculum design and development.

Verónica Perales Blanco (PhD) is teacher at the Arts School and also at the School of Communication, University of Murcia. Working on Transmedia Narratives. **Fred Adam** is a freelance Art director expert in Mobile Learning and Spatial Narratives, currently working with scientists in Australia and the United States. Founder of GPS Museum. Both are artist members of Transnational Temps collective (Art+Technology+Ecology) and part of the Research Group on Communication, Culture and Technology (University of Murcia, Spain).

Bob Coulter is director of the Litzsinger Road Ecology Center, a division of the Missouri Botanical Garden focused on educational research and development. He has served as PI/PD for four Federal grants focused on game development. Previously he was an award-winning elementary school teacher.

Ross Stauder has been designing games on mobile and computer platforms for almost four years. When he is not designing games he enjoys playing soccer, building robots and playing games rather than designing them. He hopes one day either to be a computer coder and work at Google, or to be an engineer, most likely a robotics engineer.

Jameela Jafri has spent 15 years in the field of science education, working as both a high school science teacher and developing high-quality science, technology, engineering, math (STEM) programs for out-of-school time (OST) education. In 2010, she was awarded a Fulbright Fellowship to examine perceptions of science among underprivileged women in Damascus, Syria. Jameela directed girls' programming for Project Exploration, a science education nonprofit organization in Chicago. She then served as STEM advisor for After School Matters, Chicago's largest provider of out-of-school time programs for high school youth. Currently, Jameela is program design manager at After School Matters, where she oversees the design and implementation of strategic enhancements and initiatives to refine and scale quality programming. Jameela holds a master's degree in secondary science education from Teachers College, Columbia University and a bachelor's degree in biology from Barnard College, Columbia University. She lives in Chicago with her husband.

Gabrielle Lyon is a nationally-recognized non-profit leader, educator, and public speaker on education reform with a background that includes founding and leading award-winning organizations and initiatives focused on leveling the playing field of educational opportunity for underserved youth - particularly in science and technology. She synthesizes data-driven social-justice work with education, championing the belief that high-quality educational opportunity can and should be accessible to everyone, especially those to whom it has historically been closed. In 1999 Lyon cofounded Project Exploration, a high-impact nonprofit dedicated to changing the face of science for underserved minority youth and girls. As the Vice President for Education and Experience at the Chicago Architecture Foundation Lyon is responsible for leading the organization's thinking on how to best enable youth, educator, mentor and family communities to experience the built environment and design thinking through in-person and online experiences

Stephanie Madziar lives in Chicago, Illinois. She has been teaching middle school science for seven years in a Chicago Public School and is also an instructional leader helping coach and develop three other science teachers. Stephanie was a Teaching Fellow for Project Exploration through the National Summer Learning Association *Summer Pathways for Innovation*. She is very enthusiastic about teaching her students about native bees.

Rebecca Tonietto is a PhD candidate in the Plant Biology and Conservation program at Northwestern University, jointly offered with the Chicago Botanic Garden. She studies native bee communities in restored and urban systems, and is interested in native bee conservation. She has worked with Project Exploration's Sisters 4 Science program since 2008.

Juan Rubio is an expert in educational technology who secures funding, develops, and manages programs for youth in underrepresented populations. He creates programs that incorporate a wide variety of digital media, such as video games, virtual worlds, and social media, to give students a voice about issues that matter to them. Currently, he is the Associate Director of the Online Leadership Program for Global Kids, a youth development non-profit. He has also designed curricula for other professionals in cultural institutions such as Tribeca Film Institute, New York Department of Education, Brooklyn Public Library, and Carnegie Hall. He has a Master's degree in Media Studies from the New School University in New York City and studied film at Howard University School of Communications in Washington D.C. Originally from Honduras, he is fluent in Spanish.

Angélica M. Torres, Ph.D., led Technovation Challenge at Iridescent as Director of Educational Technology in New York in 2012 and took the program global as Senior Director in 2013. Angélica's passion is for unearthing hidden potential and bringing different groups together to innovate and better the world. She trained as a physical anthropologist at New College of Florida and Yale University. She was an Edward Zigler Social Policy Fellow at Yale and the first Judith Gueron Methodological Innovation Social Policy Fellow at MDRC for her work on early childhood environments. She spent her own childhood in Puerto Rico and now lives in Dallas with her husband and son, where she writes and consults.

Gianna May is currently a graduate student in the History Department at the University of New Mexico. She is studying 20th century Southwest North American history with a focus in women's history. Her research interests center around medicine in the Southwest and the intersection of traditional and professional healthcare at the turn of the century and how the medical field interacts across categories of race, class, and gender. Gianna continues to work with games as a way to facilitate learning and enhance a museum space. She is currently working on attaining museum certification in order to further her work with video games in museum spaces and plans to build more educational games in the future. For more information on Gianna's current work, feel free to check out her website at http://www.giannamay.org.

Ryan Rieder is pursuing his PhD in the Instructional Technology division of the Patton College of Education at Ohio University with a focus on technology and language learning. Currently, he is the head of ESL at Hocking College and works as a graduate assistant at Ohio University. Previously, Ryan taught EFL in Izmir, Turkey and Aleppo, Syria and Arabic as a Foreign Language (AFL) at Ohio State University. As a graduate student at Ohio State University, Ryan earned his M.A. in Near Eastern Languages and Cultures with a focus on Arabic and Islamic studies. During his time as an undergraduate student, he majored in History with a focus on the Middle Eastern and Russian histories. Also during his undergraduate years, Ryan studied Arabic at the University of Los Angeles California (UCLA). His research will include integrating technology with language learning.

Tamala Soloman

Dr. Christopher C. Blakesley specializes in the intersection of narrative, gameplay, learning, and technology for education. He currently manages an Executive MBA curriculum as Assistant Dean of Instructional Design at the Jack Welch Management Institute at Strayer University.

Jennifer McIntosh is the Interactive Education Program Manager at the National Air and Space Museum, Steven F. Udvar-Hazy Center.

Rebecca Fischer is a graduate researcher pursuing her PhD in Instructional Technology at Ohio University in Athens, OH. She comes to the field of educational technology from a background in computer science. She uses her technical expertise and skills to research how games can make a difference in learning. Rebecca looks to leverage the power of mobile games in new ways to help create engaging learning routes and provide an experience that has more impact than a traditional lecture.

Acknowledgements

There are so many people who have done so much to make a large effort like this possible but who are not listed as part of the official credits. I will try my best here to name the names of at least a few of those responsible.

You also have seen the names of the editors and authors of this volume, and hopefully read their inspiring words. I praise my co-editors and our authors for their incredible, inspiring work that gave them something to write about here, and the determination to see this work, through all the comments and revisions, to the end. Thank you for sharing your lives with me and our readers. Thank you for your patience in waiting, revising, re-revising, and waiting some more. Thanks to Seann Dikkers, John Martin, and Breanne Litts especially for all the time spent meeting over this book, planning it, putting it together, and giving me the confidence to continue when we got to tough spots along the way. Thanks too to the families, students, departments, and other support networks that are at most a step away from the actual words in this book; everything we have contributed here is a reflection not only of our relationships with you, but the time we steal away from you to produce these words.

Being involved as we are with many new technologies, we could not do what we do without the creative effort that goes into the creation and articulation of these technologies. At a basic level, these are the devices and basic software packages, and the networks that allow us to create with these tools ourselves. At a more specific level, we are lucky to have software and expertise generated with application to learning in mind. Just as Papert and others put together Logo and gave it to teachers and young people decades ago, much of the work done in this book would not be remotely possible without software generated for the public good. ARIS, Taleblazer, Traveler, and App Inventor are the principal titles you've seen mentioned, but there are others too. Their creators and supporters are too numerous to mention here, but they deserve immense thanks for what they make possible. They not only deliver us tools, but are responsible for the creation of ecosystems, places for the creation of new meaning by inviting newcomers into the creation process itself. ARIS of course holds a place dear to my heart due to my extensive involvement with it over the last several years. There are dozens of people whose contributions to ARIS have been essential, but without David Gagnon at the center, none of them alone would have meant much. But ARIS is not the only platform with a long-lasting, deep connection for me. The first piece of software that gave me the ability to become a mobile game designer—to realize the dream that I'd always had but never felt equal to pursue—was another piece of MIT's educational software empire: MITAR, a project begun by Eric Klopfer and later led by Judy Perry (I don't know if this is fully accurate, but I think of MITAR having gone underground for a few years to re-emerge triumphantly as Taleblazer). Their determination (and that of others who worked on the project but whose names I don't recall or know) to create an authoring tool useable by non-programmers to make geolocational games inspired me and a generation of educational designers to think big when it came to mobile. The later work at UW-Madison, MIT, and Harvard in AR game design, not to mention that done by the same personnel but who moved to new locations to start AR game research there, owes a lot to MITAR and its authors.

Hardware and software are not the only technologies and contexts influential for us. The first MML book did a nice job of acknowledging some of the more general intellectual debts we have accrued in doing this work. To them I would obviously add Seymour Papert and those whose projects were so thoughtfully described in that previous volume. Those earlier pioneers have directly influenced much of the activity in these last pages. Certainly we have already mentioned, in our chapters themselves, some of the thinkers and doers whose foundational insights were essential to our endeavor. We asked everyone involved to limit their citations to those few most pivotal in their own work, so please *do* follow up on them. Rather than reprise our list of references here, I would like to personally thank some of the people whose hard work and help have been provided personally, but who otherwise might go unnamed.

First, I have a long yet incomplete list of people from Games+Learning+Society (GLS), beginning with Jim Gee. His insights into literacy, learning, and games are of course fundamental to our work and that of many others. But Jim also started GLS at UW-Madison, a group through which all the editors of this book have now passed. The remarkable thing about GLS is the diversity, talent, and enthusiasm of its members and leaders over the few short years it has been around. We are not the only ones to have been transformed by that fire. There's a lot that Jim has done to make this work possible, but creating something like GLS is something quite rare, and I feel lucky to be a part of it.

Kurt Squire is one of the current leaders of GLS, but my gratitude stems from things he did earlier in his career. Like Jim, Kurt's thinking on games and learning is foundational. But about a decade ago, he personally welcomed me into the world of games and learning; he believed in and encouraged me when there was really no good reason to do so. I got my start in designing educational technology and games for learning in a course he taught. It was an incredible incubator. There were at least a dozen people who learned to trust in their creative abilities in that semester. A year later, he asked me to help design mobile AR games for a large grant he shared with Harvard and MIT (The ARGH project). This is where I first used MITAR (Eric Klopfer was the PI at MIT), learned more than I could have thought possible, not only about the research and design of place, mobile, games, and learning, but teamwork, photography, Milwaukee, lakes, and life generally. Kurt put together a fantastic team in Madison, each of whom deserve mention here: Mark Wagler, Jim Mathews, Ming Fong Jan, Dani Herro, Christine Johnson, and John Martin (who you now know). We like to say that you learn a lot when you make games; it is this experience, making and running games with these people that is the example I have in my mind that embodies this maxim, without peer. Although Kurt shared and made us of his deep knowledge of games, learning, and mobile, he also gave us an incredible amount of freedom to develop ourselves and our ideas on this project. He did not treat us like lackeys despite our station and (in my case—he took a big chance on bringing me into that group) inexperience. He did something very similar in supporting David Gagnon, Seann Dikkers, Chris Blakesley, and Kevin Harris as they began work on what would become ARIS, and in many, many other instances. Kurt is one of the most welcoming, selfless, giving people I know. Being a teacher is ultimately about learning to share, and it was from him I learned how to share. When I work on ARIS, mentor students, or am writing this book, I am looking for ways to pay forward what he gave me.

While I cannot mention every single person who has been a part of GLS or attended their conferences, I probably should. The truth is that this collective has nourished an incredible amount of talent and good will. Their annual conference has ruined academics for me. Each year I am rejuvenated by attending. The cynicism and pettiness that is too often a hallmark of scholarly pursuits at the higher levels simply melts away as I arrive to encounter so many vibrant, enthusiastic people. The people of GLS have become my closest friends. Together they set an example for scholarship at its very best. Groups like this make not only easier to get through the days but fill one's work with meaning and direction. Three final special thanks from among their ranks: Constance Steinkuehler, whom I first knew as a student in the program. More than anything, I am thankful for her showing me what confidence looks like from the inside. Her indefatigable can-do spirit is infectious. This is especially important when you are studying not only education—already low on the totem pole of academic entelechy—but games to boot. A close second is introducing me to Katamari Damacy. The leaders of GLS have variously shown me how to play new games, ones I would not have played otherwise. It is a microcosm for the maintenance of a vital curiosity, to explore and always be trying new experiences and ideas. Katamari is special though because it is the game I most like to share with others. The joy she shared with me is something I have shared with everyone in my life, not just scholars of games and other students. It probably sounds like a small thing, but it isn't.

I would also like to single out Elizabeth Gee (formerly Hayes). I wrote a chapter for *Learning in Video Game Affinity Spaces* which she coedited with Sean Duncan. They were both kind and thoughtful editors, but it was Betty's close yet encouraging attention to my poorly written text that has made me a much better writer over the years and has helped me to understand the essential role an editor plays in producing quality writing. She was certainly my inspiration as I worked on this book.

And lastly from GLS, but not last in my heart: Ben Devane. I worked with him on that first game design project in Kurt's course, and later took over his job on the ARGH project. He let me come in on his game design for *Hip Hop Tycoon*. Ben was my first peer in GLS. Outside these projects we were close friends and it was with him whom I formed much of my thinking about games and learning, through many long arguments. Without his help, I never would have gotten started.

Finally, I'd like to thank a couple more people who have been directly involved in this book finding its way into your hands. Everybody at ETC Press and Drew Davison in particular are excellent. I can't believe how easy going and yet entirely professional they have been to work with. They make it look so easy to do what they do. I'd also like to thank Sarah McKinney, my wife, for being my editor on this project. If this book is accessible to those outside our little educational technology bubble, she deserves much of the credit.

Chris Holden
Albuquerque, NM
February 24, 2015

Printed in Great Britain
by Amazon